VICE

VICE

*Dick Cheney and the Hijacking
of the American Presidency*

Lou Dubose

and

Jake Bernstein

 RANDOM HOUSE / NEW YORK

Published in the United States by Random House, an imprint of The Random House
Publishing Group, a division of Random House, Inc., New York.

RANDOM HOUSE and colophon are registered trademarks of Random House, Inc.

ISBN 1-4000-6576-3

Printed in the United States of America on acid-free paper

www.atrandom.com

2 4 6 8 9 7 5 3 1

First Edition

Book design by Susan Turner

To Molly Ivins,
a generous friend, wise and witty colleague,
and professional exemplar without peer

and
To Eve, thank you for being

CONTENTS

INTRODUCTION

Dick Cheney—bald, gray, avuncular—standing beside Texas governor George W. Bush in a packed hall on the University of Texas Austin campus in July 2000 was the precise image the campaign intended to convey. Bush had wrapped up a brilliant and often brutal primary campaign, yet it was hard to take him seriously. Despite months of foreign policy homeschooling, the gaffe-prone governor continued to make careless mistakes like calling Greeks "Grecians," Timorese "Timorians," and Kosovars "Kosovarians." He told reporters that he didn't like to read long policy papers. There were press reports of hours of required "downtime" in the afternoon, following his long jog around Austin's Town Lake. In six years as governor of Texas, Bush had failed to convince the nation that he was no longer the volatile, irresponsible first son of a political dynasty. In fact, he was perceived as a lightweight.

By selecting Cheney, Bush brought to the ticket the experience, gravitas, and wisdom he couldn't provide himself. Cheney had served three presidents, had spent ten years in Congress, and as secretary of defense had coordinated the first Gulf War. He was Bush père's preferred candidate, the Washington insider who would provide adult supervision in the White House. Nothing exciting, just competent and steady. Dick Cheney was the safe, reassuring presence whose experience would ensure that public policy, in particular foreign policy, would not careen off track.

It's unlikely that anyone watching Bush embrace his running mate on that sticky July day in Austin anticipated the power Dick Cheney would wield as vice president. Hidden was the foreign policy course Cheney planned to chart for Bush, which would lock the administration into a legacy forever defined by the war in Iraq. And while Cheney was a private man, the press had yet to realize the thick veil of secrecy behind which he would operate.

Over the course of six difficult years, Dick Cheney has become the most powerful vice president ever to occupy the office, exercising authority that often subsumes the president's. Sources who speak about him do so at great risk and usually prefer "off the record" or "background only." "You do not want to be on the Dick Cheney blacklist," says a former congressman. He has become a shadow executive who spends too much of his time in what the media refer to as "an undisclosed location" and is so obsessed with privacy that while the White House, the Pentagon, and even American troops in Iraq are visible on Google Earth's satellite mapping photos, the satellite image of the vice president's residence in northwest Washington is obscured.

"Cheney has the foreign policy portfolio," says a lobbyist who served in the administration of the senior Bush. "Cheney has the Iraq portfolio. And he has the Congress portfolio. I don't know what's left." The answer is "Not much." Six years after the governor of Texas selected the CEO of Halliburton as his running mate, his presidency has been defined by foreign policy, and Dick Cheney has done the defining.

"I didn't pick Dick Cheney because of Wyoming's three electoral votes," Bush said to the cheering campaign supporters who had been bused onto the University of Texas campus. "I picked him because he is, without a doubt, fully capable of being the president of the United States."

In a very real sense, that is what has come to pass.

VICE

ONE

A Man, a Plan— and Names Named

By mid-April 2001, Dick Cheney had been vice president of the United States for less than three months. But he was already deeply involved in a series of secret meetings in his West Wing office. When more space was needed for these energy task force meetings, an employee on loan from the Energy Department would schedule the ornate Vice President's Ceremonial Office in the Eisenhower Executive Office Building. The aide would also send out an e-mail designating precisely who would be allowed to attend the meetings the vice president was chairing. The April 17 list was a short one. Dick Cheney had quietly cleared his schedule to meet with a friend from Texas.

It's not likely that Dick Cheney knew at the time that Enron was collapsing. But Ken Lay knew. The Enron CEO knew that the company he built had more liabilities than assets, a grossly inflated book value, and earnings statements that had little to do with actual earnings. The last best hope for the Houston-based energy giant lay in the unregulated electricity markets out west. Enron's traders were gouging the California market, taking power plants off-line to create shortages, booking transmission lines for current that never moved, and shuttling electricity back and forth across state lines to circumvent price controls. Squeezed between what it cost them to buy power from Enron and what they could charge on the regulated retail market, one of the state's two largest utility companies had filed for bankruptcy and the other had signed on to a government bailout. California was in an energy crisis unlike anything it had ever experienced. Governor Gray Davis was pleading for rate caps that would provide relief for the state's devastated utility companies and the consumers enduring rolling brownouts and soaring utility bills. And Enron CEO Ken Lay was flying to Washington to talk to Dick Cheney.

The vice president was waiting. Lay handed him a three-page memo outlining Enron's recommendations for the new national energy policy Cheney was developing. Most of what Enron asked for would be included in the report the vice president's National Energy Policy Development Group would release the following month. One of Lay's recommendations was urgent, because it related to the California energy market: "The administration should reject any attempt to reregulate wholesale power markets by adopting price caps."

The following day, George Skelton, a reporter at the *Los Angeles Times*'s Sacramento bureau, got an unexpected call from a woman in the vice president's press office asking Skelton if he wanted to interview Dick Cheney. Skelton says he thought the call might be the beginning of a campaign to make some inroads in the state Al Gore had swept in 2000. But Cheney wanted to talk energy. That was fine with Skelton, because at that time energy was the biggest story in the state. Cheney wasn't the least bit tentative. "Price caps provide short-term relief for politicians," he said. "But they do nothing to deal with the basic, fundamental problem." Skelton pushed a little. Would the administration support temporary price caps to get the state through the summer?

"Six months? Six years?" Cheney said. "Once politicians can no longer resist the temptation to go with price caps, they usually are unable to even muster the courage to end them . . . I don't see that as a possibility."

California's governor, both U.S. senators, even Republicans in California's House delegation were begging the administration for price caps, or for some relief for utility rates that were forcing small-business owners to close their doors. But Cheney had already told Senator Dianne Feinstein that one of the lessons he learned in the Nixon administration was that price caps don't work. Now he was calling a reporter to defend a position Ken Lay had laid out for him a day earlier. "Frankly," Cheney said, "California is looked on by many folks as a classic example of the kinds of problems that arise when you do use price caps." The vice president was such a free market zealot that he saw no government role in a utilities market that was savaging consumers. This was policy advocacy so fast and efficient that it seemed reflexive. Cheney heard from Ken Lay on Monday and called George Skelton on Tuesday, and Lay's position on price caps was laid out under the vice president's name in the *Los Angeles Times* on Wednesday.

The public was not aware of Lay's visit to the White House. It's not known whether Lay told Cheney that Enron was in trouble. The vice president refuses to answer the question, and Lay's death in July 2006 while awaiting sentencing for bank and securities fraud suggests we'll never know. But Cheney knew that in less than a year the wholesale cost of one megawatt-hour of electricity in California had jumped from $30 to $300—up to $1,500 at peak demand times. It was also widely reported that profits earned by power producers and marketers like Enron were up 400 to 600 percent.

Cheney did not prevail—in part because the administration didn't have all its Federal Energy Regulatory Commission appointees in place. And in part because the situation in California had become so desperate. Several days after Cheney and Lay met, the Federal Energy Regulatory Commission ignored the vice president's arguments and imposed price caps on energy traders working California. The wildly fluctuating markets were brought under control. FERC had pulled the plug on Enron's California trading schemes, cleverly named "Fat Boy," "Death Star," and "Get Shorty."

Enron collapsed six months later.

George Skelton never again heard from the vice president and says he didn't expect to. But Cheney, who goes out of his way to avoid reporters and had organized energy task force meetings that were totally insulated from the press, had succeeded in getting Lay's message out almost immediately—to the largest readership in the state of California.

President George W. Bush had created the National Energy Policy Development Group ten days after he took the oath of office. It was Dick

Cheney's idea, his big push to create a national energy policy and fix policy decisions he believed for too long had been made by the Environmental Protection Agency. The terrorist attacks of September 11 were more than eight months in the future, and Bush senior adviser Karl Rove had decided that a president who had lost the popular vote and been put into office by the Supreme Court should govern as if he had a mandate. Bush's understanding of Washington was limited to a short run as loyalty enforcer in his father's administration. As governor of Texas, he had been famously disengaged from public policy. But his vice president had served in three presidential administrations, had spent a decade in the U.S. House of Representatives, and had been secretary of defense during the first Gulf War. Bush named Cheney chairman of the energy task force, which also included the secretaries of Treasury, Commerce, Interior, Agriculture, Energy, and Transportation, EPA administrator Christine Todd Whitman, FEMA director Joe Allbaugh, and the White House deputy chiefs of staff for policy and economic policy. It was the first policy initiative the Bush administration would undertake. Its process and content would be shaped by the vice president—and, as it turned out, by the oil, gas, mining, and utilities interests he invited in—and it would all be done in secret.

No one paying attention to national politics could have been surprised to see oil and gas interests writing Dick Cheney's energy policy. This is a fossil fuels administration; both men were bona fide members of a small fraternity of Texas oilpatch executives. Bush had spent ten years in the state's Odessa Permian Basin oilfields, losing millions of dollars invested by others in his company but walking away with about $1 million for himself. Cheney left the Dallas-based oilfield construction and service giant Halliburton to join the Bush ticket in 2000 with approximately $45 million to show for his five-year effort.

Both men knew Ken Lay well; Bush had a closer relationship.

By the time Bush took his oath of office in January 2001, Lay and his Enron executives were Bush's largest lifetime political backers, with more than $775,000 invested in his two campaigns for governor in Texas. Enron took an equity position in the Bush-Cheney presidency when it put $1.7 million into Republican races in the 2000 election. There was more than money. During the Florida recount and the weeks of litigation that followed, the Bush-Cheney political and legal team flew to Florida and Washington on Enron (and Halliburton) corporate jets, while Al Gore and his guys were booking coach. So after the inauguration, Lay and Enron vice president Robert Shapiro got face time with Cheney, and four other Enron officials also got into energy task force meetings with the vice president. If six executives from one company seemed excessive—well, as Cheney press aide Mary Matalin said, to make energy policy, you talk to energy experts.

Dick Cheney talked to energy experts, as the vice president's visitors' log began to look like the American Petroleum Institute membership list. This was no coincidence. Ten days before the inauguration, an oil and gas lobbyist on the administration transition team had invited a group of industry executives to the API's Washington offices to draft a wish list. A month later, the same lobbyist, Steve Griles, was named deputy secretary of interior and assigned to work with Cheney's energy task force. The energy executives Griles had called over to the API offices were suddenly presenting position papers to the energy task force.

Two months in office and Dick Cheney was back in his professional and social milieu. Conoco CEO Archie Dunham knew the vice president from the years they spent together on the Union Pacific corporate board, and from business dealings between Halliburton and Conoco. That, and the size of his company, was enough to get Dunham a private meeting with Cheney, and access to the task force. Dunham pushed for the acceleration of oil and gas exploration and the relaxation of environmental rules slowing construction of refineries and pipelines. He also wanted an end to unilateral U.S. sanctions that kept American oil companies out of Iran and Libya, an economic realpolitik argument Cheney had made as Halliburton's CEO. Robert Allison of Anadarko Energy led a delegation of oil company executives into Cheney's office to lobby for opening up more federal land for oil and gas exploration. British Petroleum's Lord John Browne and other BP executives used their meeting with Cheney to discuss foreign markets. Electric utility giant Exelon had two chief executive officers; both of them, Corbin A. McNeill, Jr., and John W. Rowe, met with Cheney. Also representing electric utilities were Mark Racicot and Haley Barbour, both of whom had been heavily involved in the Bush-Cheney campaign. Racicot was Republican National Committee chair, a gig that Barbour had just given up.

The energy task force did its work behind a veil of secrecy that has become the signature mark of the vice president. Staffers were warned to safeguard all information about who attended meetings. The few members of Congress who met with the task force did not brief their colleagues back on the Hill. Some lobbyists, such as Haley Barbour, were met at the curb and escorted in. There were no press releases.

"It was like a black hole for information," said one Capitol Hill staffer. "Information went in, but nothing escaped." "Near-Nixonian secrecy," wrote Joshua Micah Marshall in *The New Republic*, hitting upon the etiology of Dick Cheney's obsession with secrecy. The vice president was in charge. Considering that only oil and gas executives and lobbyists were writing the nation's energy policy, he had to keep the process closed to the public, the press, and even the Congress. It was secrecy befitting the Kremlin, complete with reporters furtively watching cabs and limos, a reclusive and secretive executive, and a small cabal of corporate executives in control of public policy.

Accounts of committees drafting energy policy aren't the sort of stories that grab the attention of newspaper readers. Nor do they provide the "white girl missing" excitement that animates the twenty-four-hour cable TV news cycle. So it's not surprising that one of the defining events of the Bush-Cheney presidency never really captured the imagination of the public. It was an important story to miss. Something was happening here that was far larger than oil and gas executives writing energy policy. The fight to keep secret the participants and deliberations of the National Energy Policy Development Group was the beginning of a power grab undertaken within days of the inauguration of a president and vice president who months earlier had lost the popular vote. In one bold stroke, Dick Cheney was rewriting the extraconstitutional rules that divide power between the presidency and the Congress.

Cheney's assault on the constitutional division of powers began with his response to what appeared to be a routine letter from a member of Congress. In this instance, Representative Henry Waxman's request for names and minutes of energy task force meetings was turned over to the Government Accountability Office after the vice president refused to comply. Some level of disagreement between a new administration getting its bearings and minority committee members in the House was expected. What wasn't expected was that Waxman's request—a routine exercise of congressional oversight—would push the two branches toward a constitutional crisis.

The official who would press Waxman's demand was David Walker. The comptroller general of the United States and head of the Government Accountability Office is a centrist Republican who had worked in Ronald Reagan's Labor Department, then as an executive for two accounting firms. (He spent ten years as a partner at Arthur Andersen, departing four years before its collapse in the Enron scandal.) There is an earnestness about him, which becomes more evident when he describes himself as "the chief accountability officer of the United States government." Appointment to the position of comptroller general involves an odd process. The leaders of both houses of Congress send the names of three candidates to the president, who selects one. Then the Senate votes to confirm. Walker and two co-finalists emerged from a pool of sixty applicants when Bill Clinton selected him in 1998. The fifteen-year term Walker would fill is the longest fixed term of any federal appointee. It insulates the comptroller general from political pressure and encourages a strategic, long-term approach to the issues confronting his office.

The Government Accountability Office is often described as the watchdog of the federal government. The term particularly suits the organization under Walker's leadership. He tells reporters he represents 535 clients: all the members of the United States Congress. Reports issued by the agency are the gold standard of nonpartisan government audits. Walker has undertaken his own speaking tours, delivering grim, statistically grounded warnings about the federal deficit, Social Security, and the fiscal irresponsibility of the Bush tax cuts. Short, bald, always in a business suit, and speaking with actuarial certitude in a Jim Lehrer monotone, David Walker is as unflappable as Dick Cheney. When he took up Henry Waxman's request, the government's watchdog was challenging Dick Cheney's attack dog—David Addington.

Addington is an authoritarian Republican, who began his career at the CIA after graduating from Duke Law School. He joined the minority staff of the House Intelligence Committee in the eighties, where he connected with ranking minority member Dick Cheney. When President George H. W. Bush appointed Cheney secretary of defense in 1989, Cheney took Addington along with him. He is a distinct breed of lawyer, who like Attorney General Alberto Gonzales seems to believe that his first responsibility is to make the law work for his client. Since 2001, Addington's sole client has been Dick Cheney. Addington was Dick Cheney's staff legal counsel—until Scooter Libby was indicted and Addington replaced him as the VP's chief of staff. David Addington is as private as David Walker is public.

Addington is also a proponent of the unitary executive, an extravagant vision of the presidency that would allow the president to reinterpret or ignore laws passed by Congress, particularly in times of war. Like his boss, David Addington is a man on a mission to expand the power of the executive. He found, or created, an opportunity to do so in the National Energy Policy Development Group. The group should have been subject to FACA, the Federal Advisory Committees Act. FACA requires transparency when the government allows private parties to shape public policy. Addington devised a scheme to circumvent FACA and eliminate the transparency that Dick Cheney considers an intrusion into his business: Any time a group of lobbyists would sit down to create public policy, at least one government employee would be present. It was as bold as René Magritte's near-photographic representation of a pipe over the inscription *ceci n'est pas une pipe*—"this is not a pipe." Fifteen oil industry lobbyists meet in the Executive Office Building and one midlevel bureaucrat from the Department of Energy steps into the room—and voilà: *ceci n'est pas une foule de lobbyists.* Because one government employee sat in with every group of lobbyists, a committee of outside advisers was not a committee of outside advisers. The vice president would chair the entire working group, creating a penumbra of executive privilege, a second mechanism to keep the process closed. "The whole thing was designed so that the presence of a government employee at a meeting could keep the Congress out," says a congressional staff lawyer. It was also designed to avoid press scrutiny.

For Paul O'Neill, the first treasury secretary in the Bush-Cheney administration, the energy group's structure was a warning of the insularity of a White House in which Dick Cheney served as co-president. O'Neill is a former Alcoa CEO who had worked in the administrations of Nixon, Ford, and the first President Bush. His experience taught him that working groups perform best when government officials are encouraged to mix it up with experts from private industry—and when there was nothing to hide from the press and the public, unless national security issues were discussed. Cheney and Addington had created a task force exclusively staffed by government employees, so they were not subject to the federal transparency statute. But lined up outside the door were the "nonfederal stakeholders" actually making the policy: energy industry executives and lobbyists presenting detailed energy policy papers. It was all give and no take. According to O'Neill, that's the way Cheney wanted it. No transparency. No accountability. Five years at Halliburton had made the vice president an energy expert in his own right. If he didn't know the answer, he knew who did. In Ron Suskind's *The Price of Loyalty*, O'Neill says Cheney frequently complained about information released in the name of open government being used against you by "political enemies."

To Dick Cheney, the political enemy was a persistent congressman from Los Angeles. Henry Waxman was one of the reform Democrats elected to Congress in 1974, three months after the resignation of Richard Nixon. During Cheney's nine years in the House, Waxman served in the party that dominated Congress. When the Republicans won control of the House in 1994, Waxman adapted to minority status. As the ranking minority member of the House Government Reform Committee, he funds and directs a special investigations team focused on fraud, waste, and conflicts of interest. The French daily *Le Monde* described Waxman as *"l'Eliot Ness du Congrès."* In the summer of 2001, Waxman turned his attention to Cheney's energy task force. Waxman and John Dingell, a Michigan Democrat who has served in the House since 1955, sent the vice president a formal request for the names of participants in the energy group meetings and their working notes. Cheney adviser Mary Matalin was contemptuous, accusing Waxman of engaging in a "politics of destruction"—perhaps a bit excessive considering that Waxman was requesting information regarding the vice president's compliance with a federal law.

When the vice president refused to turn over the names, Waxman and Dingell asked the GAO to get the list. David Walker made an initial request and received a firm no from David Addington. When Walker sent a demand letter, Addington again refused, even though Walker had scaled back his request—"out of respect to the vice president." Waxman and Dingell wanted both the names of participants and notes from the meetings; Walker was asking only for a list of the private parties who met with Cheney and the energy task force. On July 26, 2001, ABC's *Nightline* anchor Ted Koppel asked Cheney about meetings with his "pals" from the oil business. "I think it's going to have to be resolved in court, and I think that's perfectly appropriate," Cheney said. "I think, in fact, this is the first time the GAO has ever issued a so-called demand letter to a president/vice president. I'm a duly elected constitutional officer. The idea that any member of Congress can demand from me a list of everybody I meet with and what they say strikes me as—as inappropriate, and not in keeping with the Constitution." The vice president was deftly turning a request for records into a constitutional struggle between the legislative and executive branches. Cheney also used another *Nightline* interview to shut down any prospect of negotiating with Congress, telling Koppel the dispute would have to be resolved in court "unless [Waxman] decides he wants to back off."

Walker prepared to file suit, then put his plans on hold after the September 11 attacks and the war in Afghanistan. Cheney stayed in the fight, turning up the heat on Fox News, the media outlet where he feels most at home. "They've demanded of me that I give Henry Waxman a list of everybody I met with, of everything that was discussed, any advice that was revealed, notes and minutes of those meetings," Cheney said in a January 2002 Fox News interview. Not only was Cheney personalizing the fight, he was lying—as was his press flack Matalin, who continued to voice the same complaint long after Walker scaled back his request and was asking for only the names and schedules of private parties who participated in the process of drafting energy policy.

"What I object to," Cheney told Fox anchor Tony Snow (who would become Bush's mouthpiece four years later when the administration was in free fall), "and what the president's objected to, and what we've told the GAO we won't do, is make it impossible for me or future vice presidents to ever have a conversation in confidence with anybody without having, ultimately, to tell a member of Congress what we talked about and what was said. You just cannot accept that proposition without putting a chill over the ability of the president and the vice president to receive unvarnished advice."

"A bogus, specious, absurd argument," says Bruce Fein during an early morning interview at the Washington, D.C., University Club. Fein is a constitutional lawyer who worked in the Reagan administration and also worked closely with Cheney on the Iran-Contra Committee when Cheney was in the House. "I would worry about giving advice to the vice president because it would leak out? That's how you make money in this town. You want it to get out." Fein is one of a growing number of conservative Republicans alarmed by the Bush-Cheney administration's contempt for the Constitution evident in unauthorized wiretapping, the suspension of habeas corpus, and using presidential signing statements to ignore laws passed by Congress. He wonders where they came up with the idea that executive privilege could be used to protect people speaking to the president. "The president himself can waive privilege any time he wants to," Fein says. "So how are the advisers protected?"

Executive privilege is an established legal doctrine that allows a member of the executive branch to withhold information to protect national security or the functioning of the executive branch. Fein, who earns his living arguing constitutional issues in federal court, is unconvinced by the administration's novel privilege argument—probably because he spends too much time reading Hobbes, John Stuart Mill, and the Federalist Papers, the latter quoted at length over the course of a long interview. The vice president's privilege argument is so novel that its antecedents won't be found in any of these foundational texts. Yet, it was clearly articulated in a White House press conference by Zern Jenner twenty-six years earlier:

> A President has to have complete candor and objectivity from those who assist him. Otherwise he is not going to explore all the alternatives and consequences of a decision before he makes it, and he's going to end up making some bad decisions. Now if the President's advisers can't be sure that what they say to him will be confidential, they're not going to deal straight with him. People just don't work that way. When they know they're speaking for the public record, they shade the truth because they worry about how their statements will appear.

If Zern Jenner's name is not familiar, it's because Lynne Cheney's novel *Executive Privilege*, in which he appears as president, was not a big seller. President Jenner is a character informed by Dick Cheney's brief time in Gerald Ford's White House. Confidentiality and executive privilege were issues that Cheney had been pondering since the Ford administration ended in 1976.

With Cheney refusing to budge, David Walker sued him in February 2002. It was the first time in its eighty-year history that the GAO had sued an elected official. "They had Ted Olson appear in district court to represent the vice president," says one lawyer close to the case. "Ted Olson is the solicitor general. He's their Supreme Court guy. He doesn't get involved at the district court level." Olson's appearance, and Cheney's overheated rhetoric, brought enormous pressure to bear on the judge, John Bates, who had been on the federal bench for less than a year. Bates, a Bush appointee who had worked for Special Prosecutor Ken Starr when he was investigating Bill Clinton, ruled that the GAO had no grounds to sue because there had been no vote by a congressional committee to request or subpoena the documents.

Bates's ruling creates a legislative catch-22 for Democrats. By House rules, all committee chairs are members of the majority party. And all committees reflect the partisan balance of the House. That Republican committee chairs refuse to issue subpoenas to the White House is not an overstatement. Through the sixth year of the Bush-Cheney presidency, despite regular reports of corruption, leaks, and nearly criminal incompetence, the lead oversight committee in the House has issued a total of five subpoenas regarding the White House and the Republican Party. During the eight years Clinton was in office, the same committee issued more than 1,052 subpoenas.

Walker did not appeal, citing the cost of a protracted court fight. He tried to contain the damage, telling reporters that Judge Bates's ruling applied only to the specifics of this case. Cheney knows better—as do serious students of the presidency and Congress. Brookings Institution congressional scholar Thomas Mann sees the decision as a big win for the Bush-Cheney administration and a big loss for the Congress.

"President Bush and Vice President Cheney have an extreme and relentless executive-centered conception of American government, and it plays out every day, and there are dozens of fronts in this effort to strengthen the presidency," Mann said. "Power naturally gravitates to the presidency in times of uncertainty. But people are going to question putting all of our trust in an unfettered presidency."

Not only the presidency—the vice presidency. This was a decisive win for the vice president. He never revealed his list of contacts, and his constitutional power was expanded. A political consultant who worked in the George H. W. Bush administration says presidents will always fight to protect their memoranda. "But these guys believe that any time you can roll back the legislative branch, you do it. And they get away with it." Bruce Fein takes it further: "Now they have a precedent they can hold over Congress's head. Like a loaded gun. Forever."

So what was Cheney hiding?

"This was not about national security," says Tom Fitton, president of Judicial Watch, a conservative public-interest law firm that spent much of the 1990s suing the Clinton administration. "This was about an undersecretary talking to a lobbyist." In Judicial Watch's law library, Fitton lays a stack of files on the table. Judicial Watch lawyers used a back door approach to obtain some of the energy task force documents. They sent Freedom of Information Act requests to the federal agencies that worked with Cheney's energy group. The president and vice president are exempt from FOIA, but federal agencies are required by law to open their file cabinets to the public and press. When the agencies—backed by Attorney General John Ashcroft's blanket promise of legal defense—refused to turn over any documents, Judicial Watch sued, and prevailed. (As did the Natural Resources Defense Council. Because of the similar demands, the two suits were consolidated.) The only public documents related to Cheney's energy group, other than those leaked to reporters, were obtained by Judicial Watch and the NRDC. It required two years of litigation—enough time to get past the 2002 elections—and an order from a federal judge to force the release of the records. Yet only a fraction of the task force records were released, as most are under the control of the OVP—the Office of the Vice President.

Among the documents released are a number of pages that demonstrate what Cheney is hiding. Perhaps the most stunning of all the documents obtained by Judicial Watch are maps of Iraqi oilfields, with a long list of corporate "suitors" for each oilfield. Why were the vice president and a group of oilmen poring over maps of Iraq long before there was any pretext to invade the country? Iraq's oil was technically embargoed and under U.N. control—why make plans for divvying up its oil reserves?

Most likely because this fit into a larger scheme Cheney had supported for years. For more than a decade, the vice president had been involved with a small group of conservative foreign policy hawks, who as they came together to advise George W. Bush began to refer to themselves as "the Vulcans." Among the hard-liners in this decidedly hard-line group are Paul Wolfowitz, Richard Perle, Donald Rumsfeld, and Dick Cheney. Six of the Vulcans—Cheney, Rumsfeld, Wolfowitz, Colin Powell, Richard Armitage, and Condoleezza Rice—ended up in the Bush-Cheney administration. Armitage and Powell represented the most moderate faction of the so-called Vulcans. The public first began to hear of some of the Vulcans in 1998, when associates of a small think tank known as the Project for the New American Century went public with their proposal that Bill Clinton invade Iraq. Perle, Wolfowitz, Douglas Feith, and *Weekly Standard* editor William Kristol did the big thinking on the plan to take military action against Iraq and turn it into a model democracy that would transform the Middle East. Cheney, while not a member of PNAC, had signed the group's statement of principles and was a supporter. (As events played out, the PNAC motto might as well have been "Small Group, Big War.")

Fitton's conservative instincts led him to doubt that Cheney was looking at Iraqi oilfields in preparation for war. But Fitton is bothered by the fact that there is no way to know. "We don't know because we weren't given the context," he says. "We have no way of knowing what they were deliberating."

Actually, there is some context. As Cheney and his task force studied maps of Iraq, administration officials were also calling in oil ministers from friendly Persian Gulf states surrounding Iraq. No one seemed to notice or report the facts and the context. While Saddam Hussein was in power in Iraq, and the country's oil revenue was under U.N. control, the vice president of the United States, U.S. Department of Energy officials, and Persian Gulf oil ministers were discussing the disposition of the region's petroleum reserves. The names and dates of visits from Middle Eastern oil ministers were obtained through the NRDC requests in the FOIA lawsuit. The lists of meetings with Persian Gulf oil ministers, and the maps obtained by the NRDC, were all included in Department of Energy files released long after a federal judge ordered them turned over to the plaintiffs—and after Bush and Cheney started the war in Iraq.

American vice presidents and presidents have studied Middle Eastern oil maps since before the Saud clan beat the Arabian Peninsula into one sovereign petroleum monarchy. And there were oilfield maps of other countries. The United Arab Emirates, for example. And Iran, which raises another huge set of issues. Earlier, as CEO of Dallas-based oilfield construction giant Halliburton, Cheney was making the argument that State Department sanctions keeping U.S. energy companies out of Iran and other state sponsors of terrorism were unfair to American business and should be lifted. The Iranians desperately wanted U.S. oilfield technology, and Cheney wanted to provide it. The Bush Doctrine, however, which would become more hardened after the September 11 attacks, would keep U.S. business interests out of Iran. Iran's maps were useful only within the context of a plan for regime change.

The focus on the Iraqi oilfield maps on the eve of an unprovoked war suggests that preliminary war planning was under way in the first three months of the Bush-Cheney administration, well before the September 11 attacks that Cheney and Bush were to use as the justification for the invasion. In fact, those plans had already been developed by Paul Wolfowitz. First securing, then unlocking Iraqi oil could only serve the interests of the United States. There was, after all, euphoric prewar speculation in the business press about the positive effect Iraq's oil would have on world markets in the long run. And Assistant Secretary of Defense Wolfowitz predicted that rebuilding Iraq would be paid for by tapping into Iraqi oil reserves. Some things don't work out as planned.

There is more the administration did not want made public.

Small embarrassments, such as task force executive director Joseph Kelliher e-mailing natural gas lobbyist Dana Contratto to ask what he would do about natural gas policy "if you were king, or Il Duce."

And a "fill-in-the-blanks" executive order drafted by the American Petroleum Institute, under a heading that read:

Executive Order _____
Energy Policy
March _____, 2001

On May 11, 2001, the draft became Executive Order 13211, which included, verbatim, the policy that American Petroleum Institute federal relations director Jim Ford spelled out, even if it was executed in May rather than March. Using the president as cover, Ford cut through government regulation and exempted certain industry acts from judicial review.

There were larger issues. On March 1, Irl F. Engelhardt and Fred

Palmer, the CEO and vice president of Peabody Energy, met with task force director Andrew Lundquist, Secretary of Energy Spencer Abraham, and Bush economic adviser Lawrence Lindsey. Peabody, the world's largest coal company, was preparing a stock offering. Coal policy recommendations in the task force report would influence the market's response to Peabody's IPO. On March 16, the task force released its report, hyping the use of coal. On March 21, Peabody went public, raising $420 million—$60 million more than analysts had predicted. The task force was, in effect, flogging a stock offering.

There were other embarrassments.

The EPA representative on the task force had blocked the recommendation of a procedure called hydraulic fracturing. "Fracking" involves high-pressure injection of chemicals into gas formations to break up rock and move the gas to the wellhead. It also contaminates aquifers used for drinking water and irrigation. In response to EPA concerns, fracking was pulled from the draft version of the report. It was reinserted in the final report. Halliburton is the nation's leader in hydraulic fracturing.

Many of the lobbyists and executives who made it to the task force table were major Bush-Cheney contributors, engaging in what looked like pay-to-play government. But the only "lobbyists" whose names and photographs the task force released to the press were representatives of environmental groups, all brought in on one day as a response to criticism that the environmental community was being shut out.

Four years after the task force went out of business, the secrecy and dishonesty continued to dog the vice president and his corporate clients, as executives for the major oil companies all told a Senate committee that they had not attended or didn't recall attending task force meetings. But after a Secret Service visitors' log that included their names was leaked to *The Washington Post*, and New Jersey Senator Frank Lautenberg announced that he was referring their testimony to the Justice Department, their memories improved so much that they amended their testimony.

Yet the task force's most far-reaching policy change was coldly executed by Dick Cheney himself. In one bold move, the vice president killed the environmental centerpiece of George Bush's presidential campaign. Bush had repeatedly promised that if elected, he would cap emissions of carbon dioxide, one of the known causes of global warming. After he took office, he turned the campaign promise into policy. Bush directed his EPA administrator Christine Whitman to move toward the carbon caps. "George Bush was very clear during the course of the campaign that he believed in a multipollutant strategy, and that includes CO_2," Whitman said on CNN's *Crossfire*. White House senior adviser Karl Rove, who was standing beside Bush when he made the CO_2 pledge at an Austin press conference in 1999, confirmed that the president was committed to reducing CO_2 emissions. Bush treasury secretary Paul O'Neill was even more dramatic, observing that on "nuclear holocaust and global warming, there is no second chance."

Bush stuck by his policy even as his fellow Texans in the House, Tom DeLay and Joe Barton, attacked it. At a Group of Eight summit of industrial nations in early March in Italy, EPA director Whitman repeated the president's position. But while Whitman was speaking in Trieste, the vice president was at work in Washington. On March 1, Cheney received a personal note, released through the Natural Resources Defense Council's FOIA suit, from lobbyist Haley Barbour: "Regarding Cheney Energy Policy & Co."

"A moment of truth is arriving in the form of a decision whether this Administration's policy will be to regulate and/or tax CO_2 as a pollutant," Barbour wrote. "Demurring on the issue of whether the CO_2 idea is eco-extremism, we must ask, do environmental initiatives, which would greatly exacerbate the energy problems, trump good energy policy, which the country has lacked for eight years?"

Cheney's response to Barbour was almost as quick and reflexive as his response to Ken Lay's call for help in California. Cheney received Barbour's memo on March 1. Bush had already announced the U.S. withdrawal from the Kyoto environmental accords, but Whitman was telling the press the president was still committed to a "multi-pollutant" bill that would cap CO_2 emissions. On March 8, an angry and embarrassed Whitman showed up at the Treasury building for a breakfast meeting with Paul O'Neill. She had in hand a letter from four Republican senators—Chuck Hagel, Larry Craig, Jesse Helms, and Pat Roberts—regarding the Kyoto Accords and the regulation of carbon dioxide. The letter made it clear that the carbon caps were in serious trouble in the Senate and the Kyoto Accords were dead. The letter had been faxed to her from Hagel's office two days earlier.

O'Neill was suspicious about the emphasis, the tone, and the language in the letter. It read like words "right out of Dick Cheney's mouth." They were. In the documents released to the NRDC is a copy of Chuck Hagel's floor speech on carbon dioxide caps, from the files of the Energy Department. Hagel was working in concert with Cheney, according to Suskind's book—and to a Senate committee source. The vice president was undermining and making a fool of Whitman. On March 13, Whitman arranged a private meeting with Bush to discuss carbon dioxide caps. She began by reminding him of the scientific evidence and of the international cooperation she had been working to build on environmental issues.

Bush interrupted her. "Christie, I've already made my decision." He said he had written a letter to Hagel, agreeing to drop the carbon dioxide caps and withdraw from Kyoto. According to O'Neill's book with Ron Suskind, as Whitman left her Oval Office meeting with the president, one of the secretaries in the atrium said: "Mr. Vice President, here's the letter for Senator Hagel." Cheney picked up the letter and left to meet with Hagel on Capitol Hill, where Cheney made a speech to the Senate Republican Conference. The topic of the speech was the reversal of policy on CO_2 emissions.

O'Neill saw in the killing of Kyoto and the CO_2 caps the same tactics Cheney had used when the two men served together under Presidents Nixon and Ford: "Quietly select an issue, counsel various participants, manufacture the exchange of seemingly impromptu letters or reports . . . then guide unfolding events toward the intended outcome."

It was by O'Neill's observation a "clean kill," done in the style of Dick Cheney. No fingerprints. No accountability. Cheney collaborated with four senators who were working against White House policy, then persuaded the president to join them.

A few fingerprints were later found when a federal judge ordered the release of the Barbour memo. And because Christine Whitman happened to be departing the White House as the vice president walked out, she saw the smoking gun in his hand.

What occurred in early 2001—in the vice president's offices in the Executive Office Building and out of the public eye—is remarkable. In the place of an open process that might have considered sustainable and renewable energy (and conservation, which the vice president described as a "private virtue"), a government-sanctioned industry cabal drew up a plan for more oil, gas, coal, and nuclear power, with far fewer protections for the environment. A smaller cabal considered the oil reserves they could liberate in Iraq. The 163-page report the group produced was illustrated with color prints of wildlife and even fly fishermen. Among its one hundred recommendations were more refineries with fewer environmental restrictions, 1,300 to 1,900 new power plants, and more natural gas pipelines. "Reality is not 'Well, gee, we can conserve ourselves out, we don't have to produce any more,' " Cheney said after the report was released.

The documents that Judicial Watch and the NRDC obtained are the only public record of a policy conducted behind what Fitton describes as disturbing secrecy. The secrecy in this case was essential. In four months of meetings in early 2001, industry interests created a national energy blueprint that could not bear the public embarrassment that would come with connecting each initiative to its industry sponsor. "There's nothing conservative about secrecy," says Fitton.

When the names and affiliations of those who met with Cheney regarding energy policy are examined in the light of day, one thing becomes clear: The secrecy in this case was essential. It has become operational policy for a government colluding with powerful corporate sponsors. It's also a personal fetish of Dick Cheney. "I had one lawyer tell me the vice president is against *all* Freedom of Information Act requests," says Fitton. The lawyer was Shannen Coffin, who was co-counsel with Solicitor General Ted Olson when he defended Cheney against the GAO suit. When Scooter Libby resigned as Cheney's chief of staff, to be replaced by David Addington, it was Coffin who took Addington's place as legal counsel to the vice president.

Unless Dick Cheney is the Republican nominee in 2008 and succeeds George W. Bush, this administration will move on and policy will change. The Congress will respond to the hot reality of global warming. The EPA will deal with the environmental hazards of fracking. Another president will begin to pick up the pieces of what remains in Iraq. Yet the structural changes Dick Cheney forced on the government will remain with us. The drastic reinterpretation of the Constitution and the new rules that govern the relationship between the executive and legislative branches will be hard to undo.

Cheney had done far more than rewrite the constitutional guidelines that govern the balance of power between the two branches. He seized the power of Congress by what might be described as an act of adverse possession. Then he and his legal counsel, David Addington, went to court to create the case law that makes the new guidelines the legal precedent Bruce Fein describes as a gun held to the head of Congress.

"It was a signal to the nation and certainly to everybody in this town that this is the way things are going to be done," Fitton says. "They refused to release the information and litigated this to the hilt. . . . It was a strong signal at the very beginning."

For Cheney, the beginning was thirty years past—in the collapsing administration of Richard Nixon and the brief presidency of Gerald Ford. The present would be devoted to creating a vice presidency insulated from any accountability—from the Congress and even from the president with whom he shared executive power.

TWO

The Education of
Richard B. Cheney

O n September 29, 1974, thirty-three-year-old Dick Cheney, still fit
and with a full head of hair, was personally presented to President
Gerald Ford as his new deputy chief of staff. Cheney would later describe
it as the day he and Donald Rumsfeld "took over at the White House."

"We moved in on a weekend and the president happened to be in the
Oval Office on that Sunday," Cheney reminisced, before describing how
Rumsfeld brought the commander in chief over to meet his new staffer.

Cheney may have arrived in the West Wing by invitation of the forty-
two-year-old Rumsfeld, Ford's new chief of staff, but over the course of
the next two years, the apprentice would replace the master and become
the youngest White House chief of staff in the history of the United
States, the leader of a national presidential campaign, and a voice in the
president's ear as the nation strove to recover from the madness of
Richard Nixon. The path to understanding the most powerful vice presidency in American history begins with the education of Richard B.
Cheney in the Ford White House.

"No president in modern times had ever taken office in more challenging circumstances," Cheney has said about Ford. The echoes and in some cases the amplification of the issues surrounding Nixon's collapse and Ford's resulting tempestuous two-year term are everywhere to be found in the administration of George W. Bush: the dramatic expansion of executive power, the debates on wiretapping and the CIA, an obsession with secrecy, attacks on the media, leaking sensitive information to strike at bureaucratic opponents, and even the current disregard for environmental protection. A common thread through it all is Dick Cheney.

Cheney's astonishing streak of professional luck began in 1968, when he won a fellowship from the American Political Science Association (APSA), which sent him to Washington, D.C., the place where he would spend most of his adult life. More important, it put him in the office of Wisconsin Republican congressman Bill Steiger, a strong supporter of the APSA fellowship program. Steiger was one of the giants of the House, according to congressional scholar Norman Ornstein: "He had a tremendous impact on policy even though he was a Republican in a Democratic Congress." In a move that would be unthinkable today, the congressman put his avidly curious student at a desk right inside his office, so Cheney could observe everything Steiger did.

There are two versions of the story on how Cheney came to the attention of Donald Rumsfeld. A four-term Republican congressman from Illinois, Rumsfeld had resigned his seat in 1969 to accept a Nixon appointment to run the Office of Economic Opportunity, which had been created by Lyndon Johnson to coordinate the war on poverty. Looking to get a running start, he sought advice from his friend and former colleague Steiger. The man-of-action version of what happened next has Cheney spying Rumsfeld's letter on Steiger's desk and then taking it upon himself to write a ten-page policy memo on running a federal agency. The memo so impressed Steiger that he passed it on to Rummy. A more plausible version has Steiger (who died in 1978) assigning Cheney the task of collecting information on the OEO for Rumsfeld. Whichever version is correct, Rumsfeld regarded Cheney's report so favorably that he hired him to be his executive assistant.

The politically ambitious former fighter pilot had insisted that Nixon grant him the title of Assistant to the President, in addition to his OEO responsibilities. Cheney dutifully followed his new boss as he split his time: mornings and evenings at the White House and the rest of the day at the OEO. But Cheney was still on the second floor, where staff had offices, not where decisions were made. "I had an intellectual understanding of the range of things the president had to deal with—but I really didn't have an emotional feel for it until you sit here and see him—what he has to do in the course of a day," he said in a 1975 interview.

Cheney's hopes of getting any closer were sidetracked when Nixon, who found Rumsfeld a tad too eager, sent him away to be ambassador to NATO. Rumsfeld offered a posting in Brussels to his faithful deputy Dick—who, after the OEO, had played the same role for Rumsfeld at the Cost of Living Council—but Cheney declined. Now with two daughters to support, he instead joined friends who ran a small institutional investment advisory firm called Bradley Woods and Company. Working at the firm allowed Cheney to stay in Washington, and available. He signed on as vice president at the company and spent most of the next eighteen months preparing research papers on Nixon's economic program and the energy business.

On August 8, 1974, the night Richard Nixon went on nationwide television to announce his resignation effective the following day, Cheney received a call from Brussels. Rumsfeld's secretary wanted to know if he could meet the ambassador's flight at Dulles airport the following afternoon. Cheney knew that if his patron had a place in the new administration, so did he. The younger man had impressed Rumsfeld with his work ethic, intelligence, and loyalty. Before going to the airport, Cheney—removed from the political fallout—watched Nixon's emotional departure. When Rumsfeld disembarked, a White House messenger met him with a letter from Ford. It asked him to come straight to the White House to lead the change in administrations. At about 2:00 P.M., two hours after Ford was sworn in and declared that "our long national nightmare is over," the two men rode into town. Rumsfeld asked Cheney to take a leave from work and help with the transition.

The transition team attempted to meld what was left of Nixon's administration and Ford's staff. Some on the Ford side, like his longtime aide and speechwriter Robert Hartmann, argued that by design, the Nixon people retained control. "The Nixon-to-Ford transition was superbly planned," Hartmann wrote in his book *Palace Politics*. "It was not a failure. It just never happened." Cheney remembered that Ford allowed them to make staff changes on the domestic side but not in the foreign policy arena. When it came to national security, Secretary of State and National Security Advisor Henry Kissinger ruled. "We lived with these conflicting objectives," Cheney recalled. "We had to emphasize continuity, on one hand, and change on the other."

Their work on the transition lasted ten days, and then Rumsfeld went back to NATO and Cheney returned to Bradley Woods. About two weeks later, on September 8, Ford took the most fateful step of his presidency. He pardoned Richard Nixon, before the ex-president could be indicted. A week later, Rumsfeld called Cheney in Florida, where he was on business. He asked Cheney to meet him in D.C. that weekend. On Saturday, Rumsfeld confided to his protégé that he had a private meeting with the president scheduled for the next day. He believed that Ford would offer him the chief of staff position. If that turned out to be the case, would Cheney be his deputy? Cheney told him he could wrap up his affairs at Bradley Woods within two weeks.

Rumsfeld and Cheney worked out a deal that benefited them both. Cheney would be Rumsfeld's surrogate. When Rumsfeld went on trips alone or with the president, Cheney would make the decisions at the White House and operate as if he were chief of staff. The young man would also have his own opportunities to take presidential trips as chief of staff. This way, Cheney would get plenty of face time with the president. Rumsfeld would later claim that the arrangement allowed the top staff to "lead relatively normal lives." Cheney didn't want a normal life; he wanted to live, eat, and breathe the White House. Most important for the political futures of both men, their understanding allowed Rumsfeld to train a loyal successor so that if Ford shook up his cabinet, Rummy could slide into a cabinet position without a hitch. When that time came, Cheney opted not to continue Rumsfeld's deputy system.

President Ford—universally acknowledged as a friendly, genial, and trusting man—held Rumsfeld in such high regard that he apparently accepted the presence of the inexperienced Cheney without question. "I was always amazed that he was so amenable to having such a relatively young stranger—I think I was thirty-three at the time—come in and all of a sudden become part of his inner operation," Cheney recalled.

Cheney would describe the qualities he admired in Ford in a speech in 1986. Today, the description casts Ford as a sort of anti–George W. Bush. "He was a man who was able to sit down and listen to debates. He never cut off an individual's access because that person disagreed with him. He relished the give and take of political dialogue. I think that's very important," Cheney said. "His knowledge and grasp of government and political issues was just enormous."

Cheney made the most of his access. He is widely acknowledged to have participated in every major administration decision. When Cheney became chief of staff, his contribution moved from the periphery to the center, but his input was often hidden. He would be the one to gather up everyone's views and carry them into the Oval Office as an honest broker, not an advocate. If he had an opinion, Cheney would deliver it orally to the president. He learned how to operate this way from Rumsfeld: Never write anything down if you can avoid it. "Both these guys were crafty," remembers James Cannon, who served in the Ford administration alongside Cheney and Rumsfeld. "You never spotted their fingerprints."

Cheney has reprised the role of private counselor to the president in the Bush administration. It's an arrangement that allows him to avoid exposing his positions to scrutiny and thus criticism. The secrecy Cheney created for himself in the Ford administration continues to this day. It appears that before leaving the White House in January 1977, he took many of his papers with him, instead of donating them to the Ford Library as most other officials did.

Cheney would argue years after the fact that Ford's pardon of Nixon was the correct decision, just poorly timed. It contributed to a Democratic landslide in the 1974 midterm election. The Republicans lost more than forty seats, ushering in a historic reform Congress that changed the balance of power in Washington. "Almost immediately after the president came to power, as a result of the election in November of 1974, we found ourselves outnumbered about two to one in both the House and the Senate," recalled Cheney. "I thought [the pardon] should have been delayed until after the 1974 elections because I think it did cost us seats. If you say that that is a political judgment, it's true, but then, the presidency is a political office. If we had had twenty or thirty more House Republicans during the two years of the Ford presidency, we would have been in much better shape than we were from a legislative standpoint." Even back then, there was no distinction between politics and governing for Cheney.

Dick Cheney was about to learn firsthand the restrictions an emboldened Congress, in this case a veto-proof Congress, can impose on a president. He would spend the rest of his career working to restore the Nixon
vision of an all-powerful executive, by undoing the Watergate reforms
that came out of the activist Congresses of the early seventies. "You've got
Cheney sitting there at the time that Congress is taking on the imperial
presidency," observes Nixon lawyer John Dean in an interview from his
home in California, "and apparently it was a trauma he never got over."

In response to the pardon, the Senate passed a resolution by a vote of
55 to 24 urging the president not to issue any more pardons "until the judiciary process has run its full course." The House introduced well over a
dozen bills and resolutions calling for formal inquiries into Ford's pardon.
The Monday after Rumsfeld and Cheney "took over" the White House,
Ford stunned congressional leaders by agreeing to testify before the
House Judiciary Committee to explain why he had pardoned Richard
Nixon. "It was only the second time in history that the president had ever
done that," Cheney noted in a 1986 interview, citing Abraham Lincoln as
the other president. (Lincoln had testified before the House Judiciary
Committee in 1862 over the matter of the leak of his annual message to
the *New York Herald.* But Cheney was wrong: both George Washington
and Woodrow Wilson had also testified to Congress, although the latter
had legislators come to the White House.) Ford's staff, particularly departing chief of staff Al Haig, begged him to reconsider. The image of
Ford, hat in hand, testifying before Congress offered startling evidence of
how weak the executive had become. Dick Cheney would never forget it.

Cheney would describe this period as "a series of institutional con-
frontations" that "led repeatedly to efforts on the part of the Congress to
impose limitations and restrictions on the president. . . . The main concern in the Congress often seemed to be to find ways to restrict presidential power so that future presidents would not abuse power the way
Lyndon Johnson had allegedly abused power in Vietnam or Richard
Nixon had abused presidential power in the Watergate affair."

Cheney particularly objected to the War Powers Resolution, passed in
1973, which restricted the president's ability to send U.S. troops into
combat without congressional approval. Since leaving the Ford administration, Cheney has counseled two Bush presidents that they didn't need
the consent of Congress to attack Iraq, arguing that war-making is the

prerogative of the commander in chief. But war powers would be just the beginning of congressional reforms that would last a little more than a decade and cover everything from intelligence to clean water and government in the sunshine.

Cheney exerted his influence to push Ford away from some of the groundbreaking environmental regulations passed during Nixon's presidency. Searching for a reason Ford had refused to enforce the Clean Air Act for new coal-fired power plants, Russell E. Train, the head of the Environmental Protection Agency at the time, saw Cheney's handiwork. "It seemed likely that Dick Cheney was responsible for the way the White House dealt with the matter," Train wrote in his 2003 book, *Politics, Pollution, and Pandas*. (A quarter of a century later, states were lining up to sue the Bush-Cheney administration for its refusal to impose Clean Air Act standards on coal-fired power plants.)

A battle over the Freedom of Information Act was one of Cheney's first big policy fights under Ford. Although the law was passed in 1966, congressional hearings in the early seventies revealed that FOIA, designed to make government records accessible to the public, wasn't working. Agencies took too long to produce documents, charged exorbitant fees for searching and copying, and forced too many requesters to go to court to procure them. Watergate taught the Congress and the public that it was incumbent upon them to watchdog the federal government. It would be a lesson forgotten by the time the Bush administration, under Cheney's guidance, dramatically curtailed the public's right to obtain government information.

In January of 1974, Pennsylvania Democratic representative William Moorhead and New York Republican representative Frank Horton sponsored amendments designed to improve FOIA's effectiveness by expanding the definition of who was covered and imposing time frames for how quickly agencies had to comply to requests for information, as well as to litigation, if a requester sued to overturn a denial. By the time Ford took office, the amendments had reached a Senate-House conference committee, meaning that the bill was nearing final passage. The CIA, Defense, Treasury, Civil Service, and Ford's staff all urged a veto. As did Cheney. What particularly bothered them was a provision that allowed for a judicial review of what the government was allowed to keep secret. It was an unacceptable check on the executive branch. Efforts at compromise failed to appease the administration. On October 17, 1974, after Congress passed the legislation over the president's objections, Ford vetoed the FOIA amendments.

In the three and a half months of his presidency leading up to the FOIA veto, Ford had vetoed thirteen bills. Congress had overridden only one. On November 20, the House and then the Senate the following day voted to override Ford's veto of the FOIA amendments.

Nearly thirty years later, in 2003, Attorney General John Ashcroft issued a directive to federal agencies that encouraged them to deny requests for documents under FOIA. Cheney had put in place a cabinet that would share his obsession with secrecy. As for his own activities, he would give new meaning to Al Gore's claim that there was "no controlling legal authority" over the Office of the Vice President. Exploiting a loophole in the Constitution, which places the vice president as the presiding officer of the Senate, Cheney's lawyer David Addington has argued that the OVP is not an "agency of the executive branch," but instead a creature of Congress, and thus is not required to disclose information under FOIA. (Congress is exempt from the disclosure rule.) Yet the OVP is not covered under Senate ethics rules either, so Cheney refuses to reveal detailed information about the OVP's operations, such as a breakdown of its budget, staff duties, and activities such as travel on corporate jets. While the 2003 Ashcroft directive mandated that federal agencies provide the number of documents they've classified, Cheney's office has declined to do so.

Cheney's hypocritical relationship to unofficial government disclosures—he has an extreme aversion to leaking of information by others, but is willing to leak himself if it suits his purpose—dates to the Ford administration, which leaked more than the *Titanic* after it hit the iceberg. In a National Security Council meeting held in the cabinet room a week after Rumsfeld and Cheney arrived, Ford fumed about the number of classified documents appearing on the front pages of newspapers. "I've been told that *The New York Times* has so much classified material, they don't know where to store it," groused the president. "This is unforgivable."

With Rumsfeld's prompting, Ford admitted that the problem was a managerial one. He asked his department heads to stop the leaks at the source before a reluctant FBI had to get involved. But in reality, the trouble began with Ford. His hybrid administration was at war with itself, and he seemed incapable, or perhaps unwilling, to stop it. More often than not, leaks in the administration were designed to embarrass one side or the other in a constant gamesmanship for control.

Some observers believe that Ford tacitly encouraged the factionalism in order to control outsized members of his administration, especially Henry Kissinger. The former House minority leader, whom Nixon had appointed to replace a disgraced Spiro Agnew, knew that despite his long service on the House Committee on Intelligence, the world believed he had little foreign policy experience. In the beginning, he relied on Kissinger to assure other nations that there would be continuity. But as Ford became more confident, and Kissinger too solicitous to Russia for the Republican right's taste, leaks that undermined the secretary of state increased.

Both Rumsfeld and Cheney believed Kissinger was too soft on the Soviets, too quick to make concessions in order to preserve détente. A July 8, 1975, memo from Cheney to Rumsfeld, initialed by the president, illustrates the conflict. It also demonstrates how a young deputy chief of staff with no foreign policy experience had no reservations about going after an institution like Kissinger. The secretary of state had advised Ford not to meet with Soviet dissident Aleksandr Solzhenitsyn, a foe of détente, for fear of upsetting talks with the Soviets. Cheney disagreed. "Seeing [Solzhenitsyn] is a nice counter-balance to all of the publicity and coverage that's given to meetings between American Presidents and Soviet Leaders," wrote the thirty-four-year-old Cheney. "Meetings with Soviet Leaders are very important, but it is also important that we not contribute any more to the illusion that all of a sudden we're bosom-buddies with the Russians."

In the memo, Cheney also advised that the discussion about a Solzhenitsyn visit should be held "with a very small group, so that we don't have the kind of leaks we did last time."

Presidential speechwriter Hartmann, who admits that he leaked himself, credits Rumsfeld with a mastery of the "calculated leak." "Rumsfeld would only personally leak the stories that reflected positively on him," Hartmann recalls. He left the negative leaks designed to damage and attack opponents to his deputy. "Cheney was the abominable No-man," jokes Hartmann in an interview at his home in Bethesda.

Cheney also found novel ways to use the media to attack his administration rivals. *New Republic* columnist John Osborne recalled that during a flight from Peking to Jakarta, Cheney, at that point chief of staff, stood silently by as Press Secretary Ron Nessen openly challenged the press corps on Air Force One for being too lenient on Kissinger. "Cheney never uttered a word of disapproval of Nessen's conduct, then or later," Osborne noted.

Former Nixon counselor John Dean believes that when the inexperienced Cheney became chief of staff, much of the leaking—everything from anonymous snipes about who was up or down to policy disputes played out in public—involved staffers who were "pissed and disgruntled" at the young man. "The people I knew who were still there were very disenchanted with Cheney," he says. "They felt he was in way over his head."

Nearly thirty years later, Cheney would apply the lessons he learned about leaking during the Ford administration to attack Valerie Plame and Joe Wilson.

Leaking of Ford administration secrets would lead to a national intelligence crisis and a wiretapping scandal that brought with it congressional investigations and reform that Dick Cheney strenuously opposed—to no avail. On December 22, 1974, journalist Seymour Hersh offered up a Christmas gift to Ford as the president departed to spend the holiday in Vail. Hersh, who would later report on the darker recesses of the Bush administration during the Iraq War, had discovered some of the federal government's most sensitive institutional secrets. Hersh's front-page story in *The New York Times* reported that the CIA had maintained intelligence files, put together over decades, on at least ten thousand Americans in the United States. Hersh had ferreted out what was known to a select few in the government as "the family jewels," described in the *Times* as "dozens of other illegal activities by members of the CIA inside the United States, beginning in the nineteen-fifties, including break-ins, wiretapping, and the surreptitious inspection of mail."

The story began to find its way to the surface when Nixon named James Schlesinger CIA director in early February 1973. Within three months, Schlesinger discovered that the closets in his agency were brimming with "skeletons," each tucked away in its own compartment, as department heads had reported only to then CIA director Richard Helms. On May 8, 1973, Schlesinger sent a memo to all CIA employees ordering them to report any activities, current or past, which might be construed to be outside the legislative charter of the agency. By the end of the month he had assembled an ugly picture, including explosive revelations of CIA participation in assassination attempts against foreign leaders. But there was much more. The CIA had wiretapped and physically surveilled a number of reporters, including the current Fox News anchor, Brit Hume, who then worked for investigative reporter Jack Anderson. Between 1953 and 1973, CIA staff had opened American mail destined for Russia and China. It had also monitored peace groups and conducted psychological studies using psychoactive drugs on unwitting subjects.

A similar process of discovery was under way at the National Security Agency (NSA). Around the time of Rumsfeld and Cheney's arrival at the White House, Attorney General Elliot Richardson learned that the NSA had been feeding information gleaned from its electronic surveillance operations to the FBI and the Secret Service. Richardson told General Lew Allen, Jr., director of the NSA, to knock it off because it could potentially be illegal, despite Allen's protestations that it was only information intercepted in the course of "foreign intelligence activities."

In July 1974, Ford elevated Schlesinger to secretary of defense, leaving the collection of misdeeds he had uncovered in the hands of Schlesinger's replacement, William Colby, a career agency official best known for overseeing a Vietnam War–era program called Phoenix, which involved the assassination of suspected North Vietnamese collaborators. Colby quietly briefed the Intelligence Committee chairmen in the Senate and House about the family jewels before Congress voted to confirm him. Once confirmed, the new CIA director sent out a memo to all department heads with precise instructions on what was now permissible activity. And there the jewels lay, until Hersh's Christmas surprise.

Initially Cheney was only peripherally involved in the administration's response to the intelligence scandals, but that would change. The week Hersh's December 1974 story hit, one of Cheney's main tasks was coordinating the White House Christmas cards. A review of documents at the Ford Library in Ann Arbor reveals a host of small-bore duties Cheney handled in his first nine months as deputy, including remedying the dearth of salt shakers in the Residence, obtaining a new headrest for Mrs.

Ford's helicopter seat, and dealing with requests for congressional visits to Camp David. On the latter, a request from Alaska senator Ted Stevens for a tour of the facility, Cheney, ever mindful of executive privilege, wrote Rumsfeld to "strongly" recommend against allowing Congress access to Camp David. First of all, it might tip off the public to the classified nature of some of the facilities at the compound. Second, "once we start Congressional tours at Camp David, we may end up with yet another series of issues about the prerequisites [*sic*] of the White House."

Amid the picayune staff work, Rumsfeld also asked Cheney to make political recommendations, including how to energize the conservative Republican base. Cheney identified a school voucher program in New Hampshire that needed money as "a very important project that we'd like to see funded" and advocated the extension of the Voting Rights Act to the entire country so the South wouldn't feel discriminated against. When Caspar Weinberger, then secretary of health, education, and welfare, proposed a tax increase to cover the deficit in the Social Security Trust Fund, Cheney persuaded him to drop the proposal.

But on May 25, 1975, with Chief of Staff Rumsfeld out of the country, *The New York Times* dropped another Hersh bombshell. It revealed that U.S. spy submarines were tapping into Soviet communication cables inside the USSR's three-mile territorial limit. Hersh admitted in the story that his sources gave him the information in the hope that it would move policy. They believed that the submarine program violated the spirit of détente and that using satellites to obtain the same information was less risky. Rumsfeld, traveling with the president in Europe, put Cheney in charge of devising an administration response to the story. Cheney's answer was as stunning as it was predictive of positions he would take when he had real power as George Bush's co-president.

Cheney called a meeting with Attorney General Edward Levi and White House counsel Philip Buchen to discuss options. Levi, a short man with a towering intellect, unimpeachable integrity, and a nonpartisan bent, served as a bridge between the Democratic Congress and Ford, winning the president's approval for intelligence reforms over the objections of executive absolutists like Cheney. "Ed Levi was a voice of wisdom and counsel," says Jack Marsh, a Ford senior adviser who worked on intelligence matters with Levi. "His contributions have never been appreciated."

In the case of Hersh's submarine exposé, it would be Levi, the designated adult, who would rein in Cheney. Faced with the possible leak of classified information, the thirty-four-year-old Cheney's first thoughts involved breaking into the home of a reporter. Among the options the three men explored, according to Cheney's handwritten notes, were grand jury indictments, threatening the *Times* with prosecution if they didn't stop reporting classified information, and obtaining a search warrant to "go after Hersh papers in his apt." They also discussed political considerations. "Will we get hit with violating the 1st amendment to the constitution?" Cheney wrote. Ultimately, Levi put the kibosh on searching Hersh's apartment. Since the leak did not endanger the Soviet eavesdropping, with Levi's prodding, the White House decided to do nothing rather than draw more attention to it.

Fast forward thirty years to the spring and summer of 2006. *The New York Times* has exposed details of the government's warrantless domestic eavesdropping program and its surveillance of banking transactions. The Bush administration responds by threatening a criminal investigation and launching a political smear campaign—to punish the newspaper. In June, Cheney takes the opportunity of a congressional fundraising lunch at the Waldorf-Astoria in New York City to lash out at the hometown daily. "Some in the press, in particular *The New York Times*, have made it harder to defend America against attack by insisting on publishing detailed information about vital national security programs," the vice president declares.

In Hersh's submarine exposé, Cheney saw an opportunity to discourage congressional investigations into intelligence issues initially reported in the *Times*. Dealing with requests from the Senate (the Church Commission) and the House (eventually the Pike Committee) had become a daily preoccupation at the White House. "Congressional action on intelligence was like opening the door and a tsunami came through every day," remembers Marsh.

Cheney scribbled in his notes on Hersh's most recent scoop, "Can we take advantage of [the leak] to bolster our position on the Church committee investigation? To point out the need for limits on the scope of the investigation?"

One area in particular where the administration decided to fight Congress rather than cooperate has particular resonance today. On

May 15, 1975, Church Committee lawyers approached the NSA for information about Project SHAMROCK, a program begun shortly after World War II under which U.S. communications companies including AT&T and Western Union gave access to the NSA to review practically all communications between the United States and foreign countries. Perhaps not coincidentally, the NSA shut the program down the very same day the Church Committee came calling. SHAMROCK had grown so large that in 1966, the NSA and CIA created a front company in New York City just to process the intercepts. At the program's peak, the agencies were reviewing more than 150,000 messages a month.

The Senate committee's investigation focused on the review of international cables. But the House was just getting started. Efforts by two different subcommittees to subpoena AT&T were rebuffed by the administration, which declared "the American Telephone and Telegraph Company was and is an agent of the United States acting under contract with the Executive Branch." A sweeping and aggressive investigation by New York liberal representative Bella Abzug's Subcommittee on Government Information and Individual Rights resulted in increased pressure for a legislative remedy. (Abzug believed—correctly, it turned out—that NSA had continued SHAMROCK-like activities after terminating the program.)

Helping the administration resist Congress on issues ranging from FOIA to intelligence sharing was a whip-smart thirty-eight-year-old assistant attorney general named Antonin Scalia. Over the next two years, Cheney and Scalia would become friends and ideological kindred as they teamed up to defend executive privilege and minimize reform. In fact, when it came to illegal wiretapping, Scalia was so valuable to the Ford administration that when his name surfaced in the spring of 1976 as a possible chairman of the Federal Trade Commission, Ford's lawyer Philip Buchen urged the president to leave him at his post as the head of the Department of Justice's Office of Legal Counsel. Buchen wrote that "it would be a severe loss . . . if Scalia were to be asked to leave his present position." He listed seven areas in which Scalia was heavily involved, most related to executive power. Buchen included as number three: "Constitutional issues involved in warrantless electronic surveillance of all types." Scalia's value to Cheney and to the advancement of the power of the presidency would increase exponentially after 1986, when he received his lifetime appointment to the U.S. Supreme Court.

Even prior to the congressional hearings on SHAMROCK and wiretapping, Attorney General Levi had drafted a proposal for legislation regulating electronic surveillance and mail openings for foreign intelligence purposes. Levi envisioned a judicial warrant for such surveillance that would be overseen by a special court. Rumsfeld, Bush, Kissinger, and National Security Advisor Brent Scowcroft were unanimous on Levi's legislative proposal: They didn't like it. (Cheney would certainly have sided with this view, but as usual, left no fingerprints either way.) Among their many complaints summarized in a memo to the president from Buchen in February 1976 was that "the bill unnecessarily derogates from the inherent Constitutional authority of the President to conduct warrantless electronic surveillance for foreign intelligence purposes." Ford lawyer Buchen then added: "(Note: The Attorney General totally disagrees with this argument.)"

In the same memo, Levi argued that the administration had no choice. "Certain committees of Congress will move ahead with their own proposals to control electronic surveillance for foreign intelligence purposes, and only by submitting an Administration proposal can we effectively counter objectionable moves by Congress."

Ford ultimately agreed with Levi and accepted the idea of the legislation. But by that time, Congress and the White House had moved on to the 1976 election. When asked in 2006 about his position on this heated and high-level debate in the Ford administration, Cheney, the chief of staff at the time, professed not to remember Levi's proposal. It would be another president in 1978, Jimmy Carter, who would sign what would be known as the Foreign Intelligence Surveillance Act (FISA). And a little less than thirty years later, Cheney would get another crack at FISA.

In the Ford administration, Cheney received his first experience in the major leagues of bureaucratic combat—the White House. It turned out he had a natural talent for it. Cheney's perch as chief of staff allowed him to eliminate his opponents stealthily, often without having to expose himself personally. He had a great teacher and ally in Donald Rumsfeld.

Without doubt the biggest trophy Cheney and Rumsfeld put on their wall during this period was that of the head of Vice President Nelson Rockefeller.

Cheney viewed Rockefeller as a political liability and an ideological adversary, and worked to ensure that he never had a role in the administration. Rockefeller, besides being enormously wealthy, had been an accomplished governor of New York and a standard bearer for the moderate wing of the Republican Party. Ford, who was more conservative than his vice president, seemed to want Rockefeller's stature more than his ideology.

Rumsfeld and Cheney loathed Rockefeller's New Deal–style activist vision of government and his partiality for balanced budgets over tax cuts. Cheney would later argue that Ford should have realized that Rockefeller was anathema to the conservative wing of the GOP, and that picking him strengthened the likelihood that California governor Ronald Reagan would challenge the president in the primary. "He should have thought of Reagan as vice president in the summer of 1974, if you are talking strictly in political terms," said Cheney in 1986 at a seminar held at the Miller Center of Public Affairs at the University of Virginia.

Yet Ford wanted Rockefeller to have a role in his administration. He made the VP his chief domestic policy adviser, as chair of the Domestic Council, which shaped policy in areas such as health and education. The appointment created a conflict between Rockefeller and Rumsfeld, who with Cheney had persuaded Ford to veto large initiatives coming out of Congress. Cheney also warned Rumsfeld that if Rockefeller had too big a role in formulating domestic policy, he would be perceived as "the man responsible for drafting the agenda of 1976." He then went on to suggest that "the potential for conservative criticism can be reduced if it is made clear that his jurisdiction includes only domestic policy, and not economic or energy policy." This would eliminate Rockefeller's influence almost entirely, as economic and energy policy were the two main areas on which the administration would focus. Cheney might have been particularly protective of the energy portfolio because of his experience growing up in the oil town of Casper. When Rockefeller suggested a fund to support the development of alternative fuels, Cheney was quick to dismiss the idea. After Ford proposed a comprehensive energy package in 1975 that stressed conservation and limiting dependence on foreign oil, Cheney wrote memos to ensure that this was not misconstrued as an intent to reduce energy consumption.

Cheney did more than write memos to Ford. Working with Rumsfeld, Cheney took the vice president out of the White House policy process. When the vice president proposed an idea to Ford, the president would hand it off to Rumsfeld, and later Cheney, who would then ensure it died somewhere in the bureaucracy. "We built in a major institutional conflict with Nelson Rockefeller, a strong dynamic political leader in his own right," Cheney would later acknowledge. "The Vice President came to a point that he was absolutely convinced that Don Rumsfeld and I were out to scuttle whatever new initiatives he could come up with." Rockefeller was right about that.

"They were two little throat slitters," says a journalist who knew Cheney and Rumsfeld socially at the time.

Cheney would argue in 1977 that the staff structure, as he conceived it, involved "the give and take of ideas, and an idea that goes into that system has to get shot at by its enemies and its opponents—taking a man or woman who's vice-president of the United States and putting him into that has an impact . . . on the others in the process because they react to the vice-president very differently than they do to the director of the OMB [Office of Management and Budget] or their colleagues on the staff." There was no room for Rockefeller.

According to Cheney, his already strained relationship with the vice president hit bottom in September 1975, when Rockefeller opened the vice president's official residence in the old chief of naval operations' house on Observatory Hill. Ford had been its first occupant but hadn't had time to redecorate. Rockefeller finished the job, in part with his own money. "After it was all completed, renovated, furnished and so forth, he had a series of parties for virtually everybody in Washington," Cheney recalled. "He had all the press, congressmen, and administration over. Essentially, everyone in Washington over [government staff classification] GS-12 got invited to the vice president's residence—except me. I was never to attend a function there until Walter Mondale was vice president."

Ironically, Cheney would not only make the vice president's mansion his own home, he would adopt Nelson Rockefeller's operational model for the Bush vice presidency. "Cheney is now doing what he and Rumsfeld blocked Rockefeller from doing—influencing policy," marvels James Cannon, who came into the Ford administration with Rockefeller.

The final push toward irrelevance for Rockefeller occurred at the beginning of November 1975. Ford asked his vice president to withdraw his name for the 1976 reelection campaign and accept lame duck status. In what would become known as the Halloween Massacre, Ford also fired CIA director Bill Colby and Defense Secretary Schlesinger and stripped Secretary of State Kissinger of his dual position as National Security Advisor. Cheney would later say that firing the defense secretary might have been a mistake, but he never expressed any public regret over Colby. Many inside the administration, including Ford, felt that Colby had been too forthcoming with Congress and had laid bare too many CIA secrets.

The big winners of the massacre were Rumsfeld, Cheney, and George H. W. Bush. Rumsfeld finally received his cabinet position, as secretary of defense; Cheney, after only a year in the White House, became chief of staff; and Bush moved from China envoy to director of the CIA. Cheney would admit years later that his was an improbable appointment. "If you were to have sent out a search team to look for a chief of staff when President Ford was trying to replace Don Rumsfeld in the fall of 1975, you would not have picked a thirty-four-year-old graduate school drop-out for the job," he said.

Even more remarkable than a relative youngster acting as White House chief of staff was one running a presidential primary and a general election campaign. Yet that is exactly what Cheney maneuvered himself into doing, ousting sitting campaign chairman Bo Callaway in the process. "Although he kept a low public profile, Cheney had accumulated as much control as some of the better-known chiefs of staff," wrote Press Secretary Ron Nessen in his book on the Ford administration. "Some reporters privately started calling him the Grand Teuton, a complex pun referring to his mountainous home state of Wyoming and the Germanic style of his predecessor in the Nixon Administration, H. R. Haldeman."

Cheney's control of the campaign would come under heavy criticism. Despite the new chief of staff's constant efforts to move Ford to the right, Reagan decided to challenge the sitting president in the GOP primary. When Cheney assumed the role of chief of staff, the campaign was already in disarray. In the months to come, an advisory group to the President Ford Committee (PFC), which included Senators Barry Goldwater and Bob Dole, grumbled about the inability of the White House "to manage the president politically." As chief of staff, Cheney controlled the president's schedule, allowing him to serve as de facto campaign manager. Party elders' complaints of his handling of that control would continue unabated, both publicly and privately, until the end. Cheney would admit "the 1976 campaign was in many respects a series of crises all the way from [the first primary in] New Hampshire in February of 1976 when we won by 1,300 votes to the convention in Kansas City with a lot of wins and losses in between, to the final outcome in November."

To James Cannon, Cheney was in over his head. "Too bad Rumsfeld did not stay for the campaign, Ford might have won a second term," he says from his home in Georgetown. "Cheney was not as good an organizer and he was not as astute politically."

The future vice president clearly learned a number of lessons from the campaigns of '76 beyond the importance of locking up the conservative base. That spring, having won seven primaries, Ford had been in a position to put away Reagan. Then came North Carolina. Cheney would later admit that they made a tactical error in not committing more resources to the state. Rather than finish off Reagan, as George W. Bush would do to John McCain in 2000 in South Carolina, Cheney's inaction allowed the California governor to pull out a victory. Reagan's win in the state invigorated his campaign, and he went on to take a majority of the Arizona delegates and to rout Ford in Texas. Cheney would blame Kissinger for Ford's loss in the Lone Star State, because prior to the primary, the secretary of state had traveled to Africa to speak out against apartheid.

Reagan's decisive victory in Texas meant that the nomination would be decided at the national convention in Kansas City. It also made the platform committee an essential part of the process to win the nomination. Cheney would say a year later, "that platform contained in it the seeds of our demise and our loss of the nomination if it wasn't very well managed." He persuaded Ford to take positions contrary to his administration's policies, yet necessary to win conservative delegates, arguing that what was in the platform didn't really matter in the long run. In particular, at Cheney's urging, a reluctant Ford and Kissinger accepted a "Morality in Foreign Policy Plank." Proposed by Reagan supporters, its ambition was sweeping: ". . . we shall go forward as a united people to forge a lasting peace in the world based upon our deep belief in the rights of man, the rule of law and guidance by the hand of God." It was a harbinger of the neoconservativism and right-wing Christianity that George W. Bush would embrace decades later.

Cheney ran an ultimately successful operation to woo the uncommitted delegates who would select the nominee. Leading up to the convention and throughout the campaign, Cheney pushed a "Rose Garden strategy" of constant official announcements on the White House lawn that were designed to use the power of the presidency whenever possible to enhance Ford's stature, win supporters, and take advantage of earned media. He also had a secret weapon. Ford's convention delegate counter and all-around troubleshooter was James Baker III, later a Bush family handyman who ran the 2000 recount for the GOP. Baker would eventually take over as Ford's campaign manager for the final stretch.

After Ford clinched the nomination, the campaign made up some ground against Democratic candidate Jimmy Carter. Cheney loved the nonstop action, commenting to Nessen before one final campaign swing, "If you like politics, there is not anything comparable to the experience you are about to have. It's going to be a ten-day orgasm."

Then, in the second debate with Carter, Ford made a terrible gaffe that he initially refused to acknowledge, despite Cheney's urging. The president seemed to argue that the Soviets didn't dominate Eastern Europe. But as serious as the debate blunder was the reemergence of a Watergate special prosecutor investigating Ford's alleged misuse of congressional campaign funds. "Given the Nixon experience just two years before, we had no choice but just to sit back and take it," remembered Cheney. "For ten days we were dead in the water until that was finally resolved and the report [exonerating Ford] was ultimately issued."

The night of the election, Ford went to bed with the vote too close to call. The next morning Cheney chaired a meeting of the campaign staff to determine whether to ask for a recount. They decided that Carter had too much of a lead. Ford, who was hoarse and depressed, had Cheney deliver the concession message to the new president-elect.

THREE

Long Strange Trip: Washington to Wyoming to Washington

The day after Jimmy Carter took the presidential oath of office, Dick Cheney left the country. For the first time in years, he and Lynne and their two daughters went on an extended vacation. Before departing for the Bahamas he told the *Casper Star-Tribune* that he was going to "lay in the sun for ten days and think about what to do next." Those who knew Cheney knew what he would do next: move back to Wyoming and run for public office. While the family enjoyed the beach and celebrated Dick's thirty-sixth birthday, Cheney was planning his next career move.

A return to his Bradley Woods sinecure would be a lucrative way station while his plan fell into place. But a steady paycheck wasn't enough. Cheney needed campaign cash. His Nixon and Ford White House connections provided him easy access to the party's fundraising A-list. What he didn't have was a clean shot at public office. Republican senator Clifford Hansen was not going to run for a third term, but his Senate seat had already been claimed by one of Cheney's political mentors, Alan Simpson. That left challenging the state's sole congressman, Democrat Teno Roncalio, but taking on a popular incumbent would not be easy. Then in October 1977, after more than a decade in the House, Roncalio announced his retirement from politics. Two months later, on December 15, Cheney declared himself a candidate. His support would be local, but most of his campaign contributions would come from out of state—as did George W. Bush's money in a Texas congressional race he lost to a Democrat that same year.

"He had already been running the country," Wyoming native John Perry Barlow says in an interview. "Chances were that he knew how to hit the buttons and pull the levers." Barlow was the Sublette County Republican Party chairman. He knew Cheney wasn't quite running the country. But he also knew that no other candidate running for Congress had worked in two presidential administrations.

In 1978, Barlow ran the Bar Cross Land and Livestock Company in Cora. In his spare time, he wrote songs with Bob Weir, a boarding school chum from San Francisco. Weir played rhythm guitar and had helped found a band called the Grateful Dead; Barlow would become one of the band's lyricists. The antiauthoritarian streak Barlow shared with the Dead also led him to the libertarian wing of Wyoming's Republican Party. A polymath with an active life outside the Dead, Barlow would later become a fellow at Harvard University's Institute of Politics and Harvard Law School. Cheney, he says, "seemed like an incredibly smart guy."

The big issue in the state at the time was federal land use policy, says Barlow, who was also on the Wyoming Outdoor Council, a statewide environmental group. Cheney embraced a Western environmental ethic that was simultaneously preservationist and antiregulation. "It's hard to believe now that he was a conservationist," says Barlow. "He had a natural resonance toward biology. The only time I ever saw him thoroughly happy and not exercising power was fishing in my river."

Cheney spent the first half of 1978 introducing himself to a Wyoming he had left more than ten years earlier. He faced two Republican challengers in the September primary. In the general election awaited Democrat Bill Bagley, a Wyoming-born lawyer and Congressman Roncalio's former legislative assistant. Unlike most first-time congressional candidates, Cheney had the services of a national pollster, through his friendship with Bob Teeter, who had worked for the Ford campaign. Teeter's polls showed that while Cheney held a narrow lead against Bagley, he wasn't well known around the state. By mid-June 1978, Cheney had put ten thousand miles on his car, crisscrossing Wyoming in an attempt to rectify that.

Then a family history of heart disease kicked him in the chest.

On June 18, at the end of a hectic weeklong campaign swing through Cheyenne and eastern Laramie County, Cheney awoke in the middle of the night complaining of pain in his arms and back. At 4 A.M. he was admitted to Pershing Memorial Hospital in Cheyenne. The thirty-seven-year-old candidate for Congress had just had his first heart attack.

Doctors transferred him out of the intensive care unit after three days, but kept him in the hospital for another week for observation. On June 29, Cheney returned to Casper, where his campaign aide Mike Patchen told reporters that the candidate would announce his intentions after the July 4 weekend. It was a defining moment for Cheney.

Cheney scheduled a July 12 press conference to announce that the campaign would continue. "The heart attack is not a problem," he reassured reporters. "I look upon it basically, somewhat philosophically, as a warning. I suppose the Dick Cheney of today is a little wiser." Rather than a setback, for Cheney heart disease proved to be a boon. "It didn't look like weakness at all," remembers Barlow. "People felt like it wasn't as significant as it probably was."

Cheney's resilience appealed to the state's sense of identity. "They liked that he was a fighter," says Barlow. "Wyoming is a tough place. If you get thrown off the horse and kicked in the face you're expected to get back on the horse."

The campaign created a fictitious grassroots organization, "Cardiacs for Cheney," to extol the virtues of bouncing back and to address public concerns about the candidate's health. For a month, Cheney took it relatively easy while Lynne, once a state champion baton twirler, campaigned as her husband's surrogate. News coverage of Cheney's heart attack increased his name recognition. To address voter concerns, Cheney sent every registered Republican voter in the state an introspective two-page letter explaining that the heart attack had focused his mind on the importance of public service—and that he had quit smoking.

In 1978 in Wyoming, it was almost possible to meet every voter. In the final months of the primary campaign, the Cheneys set out to do just that. They traveled the state in a Winnebago driven by Cheney's dad, also named Dick. Everybody campaigned, including twelve-year-old Liz and nine-year-old Mary. Wearing a sandwich board that read "Honk if you're for Cheney," Mary would stand in front of the campaign headquarters in Casper.

That September, Cheney trounced his two Republican rivals, neither of whom could compete with his fundraising. He outspent one opponent by a factor of seven. Although Bagley had been campaigning for months, Cheney announced that polls had him leading the Democrat by twenty points. Yet he left nothing to chance. On October 25, former president Ford came to Wyoming to extol his former chief of staff. Ford spoke at a breakfast fundraiser for Cheney at the Petroleum Club in Casper, where he brought in $2,200. Afterward, Cheney and Ford appeared together at a campaign rally.

Large checks from business associations across the nation poured in: the American Dental Political Action Committee, the Amoco Political Action Committee, the Commodity Futures Political Action Fund, and the Weyerhaeuser Special Political Action Committee, to name a few big donors who began Cheney's lifetime relationship with K Street. By the end of October, Cheney had outspent Bagley by more than $30,000—the rough equivalent of a $1 million advantage by today's standards.

In an attempt to recapture some ground, Bagley went negative. At a press conference in Casper, he claimed that Cheney's salary from Bradley Woods and Co. didn't seem to correspond to work performed, which might make it an illegal campaign contribution. Bagley noted that 69 percent of his opponent's campaign contributions came from out of state, where Cheney had spent the last ten years. The Democrat questioned whose interests Cheney would represent in Washington.

Cheney was aggrieved. "I have campaigned on the issues, on my qualifications and attributes, on my hopes and aspirations for our state," he told the *Casper Star-Tribune*. "But a man's patience can only be stretched so far, and I think it's time Mr. Bagley stops talking about me and started talking about himself."

He was on leave from Bradley Woods, Cheney said. As a full-time campaigner, he and his family were living off his savings. And as to the charge that he was a carpetbagger, "If we're going to function solely on the basis that the individual we elect ought to have spent more time in

Wyoming than anybody else, we ought to go find a 104-year-old who never left the state," he said.

On November 7, Wyoming elected Dick Cheney to Congress.

"Dick wasn't like any other freshman," says a colleague who served with him and asked to remain anonymous, because his lobbying practice could be jeopardized by discussing the vice president with a journalist. "Just like [former professional quarterback] Jack Kemp arrived as a celebrity, so did Dick Cheney." Unlike Kemp's, Cheney's celebrity came from a mastery of politics. "He had worked in both the Nixon and Ford administrations," the lobbyist says. "He was someone with a lot of stature. He knew how the institution worked, and he knew what he wanted to achieve."

Cheney also had a good understanding of the workings of the House. Because he had been a legislative fellow in 1968, Cheney was better positioned than most of his colleagues, in particular because he had been assigned to Bill Steiger while Steiger was a bipartisan dealmaker on the Ways and Means Committee. Cheney could also take his cues from Donald Rumsfeld, who had brought him into the Ford administration. Rumsfeld had served four productive terms in Congress and had directed Gerald Ford's campaign for minority leader.

The House of Representatives—with 435 members, twenty-one standing committees and a multiplicity of subcommittees, and, when Cheney arrived, more than a dozen fully staffed party committees and caucuses—can bewilder a freshman. Like Lyndon Johnson before him, and Tom DeLay after, Cheney was one of those members who began an immediate ascent to power. Legislative committee chairmanships, or, for the minority party, "ranking" positions on committees, require seniority and therefore take time to achieve. Often, the shortest path to power is election as chair of one of the party committees or caucuses. By the time his second term began, Cheney had worked the Republican Conference to leverage his celebrity and understanding of the House into the chairmanship of the Republican Policy Committee. With twenty-eight members, including minority leader Bob Michel, the policy committee connected Cheney to the entire Republican Conference.

"Because we were in the minority, we had no specific leadership team. We were more like five among equals," said Mickey Edwards, who represented an Oklahoma district while Cheney was in the House. Edwards chaired the House Research Committee, at a time when party caucuses, committees, and study groups had real power. (After the Republicans took control of the House in 1994, Newt Gingrich cut funding for many party caucuses and reduced the number of committee staffers in order to strengthen the leadership and eliminate competition.) "The relative power depended upon the chair and how the chair used that power," says Edwards. Cheney used his position as chair of the Policy Committee effectively. So effectively that he quickly eclipsed Trent Lott, the odds-on favorite to succeed minority leader Michel until Cheney started working the House. Cheney's rise to power was so rapid that Lott, minority whip and heir apparent, understood that he had lost his lock on the leadership position. He left the House to run for John Stennis's vacant Senate seat. "It influenced Trent's decision to run for the Senate," says Edwards, a professor at Princeton. Pushed out of the leadership race by Cheney, Lott couldn't resist one parting shot. As he left the House, Lott openly complained that he didn't believe Cheney would be a good choice to replace Michel.

The chairmanship of the House Policy Committee provided another advantage: Cheney attended regular leadership meetings. "Cheney immediately became a core part of the establishment," says congressional scholar Norman Ornstein. "He was a leader. He came to Congress without trying to impress anyone. He never stepped out of line."

Yet Cheney was a leader in a minority conference that had almost no influence on legislation passed by the House. The Republicans had been out of power for twenty-five years and the Democrats had an overwhelming (276–159) governing majority. "There's always been this talk about how we treated them fairly," says a Democratic staffer who served in the House while Cheney did. "But we treated them like shit. They didn't matter." Republicans in the House were legislative supplicants. Cheney's entire tenure in Congress occurred while the Democrats, through the "old bull" system of committee chair*men*—the omnipotent, institutional Democratic chairs who treated their committees like personal fiefdoms—controlled the content and flow of legislation. Not only was Cheney a member of a disaffected minority party, he was a minority member of a Democratic Congress that had reasserted its power by ending the career of Richard Nixon and imposing limits on the authority of Gerald Ford— the two presidents for whom Cheney had worked.

The freshman from Wyoming was calculating rather than reactive. Despite his conservative ideology and his frustration with minority status, he was never openly associated with the partisan activists who immediately fell in behind Newt Gingrich. "What you saw was someone who was a natural leader," says Ornstein. "He was clearly on the leadership path. But it came to him." A political consultant who worked in the first Bush administration agreed. "Power came to him, he didn't go looking for power," he says.

"Newt arrived with a fully developed strategy for winning the House," says Ornstein. "Cheney felt the frustration of being in the minority. He understood where Newt came from." Yet while Gingrich would recruit and lead a small cabal of radical conservative partisans who mounted a legislative guerrilla campaign against the Democrats, Cheney maintained generally cordial relationships with the majority. Within his own conference, he served as a bridge between the Gingrich faction and the more cautious members led by minority leader Bob Michel.

"I sensed early on that he was an institutionalist," says Ornstein. "He cared about institutions. He had a good relationship with [Democratic majority leader and later Speaker] Tom Foley. He really cared about how the institution worked." Cheney, in fact, was all over the institution. He would serve on the House Interior Affairs Committee, the Ethics Committee, and the Intelligence Committee. Cheney also joined the Wednesday Group, an unofficial caucus of moderate (for the most part) Republicans, none of whom were associated with the Gingrich radicals. It was an intriguing approach. Here was a hardened ideological conservative associated with Republican moderates and following the traditional path to power. At the same time, Cheney maintained contacts with the hardright putschists plotting a takeover.

Cheney also found a social niche in the institution, in the legendary hall parties House members threw after hours in the House office buildings on Independence Avenue. Though it doesn't fit the public persona of the staid vice president, Dick Cheney was a guy who enjoyed a rowdy evening in the halls of whichever office building was designated for a Friday night hall party. Food and liquor materialized from members' offices for gatherings that would go on until early morning. "It was good fun," says a former staffer who was a hall party regular. "And Dick Cheney was fun. He was funny and witty, just like the rest of the guys, but maybe better. There were a bunch, Jerry Lewis, Jack Kemp." Asked if wives attended, the former staffer says: "Women, yes; wives, none that I remember." The hall parties took place at a time before the press began reporting on the personal lives or moral transgressions of public figures.

Asked if the Democrats had similar parties, she said, "None that you would want to go to. The Democrats were boring liberals. Dick was one of the guys. It's hard to imagine him there now." Sometimes, she says, the parties spilled over into the following day and moved out onto Chesapeake Bay, where a few members had large fishing boats that would be lashed together to form floating party barges.

The hall parties are not a slice of congressional history in which you would expect to find Dick Cheney. In any event, with the class of '94, and the arrival of the Southern Christian Republicans, the fun was over. Or at least, it was taken out of the halls.

In the House, Dick Cheney quickly found one policy issue that absorbed much of his energy. In Gerald Ford's White House, he had opposed Kissinger's engagement with the Soviet Union and his politics of détente. When Ronald Reagan was elected, Cheney was immediately drawn to the new president's overheated version of the Cold War—in particular, Reagan's pursuit of missile technology.

In the context of the grim logic of mutually assured destruction, the theory behind the MX (missile-experimental) made some sense. MAD was the understanding that if either of the two nuclear superpowers attacked the other with nuclear weapons, a mutually destructive holocaust would ensue. The U.S. military was shifting away from Strangelovian bombers circling the globe awaiting orders to obliterate Russian cities in the event of a Soviet attack. The new defense strategy would rely more heavily on intercontinental ballistic missiles. A weakness in the missile-based defense was the possibility that the Soviets might first target and destroy American missiles, diminishing the mutual part of the assured destruction. Enter the MX. First proposed in 1971 by the Strategic Air Command, it represented a new kind of destructive force. With the capability to travel more than four thousand miles, an MX rocket carried ten reentry vehicles that could spread out over three hundred miles. Each of these ten projectiles was armed with a three-hundred-kiloton warhead, twenty-five times more powerful than the bomb dropped on Hiroshima. To prevent the Soviets from knowing where the missiles were, they would be mobile, trucked around interstate highways, loaded onto rail cars, or even submerged in lakes.

Ranchers were galvanized in opposition to the MX supermissile. The MX was a seventy-one-foot-long canister that weighed 190,000 pounds, so missile-emplacement holes were a big piece of the debate, considering there would be at least four thousand and perhaps as many as five thousand. The idea of dragging four hundred missiles out of the ground at night to move them around in what critics called a "missile shell game" worried residents of the western states where the missiles would be based. It worried the Soviets, who—like the Americans—depended on satellites to count land-based missiles to ensure the other side wasn't cheating on its agreed limit. For most of his one term in the White House, Jimmy Carter struggled with the issue. In June 1979, just in time for Ronald Reagan to use the issue against him, Carter called for two hundred MX missiles and forty-six hundred soft shelters in Utah and Nevada. Once elected, Reagan proposed placing the missiles in superhardened silo clusters. Deemed tactically stupid, this idea quickly died in Congress. Reagan appointed a commission chaired by Brent Scowcroft to find a way to make the MX work. One of its members was Donald Rumsfeld. Their recommendations included a hundred MX missiles placed in existing Minuteman missile silos in Wyoming. Smaller, single-warhead rockets called Midgetmen would complement the MX. Reagan, who taunted the Soviet Union as "the Evil Empire," greeted the report enthusiastically and dubbed the MX the "Peacekeeper."

Speaker of the House Tip O'Neill opposed the missile program. The "evil" is in the White House, O'Neill said: "When you mention the peacekeeper, the president thinks it's a missile. That's not what the Lord meant." The Speaker believed that Christ's Sermon on the Mount was the greatest political speech ever made, but Cheney didn't buy O'Neill's pacifist theology. He accused the Speaker of sullying the dignity of his office. "Such comments poison national politics," Cheney said.

John Perry Barlow was one of many Americans who agreed with O'Neill and objected to "Doomsday on the Range." He saw the missiles as a move away from MAD and toward a first-strike policy. The missiles would be vulnerable in the silos, and so to avoid being wiped out they would be fired first, or placed on computer-triggered "launch-on-warning" systems. It created the Nightmare Scenario: A computer error ends civilization.

Barlow traveled to Washington to work against the MX. "I must have lobbied more than one hundred members of Congress on this, and Dick was the only one who knew more about it than I did," he recalls. *Washington Post* columnist Mary McGrory accompanied Barlow to one meeting with Cheney. McGrory sat listening to the intense debate. As she and Barlow left the meeting, McGrory said, "I think your guy Cheney is the most dangerous person I've ever seen up here." It was a sobering assessment. McGrory had covered Washington since the Depression. Yet there was something disturbing about a young member of Congress as hardened and cold as the concrete silos in which the MX missiles would be buried— and unwilling to concede a single point.

"I felt we were really arguing about the fate of the world," says Barlow. Cheney and Barlow engaged in a protracted debate that ranged from the philosophical to technically arcane questions about "circular error probable to 'MIRV' decoys." "Cheney believes the world is an inherently dangerous place," says Barlow, "and he sees the rest of the world as . . . populated by four-year-olds with automatic weapons."

Throughout his career in Congress, Cheney was an unyielding opponent of détente, or of any engagement with the Soviet Union. A missile launched in the Soviet Union would reach Wyoming in twenty minutes, Cheney said. So in addition to the MX, he wanted the Midgetman, with its single warhead, placed above Minuteman missiles already in silos in Wyoming. The Minuteman-shuffle argument was chilling. Upon launch of the Soviet missiles, all-terrain vehicles would have twenty-two minutes to drive the Midgetman missiles to secure launch sites away from the targeted silos. It was all based on a Rand Corporation study Cheney cited, justifying the necessity of an eclectic and constantly growing nuclear arsenal.

With Reagan in the White House, Cheney was an obvious pick for a congressional delegation trip to Moscow, where the cold warrior from Wyoming could look the enemy in the eye. Minority leader Bob Michel would appoint Cheney to several "codels," but a 1983 Moscow trip on which Cheney was the ranking Republican illustrated just how extreme Cheney's position was. Because he was "ranking," Cheney was invited to meet with Soviet marshal Sergei Akhromeyev, the deputy chief of the Soviet general staff. New York Democrat Thomas Downey was also invited to the meeting, at which Akhromeyev stunned the two congressmen by suggesting the Russians would consider reopening discussions of mutual weapons cuts in Europe and a one-year ban on testing the ten-warhead SS24 ballistic missile—in exchange for an American ban on testing the MX.

No member of Congress had traveled to Moscow since 1979, when U.S.-Soviet relations became strained because of the Soviet invasion of Afghanistan. On a trip that represented a thaw in U.S.-Soviet relations, Downey saw Akhromeyev's comments as a clear signal that the Soviets wanted to move ahead with strategic arms talks. In press accounts at the time, he quoted Akhromeyev saying, "If such a proposal is put forth, it would be considered at the negotiations."

Cheney wouldn't hear it. "Cheney did not want to allow the Russians to appear to be in any way reasonable," Downey says. "He doesn't believe in negotiations. He's completely rigid, states his position, and concedes nothing. There could be no negotiations when his position was: It's my way or the highway." Cheney said Akhromeyev had made no such offer.

Downey and Cheney were friends who disagreed on just about everything. Downey recalls asking Cheney what he expected of the Soviets. "I said, 'You can't expect them to accept all our terms? You can't expect them to surrender?' "

"He said, 'Yeah, yes I can.' "

Downey recalled one moment with Cheney in Moscow that he found particularly sobering. "It was a spectacular night and we walked over to Red Square. There were just the two of us and I asked him what he was thinking.

"He said, 'I think we're standing at Ground Zero.' "

There, on a cold clear night in Moscow, after a day spent in the company of Russian officials, Dick Cheney believed he was standing on the very spot over which one of the three-hundred-kiloton warheads buried in a silo in the American west might one day be detonated.

While Barlow was a persistent opponent of the MX in the early eighties, after the collapse of the Soviet Union he has no longer been as certain. Congress gave Reagan only fifty MX missiles, but his administration's weapons drive started an arms race that included an unworkable space-based defense system called the Strategic Defense Initiative (SDI), also known as Star Wars. Cheney was one of its most enthusiastic proponents in Congress. The Soviet Union's attempt to match the American military buildup contributed to its demise. "He believed that this would scare the Soviet Union into capitulating, and in a sense that and SDI did," Barlow said. "Under the frenzy of spending to keep up they actually rolled over." Barlow is not alone in this view. There is, in fact, a valid argument made by many defense analysts that Ronald Reagan spent the Soviet Union into ruin. Dick Cheney was always eager to buy into another weapons system. "An ICBM perennial," is how one former member of the House described Cheney, whose fight to keep the missile program alive spanned his career in Congress. His advocacy was a complete success. The president got his missiles. The Soviets got word that the United States had the money for a sustained arms race. And the MX's most vocal proponent in Congress got a jobs program for his constituents in Wyoming.

There was in Dick Cheney's early career in Congress a fleeting moment of the western conservationism. In the early eighties, the nation's eighty-million-acre wilderness system was under tremendous pressure from oil and gas interests. Ronald Reagan's interior secretary James Watt was eager to accommodate them. Before he joined the cabinet, Watt worked for the Mountain States Legal Foundation, a front group for industry, where he represented miners, oil and gas interests, and cattlemen working to limit environmental protections. One of many wilderness areas Interior Secretary Watt intended to open up for drilling was Wyoming's Washakie Wilderness. Situated on the edge of Yellowstone National Park, the Washakie is a remote mix of poplar and conifer stands, pristine mountain lakes, river valleys, and streams filled with native cutthroat trout. Initially, Cheney was prepared to go along with Watt and Wyoming's two Republican senators and open the Washakie to drilling.

Then Cheney received more than a thousand letters from constituents, all opposed to opening up even a small section of the Washakie to energy companies. Cheney had filed his own bill, lowering the level of protection for the Washakie. And from his seat on the House Interior Affairs Committee, he spoke with some authority, particularly regarding a designated wilderness area in his home state. After hearing from his constituents, he struck a compromise with Interior Affairs chair Morris Udall. "There is a general feeling in my state that much as we would like the economic benefits from the energy resources in the Washakie, we'd like even more to save a few acres and declare them off-limits: Yellowstone, the Grand Tetons, and the wilderness areas around the parks, which account for less than 8 percent of the state," Cheney said. "Wilderness areas should be the last places we look for energy." The result of Cheney's compromise was the creation of 883,000 acres of protected wilderness in Wyoming. "He was instrumental in hammering out a compromise in what would become the Wyoming Wilderness Act," says Barlow. The late Mo Udall, a pro-wilderness Democrat, also said the road to compromise was through Dick Cheney, and he gave Cheney credit for making the compromise possible.

Today, the Washakie, the best bear habitat in the lower forty-eight states, stands as a monument to Dick Cheney's conservationist moment. But perhaps not for long. Cheney's 2001 energy task force report calls for the opening of wilderness to oil and gas exploration. (That contradicts the legal definition of "wilderness," which precludes anything other than light recreational use and prohibits permanent structures.) Although Congress initially rejected the vice president's energy task force report in 2001, Cheney signed off on memos ordering Bureau of Land Management employees in the west to circumvent Congress by using rulemaking, rather than law, to open up wilderness areas to minerals extraction.

Consequently, drilling for oil and gas is now under way in natural areas protected since LBJ signed the Wilderness Act in 1964. Unless Cheney's policy is reversed, drilling rigs will ultimately find their way to the Washakie Wilderness Area that Cheney helped protect twenty years earlier.

As the sun rose over Managua the day before Dick Cheney took his oath of office as a freshman member of Congress, Anastasio Somoza Debayle began his daily workout: thirty-four laps around the track, ten sit-ups, then five miles on a stationary exercise bike, all under the watchful eyes of armed soldiers posted in towers surrounding the presidential residence.

As one of the most brutal dictators in the Americas finished his workout, he told *Washington Post* reporter Karen De Young that Nicaragua was under control. A day earlier, at a huge antigovernment demonstration, "only" seven people had been wounded by National Guard troops firing on the crowd—a number so insignificant, Somoza said, that it could be considered "a day without violence." This level of domestic tranquillity was achieved by a huge military presence in the city's slums, where youths described as terrorists were rounded up and jailed. Some of the kids Somoza's National Guard picked up were released. Some were later found dead. Some were never found.

Despite the physical vitality Anastasio Somoza strutted for the *Post* reporter, he was damaged goods. The United States had long propped up the Somoza dynasty. ("Somoza may be a son of a bitch, but he's our son of a bitch," FDR famously said of Anastasio's father.) In response to an increase in the brutality that had kept the Somoza dynasty forty years in power, Jimmy Carter cut off all U.S. support. It was foreign policy conducted through the prism of human rights. By 1979 the State Department was working on Somoza's exit strategy. On June 7, the U.S. ambassador in Managua met with Somoza and told him to start packing. He fled to Miami in July 1979, abandoning his country to the leftist Sandinista Front.

The Sandinistas' rise to power in Nicaragua would have enormous consequences in Washington, creating a partisan struggle that would lead to the most serious constitutional crisis since Watergate. It would also define Dick Cheney's career in the House and provide him the opportunity to expand the power of the executive branch—at the expense of the legislative. In the House, Cheney would lead the fight to fund the guerrilla campaign to overthrow the Sandinista government—a regional application of his anti-Soviet policy. Then he would seize control of his party's effort to manage the constitutional crisis created by the illegal funding of the Contras, the anti-Sandinista insurgency. And as his House career came to an end, Cheney would find in the Central American issues that divided Congress the mechanism to overthrow Democratic Speaker Jim Wright.

Reagan's 1980 rout of Jimmy Carter made bold partisans of housebroken House Republicans. After twenty-five years out of power, their moment arrived, and with it a growing sense that the beaten-down leaders of the Republican minority had been too accommodating. The moment was right for a radical conservative who understood the dynamics of institutional power, and Cheney had mastered bureaucratic infighting in the Ford administration. "If you look at his career, he loves power," says a former Democratic congressman. "He always seeks power. He's not uncomfortable exercising power. And he likes operating behind the curtain."

As Cheney acquired power in the House, it's not surprising that he remained behind the curtain. He directed his aide (and high school classmate) David Gribben to attend Gingrich's Conservative Opportunity Society (COS) meetings, where angry young reformers were planning Newt's Revolution. He also ordered Gribben to help the COS's organizational efforts—and, it's safe to assume, to keep a careful watch on what they were about. It wasn't a schedule conflict that kept Cheney from attending the meetings. The COS was Newt's group, whose members were taking far greater risks than the more accommodating Wednesday Groupers. With the great risks came the prospect of great failure.

The COSers were using tactics never before seen in the House. Aware that C-SPAN televised House proceedings as long as a member was on the floor, they began scheduling "special orders" speeches at the end of the day, when the chamber was empty and C-SPAN's cameras were at their disposal. By seizing the night, Gingrich's young Turks found an audience of millions who would watch their attacks on the Democrats, unaware that the speakers were addressing an empty chamber. They also began to create parliamentary barricades that both interfered with and revealed the Democrats' control of the legislative process. Once it became evident that Gingrich was succeeding, Cheney brought the COS discussions into his House Policy Committee—expanding Newt's institutional reach from a half dozen to the thirty members of the Policy Committee.

All the while, Cheney stayed close to Bob Michel, the minority leader Newt claimed was eager to accept the "crumbs the Democrats left on the table." (Michel was also the occasional golfing partner of Democratic Speaker Tip O'Neill, Jr., which Newt's hardened partisans found intolerable.) It would take a while for Cheney to openly embrace Newt's bold tactics.

Cheney was, however, fully engaged in the Cold War as it played out in Central America. He joined the fight to fund the Contras as soon as the Sandinistas came to power. The partisan division in the House grew more acrimonious and personal, in particular after 1982, when an amendment by Massachusetts representative Ed Boland cut off covert military aid to the Contras. By 1985, the effects of the Boland Amendment were constraining the Contras (whose appalling human rights record made them harder to sell to the American public). The American-funded insurgent movement was a motley collective of former Somoza guard members, anti-Sandinista activists, unemployed Nicaraguans who preferred being paid as paramilitaries to "fishing turtle" or picking coffee, and a few genuine democratic reformers. The more marginalized the Contras became, the more dedicated Cheney was to their cause. His colleagues—congressmen such as Henry Hyde, known for his impassioned speaking, and Texan Dick Armey, a vitriolic and aggressive debater—got the attention. But Cheney was quietly persistent, whether speaking on the floor or negotiating with senators or conservative House members he believed could help restart the flow of money to the Contras.

Former congressman Edwards worked with Cheney in trying to build support for the Contras. Edwards says Cheney was a remarkable negotiator. "We spent hours, often late into the night [on Contra negotiations]," he says. "He was calculating and careful. I never saw Dick as anything but unflappable. . . . He never raised his voice. He was so taciturn. He never said much. He was always attentive, but you never knew what he was thinking." Cheney was also hardwired into the Reagan administration. "He was on the Intelligence Committee," Edwards says. "And he had that experience in the Ford administration. I'm not the kind of member who would get a call from the White House. But Dick was."

A Democrat who sat across the table from Cheney agrees, after a fashion. "He's good in negotiating," he says, "because in negotiating with him there's no negotiating. You would have this sense that he's listening intently. But he is an ideological person who was planning his rebuttal or reaction while he appeared to be listening to you. But he won't be moved. He was always anchored by his ideology. He was also anchored by his partisan position." There was also a sense, the Democrat concurs, that Cheney represented the Reagan administration's position, namely, that the defeat of the Contras on the floor of the United States House and Senate rather than on the battlefields of Nicaragua was the fault of cut-and-run Democrats willing to accept a Soviet beachhead in Central America. President Reagan warned of communist insurgents "a two-day drive from the Mexican border"—even if the Soviet Union was on the verge of collapse and the drive from McAllen, Texas, to Tapachula, Mexico, requires four days in a car, and probably a few more in a Cuban military convoy. For a cold warrior like Dick Cheney, the Democrats' obstruction of the president's hard-line position in Nicaragua was deeply disturbing.

Washington Post columnist Mary McGrory described Speaker Tip O'Neill as a leader whose "carpet slipper rhetoric . . . causes more pragmatic Democrats to blush and the more militant to regard him as a hack." O'Neill was far too gregarious and appealing a public persona to be turned into the bête noire House Republicans needed. (He was also notoriously vindictive.) Yet O'Neill was in no way sympathetic with the Contra forces the Republicans celebrated as "freedom fighters." He was getting back-channel reports from his own unconventional intelligence network in Nicaragua: the Maryknoll Sisters. The Speaker's octogenarian aunt Ann was a founding member of the order, which does missionary work in Central America. She put him in contact with her sisters in Nicaragua, where O'Neill got a different account of the Contras. The pedestrian-level reports of bands of insurgents violating the human rights of the rural population they were supposed to be saving from communism disturbed O'Neill, and he became an impassioned opponent. In 1986, for example, he delivered a speech from the well of the House, then immediately cast his vote against a $200 million Contra aid package, a breach of House protocol, under which the Speaker votes only to break a tie. The Republicans were furious with O'Neill. But speaking with the authority of the Catholic Church, and doubled over with bonhomie, this big unmade bed of a man was an unsuitable enemy for Republicans looking to bring down the Democrats.

House Republicans got the break they were looking for when Jim Wright was elected Speaker after O'Neill retired in 1987. Wright was a hard-driving Texas populist, born poor in Fort Worth, decorated as a pilot in World War II, elected to the Texas House in 1947 and the U.S. House in 1954. Slight in physical stature, Wright was a powerful personality and intellect. Thirty-three years in the House made him a skilled legislative tactician. He was also a forceful leader and an old-school populist orator who on occasion would use the prerogatives of the chair to get his bills passed.

Wright's first term was a tour de force. He managed to get all thirteen appropriations bills passed, which no Speaker had achieved since 1954, thus avoiding the sloppy and perennial continuing resolutions that keep government in business. He enacted most of his domestic agenda, including a $12.8 billion tax increase intended to stanch the deficits Reagan had run up in two terms. In one session, in fact, Wright managed to fill the vacuum created by Ronald Reagan's lame-duck presidency. He also managed to enrage Republican House members, in particular Dick Cheney.

Cheney was justifiably angry when Wright broke precedent on one occasion, holding open and almost doubling the standard fifteen-minute voting period in order to give himself more time to muscle Texas Democrat Jim Chapman into changing his vote so a budget reconciliation bill could pass. Wright had already antagonized Republicans by sending the bill back to the Rules Committee to remove a provision that would have ensured its rejection, then adjourning and reconvening the House within a few minutes for a new legislative day because House rules prohibit considering bills under two different rules on the same day. His procedural two-step infuriated Dick Cheney and other Republicans, who would refer to the day as "Black Thursday."

"Jim Wright," Cheney told *The National Journal*'s Richard Cohen, "is a heavy-handed son of a bitch." He told another reporter that he never believed he would "miss Tip O'Neill."

Cheney's profane public mugging of the constitutional officer third in the line of presidential succession was without precedent. It even shocked his colleagues in the Republican Conference, though many of them were making the same comments in private. They had reason to worry. Richard Cohen's recap of Wright's first session said a great deal about why a group of House Republicans led by Dick Cheney were convinced they had to destroy Jim Wright:

> At a time when Members of Congress seem to move painfully slowly—or not at all—in addressing issues, Wright has often been well out front in trying to redirect the national agenda. As Speaker, his handling of such controversial issues as international trade and peace in Central America offers a dramatic change in congressional leadership.

Not only was Tip O'Neill's successor accelerating the pace of the House and passing bills that embarrassed Reagan, he was using his office to look for a way out of the foreign-policy dead end in Central America. Wright was a self-taught Latin Americanist who spoke Spanish, knew the players, and had traveled in the region. He joined Reagan in creating a peace process, which suddenly was referred to as Reagan-Wright.

Republicans, for the most, opposed the negotiations and intended to use their collapse to justify rearming and re-funding the Contras. After discussions were under way, Reagan's national security affairs assistant Colin Powell and assistant secretary of state Elliott Abrams traveled to Central America to meet with leaders of four of the five nations involved in the process—all but Nicaragua. They urged the Central American presidents to take a public stance against Nicaragua and thus undermine the peace talks.

Yet Wright kept pushing, working with Costa Rican president Oscar Arias (who would win the Nobel Peace Prize for his efforts). Wright also told the hostile factions that his office door in Washington was open to all of them. In Cheney's view, the Speaker was encroaching on the power of the executive branch—a transgression Cheney found intolerable. Cheney had seen the powers of the presidency eroded after Watergate. Ronald Reagan was a vehicle to restore that power. Jim Wright was an obstruction. Wright's open-door policy provided Cheney the opportunity to begin a campaign that would end Wright's career.

In September 1988 a group of Nicaraguan Contra leaders showed up at Wright's office asking for help with prisoners the Sandinista government had detained during civil unrest. In an interview, Wright said he found it unusual that they showed up unannounced, but he cleared his schedule. He had already sent word to the CIA that agency operatives creating civil unrest and pushing the Sandinista government to overreach in Nicaragua were violating laws passed by Congress. So Wright informed the Contra delegation that they could no longer expect CIA agitators to work on their behalf.

"That got back to Cheney and Elliott Abrams, and they were furious," Wright says. The State Department moved the Contra delegation along to the offices of the right-wing *Washington Times*. There, they told the editorial staff what Wright had revealed to them—that the CIA was provoking civil unrest in Managua. A week later, Wright was blindsided by a *Washington Times* reporter who said that several sources told him Wright had leaked classified CIA activity in Nicaragua. Wright, in fact, had conveyed in a closed meeting with the Contra delegation nothing they didn't already know.

Dick Cheney demanded that Wright be investigated. The Speaker of the House had been set up by the State Department so that Cheney could take him down. Again Cheney focused his argument on leaking. Speaking as a member of the Intelligence Committee, he cited major "institutional questions that go to the integrity of the House, to the integrity of the oversight process in the area of intelligence, and to the operation of the Intelligence Committee."

Newsday investigative reporter Roy Gutman followed the story to Foggy Bottom, where he verified that a political appointee at the State Department had sent the Contra delegation to the *Washington Times* office with specific instructions to leak the CIA content of their conversation with Wright. Cheney seized the moment and the attention of the press. He and minority leader Bob Michel filed a complaint with the Ethics Committee and demanded an investigation by the Intelligence Committee. They claimed Wright had compromised U.S. intelligence operations.

In his office at the Texas Christian University library in Fort Worth, Wright, who had been Michel's host at a golf tournament several days before the minority leader filed his ethics complaint, still seems unable to come to terms with what was done to him. "I got no warning from them. I expected him—if not Cheney, then certainly Bob Michel—to say 'Jim, can you tell us about this? What does it involve?' I heard nothing from them, except that they were requesting an ethics investigation. It was the sort of thing I couldn't imagine Bob Michel doing. We had a good working relationship, and I held him in high regard."

Michel later apologized to Wright. He said Cheney had put so much pressure on him that he acquiesced and co-filed the ethics complaint. Cheney was not yet minority whip, so Michel put the imprimatur of the House leadership on the complaint against Wright.

The filing of the complaint in September 1988 began the end of Jim Wright's career. Cheney, who assumed he would soon become minority leader, was eliminating a powerful adversary, as he had moved Nelson Rockefeller out of the Ford administration. Newt Gingrich would pick up where Cheney left off. Over the course of the following year, Wright would be accused of defending Texas S&L owners as the industry collapsed. Ultimately, he would be drummed out of Congress because friends and supporters placed bulk orders for a book he had written, which came to be construed as undisclosed campaign contributions, and because it was alleged by the House Ethics Committee that he received an undisclosed gift in the form of two apartments made available for his use by a Dallas businessman.

Wright resigned his seat in Congress on May 31, 1989, six weeks after a team of FBI agents had walked into his office and told him they were doing a background check on Dick Cheney. "I told them, 'Dick Cheney is a patriotic person who is devoted to the interests of the United States and will be completely dedicated to the president, in my opinion,' " Wright says. "That he would make a good secretary of defense." That same night, Jim and Betty Wright ran into Dick and Lynne Cheney at the Ford Theater.

"We walked in and Dick was there," says Wright. "He stood up and whispered in my ear, 'Thanks for the very nice response to the investigating committee.' "

FOUR

Covert Cover-up

On October 5, 1986, a Sandinista soldier fired a surface-to-air missile and ended Ronald Reagan's secret war in Nicaragua. The president and his covert warriors in the White House would have been better off if the entire crew of the CIA transport shot down in southern Nicaragua had died. But a "cargo kicker" dropping supplies to the Contras ignored instructions and wore a parachute. As the plane crashed into the jungle, he floated down into the arms of Sandinista soldiers waiting on the ground. The following day, newspapers around the world featured photos of Eugene Hasenfus, a down-on-his-luck construction worker from Wisconsin who had found temporary work with CIA contractors.

Two weeks later, at a secret meeting of the House Intelligence Committee, Assistant Secretary of State Elliott Abrams tried to cover the administration's tracks. Wiry and strident, Abrams was a self-declared former socialist who had embraced neoconservatism with a zealous intensity, even marrying the daughter of one of the movement's leading lights, Norman Podhoretz. In the meeting, Abrams and CIA officials assured committee members that the U.S. government was not involved in any way in supplying the Contras, according to a summary classified "Top Secret Veil." They had nothing to do with the Hasenfus trip. All U.S. officials had done was offer public encouragement, Abrams said. It was a brazen lie. The Democrats on the committee didn't believe a word of it, but the story was good enough for one of its Republican members, Dick Cheney.

"Mr. Cheney said he found our ignorance credible," read the summary written by the administration staffer taking notes that day in the secure committee room on the fourth floor of the Capitol dome.

For years Cheney had attempted to convince his colleagues that they should support Ronald Reagan's wars in Central America, but had met with mixed results at best. The Democratic Congress had been inconsistent in its support. So zealots like Abrams and Lt. Col. Oliver North took matters into their own hands. When Hasenfus went down, North, who stage-directed the Contra operation out of the National Security Council in the White House, was on his way to Frankfurt, West Germany. North was negotiating with a delegation from Iran—a country designated a supporter of international terrorism by the U.S. State Department—as part of an ongoing effort to exchange arms for U.S. hostages held by the Iranian-backed Hezbollah guerrillas. He was selling missiles to a regime that had all but declared war on America. Hasenfus's capture forced the colonel to cut short his trip and return to Washington, D.C., as the administration, from President Reagan on down, went into full public denial mode. Cheney, an ardent cold warrior, was no exception.

On November 3, the Lebanese weekly *Ash-Shiraa* published a story about a secret trip to Tehran the previous May by former U.S. national security advisor Robert McFarlane. The U.S. media picked up the story and added new details to an emerging portrait of Keystone Kops diplomacy in which North gave the Iranians a Bible inscribed by Reagan and, to sweeten the deal, a chocolate cake. The Iranians had, in response, stalled. Hezbollah released a few hostages and then picked up a few more.

Debate began within the administration over how much to reveal to Congress and the public. At the urging of CIA director Bill Casey and Vice Admiral John Poindexter, who had replaced McFarlane as national security advisor, the president agreed to downplay the extent of the administration's dealings with Iran. At the time, they believed that negotiations with Iran would continue. "Must say something because I'm being held out to dry," Reagan said, according to notes of an internal White House meeting on November 10.

The White House staff decided the president would speak to the nation and tell the American public that the talks with Iran had been about restoring normal relations rather than bartering for hostages. The day before Reagan's speech, he and other senior White House officials met with the four leaders of Congress in the White House Situation Room to give them a preview. House minority leader Bob Michel sent Cheney in his stead. At the meeting, Reagan fed the congressional leaders the same lies he would tell the American public the next night. In his address, he claimed that the weapons and spare parts shipped to Iran "could easily fit into a single cargo plane." In reality, there were more than a thousand missiles over several shipments.

Again, Cheney, the good soldier, tried to hold the line, telling *The New York Times* after the speech that he took "issue with describing the efforts as arms for hostages," and warning critics against "Monday-morning quarterbacking."

But disclosures quickly overtook denials. By the end of November, White House efforts to contain the story veered toward obstruction of justice. U.S. attorney general Edwin Meese conducted an "investigation" into the affair. The inquiry smacked of a cover-up, as Meese declined an FBI offer of assistance and failed to take notes of his interviews. During his probe, the attorney general discovered a memo drafted by North in early April 1986 that detailed how $12 million from the arms sales to Iran would be diverted to the Contras. The two strands of an illegal policy came together in that memo. Poindexter and North had missed the document during a frenzy of shredding and alterations of official records that had started in October. Among the documents they did destroy was a retroactive Presidential Finding from December 1985 that gave official authorization to the transfer of HAWK missile parts to Iran the previous November. The finding was never shared with Congress at the time, as required by law. On November 25, Poindexter resigned and the White House sent North back to the Marine Corps.

Democrat Jim Wright, elected Speaker of the House in the beginning of 1987, realized administration officials had violated a number of laws, starting with the Boland Amendments that prohibited military aid to the

Contras. North, Casey, and Poindexter had constructed a parallel foreign policy operation with third-country funding and paid mercenaries—all beyond the reach of the congressional authority enshrined in the Constitution. In the process they had violated at least four federal statutes.

Democratic congressional majorities in both the Senate and the House guaranteed that there would be hearings in what was shaping up to be the worst constitutional crisis since Watergate. It was time for Dick Cheney to advance from foot soldier to general—a commission that he instinctively felt belonged to him. He would be at the center of the successful attempt to defend Reagan, using the opportunity not only to turn defeat into victory, but ultimately to expand the constitutional role of the president to conduct foreign policy.

Months later, when Cheney finally questioned Poindexter, he addressed that first November meeting in the Situation Room. Cheney felt at home in the Sit Room, dating back to his time as deputy chief of staff for Ford more than a decade earlier. He chided White House officials for lying to him, because it was counterproductive to the cause: "The point is, if the relationship is going to work long-term, there have to be a handful of members of Congress who have enough knowledge about policy to be able to do whatever needs to be done on the Hill to support and sustain the President's efforts downtown."

When it came to blunting the investigation of the Iran-Contra affair, from 1987 to 1992, Cheney would fill that role.

Going into the 100th Congress in January 1987, Wright believed he faced a difficult situation. Both the Senate and the House had appointed committees to look into the scandal. Laws had been broken. Attorney General Edwin Meese had requested an independent counsel to investigate, and a three-judge panel of the U.S. Court of Appeals had tapped retired federal judge Lawrence Walsh. "I could see the potential for a carnival atmosphere," remembers Wright.

Some Democrats in the House were talking about impeachment, and Wright wanted to stifle that idea as quickly as possible. Both Wright and Senate majority leader Robert Byrd had gone through the trauma of Watergate, and neither had the stomach for a repeat. "That is the last thing I wanted to do," Wright says. "Ronald Reagan had only two years left in his term. I was not going to allow a procedure that would lead to his impeachment in his final year in office."

The two men decided on a first-ever joint House-Senate investigative committee. They hoped that a single committee would make the process go more quickly and thus limit the damage to the institution of the presidency. In their vision, the joint committee would be composed of senior members who would be sober enough to prevent the investigation from becoming a witch hunt. Wright remembers telling the Republican leadership, "You appoint and we appoint and we can maintain some control."

Byrd picked as his chairman Hawaii's senator Daniel Inouye, a decorated World War II veteran who had served on the Senate Watergate Committee and the Select Committee on Intelligence. Inouye, in a shrewd gesture of bipartisanship, named New Hampshire Republican senator Warren Rudman to be his vice chair, promising to share all the powers of the chairmanship with him. Rudman was one of only a few former prosecutors to sit on the committee. A supporter of the Contras, Rudman nonetheless thought the White House had improperly bypassed Congress. He would overshadow Inouye.

Wright asked Indiana conservative Democrat Lee Hamilton to chair the House side. Hamilton had an expertise in foreign policy, with service on the Foreign Affairs Committee and as chairman of the House Permanent Select Committee on Intelligence. He, like Inouye, had an abiding faith that bipartisanship was essential to the proper function of government. Wright also named several of the more powerful Democratic committee chairmen in the House. While these men provided the gravitas the Speaker sought, the time-consuming responsibility of running their own committees hindered their effectiveness in investigating the scandal.

Republican minority leader Bob Michel chose six committee members. His choices reflected a different agenda than the Speaker's. Michel selected Cheney to be the ranking Republican House member. Few were more knowledgeable when it came to intelligence issues, better positioned to understand what was at stake, and as ruthlessly partisan. According to one well-placed committee staffer, Cheney was the White House's guy on the committee, and the conduit through which the White House communicated with the Republican minority.

To accompany Cheney, Michel added several of the more ideological

House Republicans, including Henry Hyde of Illinois and Bill McCollum of Florida. Both men would go on to be key lieutenants in Newt Gingrich's revolution and House managers in the impeachment of President Bill Clinton. As early as 1987, they were ready to burn the village to the ground in order to save it from the Democrats. This time, their contempt for an institution and its established order was not focused on the executive, but on a Democratic Congress.

The Democrats began with a disadvantage that resulted from their deference to the executive. Wright had lost leverage by making it clear that impeachment was not an option. The committee ignored important evidence, including recordings of Reagan's phone conversations with foreign leaders involved in third-party funding. While his expertise was unquestioned, Hamilton's desire to be fair, and his middle-of-the-road orientation, made him an easy mark for the Republican House members, who wanted the committee to fail. Hamilton worried about the potential damage to the government from an activist investigation that would lead to impeachment. "The real question was whether Reagan would be able to govern," he recalls today.

But it wasn't enough for the Republicans that the Democrats had declared they would not pursue impeachment. Their goal was to prevent *any* damage to the Reagan administration. "It was obvious that Dick Cheney and others were more interested in protecting the president than in finding out what had happened," says Rudman today from his Washington, D.C., law firm. And Cheney had a broader agenda: to ensure that the committee would in no way diminish the powers of the executive branch.

As he had done throughout his career, Cheney lulled his enemies into underestimating him. He wasn't a table-pounder. "I never felt on his part any incivility or anger," says Hamilton, who can't recall his colleague's ever losing his temper during their meetings.

Cheney preferred to operate behind the scenes. Sometimes he would even send a proxy to the committee leadership meetings. "You saw the results of his work, but you rarely saw what he did," remembers a Democratic committee staffer. "We totally misread the guy. We thought he was more philosophical than political."

The Republicans got a big break on February 2, 1987, when CIA director Bill Casey resigned because of a lymphoma that had spread to the lining of his brain. He was a key witness. Casey had directed North to set up "the Enterprise," a secret organization run by General Richard Secord that trained, supplied, and even fought for the Contras—and in the process evaded Congress's intent to limit support for the rebel group. North would testify that Casey had suggested that the Enterprise could become a model for other covert operations around the world. Casey had been the first to propose hitting up third parties, including Saudi Arabia and Israel, for money to aid the Contras, despite the objections of Secretary of State George Shultz, who worried that "every quid had a quo." As one Democratic congressman would put it, Casey was the "godfather" of the scandal.

In April, Cheney told a UPI reporter that Casey was "one of the best CIA directors the agency had ever had." He continued: "I don't think it's fair for people to criticize the man based on speculation and innuendo, and to do it at a time when he is incapable of defending himself strikes me as in extremely poor taste."

The day after the hearings began on May 6, 1987, Casey died of pneumonia. In death he would become a helpful scapegoat for Oliver North and a resting place for missing information that would have filled out the contours of the scandal. But even in his absence, four CIA officials were eventually charged with criminal offenses. (The first Bush administration would pardon three of them and stymie the investigation of the fourth by refusing to declassify information needed for his defense—the same "graymail" tactic Cheney's vice presidential chief of staff, Scooter Libby, would use years later in an attempt to block his own prosecution.)

By early April 1987, Cheney was meeting with the Democratic leaders to discuss the logistics of the hearings. "Lee Hamilton and I bent over backwards to be fair to the Republicans," recalls Wright. Rudman represented a bloc of moderate Senate Republicans who parted company with their more partisan House colleagues. "The meetings were very, very intensive," Rudman says.

The first fight was over how long the hearings would last. The Republicans wanted it over quickly—"like tomorrow," one former staffer jokes. "Did I know Dick wanted to shorten it? Yes, I knew that," says Hamilton. The Democrats, fearful of being labeled as overly partisan for extending the proceedings into the 1988 election year, agreed to an artificial ten-month deadline to complete the investigation and issue a report. It was an invitation to the administration to stall while simultaneously burying the committee under mountains of useless information. Toward the conclusion, in the fall of 1987, committee investigators kept discovering new evidence, such as White House backup computer files. "We wanted to keep it going," recalls one staffer. "Cheney didn't want to do that." His view that the committee should stick to its schedule won out.

One of the biggest issues facing the committee was what to do about the special prosecutor. It would be impossible to obtain candid testimony from North or Poindexter if the threat of criminal prosecution hung over them. To avoid being prosecuted for their testimony, the two men would likely take the Fifth and refuse to respond. Rudman and Senate counsel Arthur Liman urged Walsh to obtain a quick conviction by prosecuting North right away for obstructing justice with his shredding party. The Republican senator thought he could get his Republican committee members to defer their investigation until after such a prosecution, thus satisfying the interests of justice and getting the whole truth into the open. The special prosecutor with the political tin ear declined. He envisioned a much longer case that would take at least a year to prepare and prosecute. "Walsh might have been more successful if he had followed our suggestion when Liman and I met with him," recalls Rudman. "But he had this grand scheme of conspiracy."

Walsh's intransigence forced the committee into a Hobbesian choice: Either abort the investigation, or grant immunity so North could testify.

Cheney argued that North should be spared having to appear before the committee in deference to the criminal case, according to Rudman. Even some Democrats felt that way. "People were all over the lot on that one," Rudman recalls.

Inside the Democratic caucus, the strongest proponent for offering immunity in exchange for quick testimony was Hamilton. "He believed that North had information no one else had," recalls one staffer. Hamilton, like the moderate Republicans, wanted a thorough airing of the details of the scandal, but he was not as keen on a criminal prosecution. As a compromise, the majority agreed to defer the testimony of North and Poindexter until the end of the investigation. With the eventual support of committee member Tom Foley of Washington, Hamilton's view carried the day.

"Hamilton was so fair-minded and balanced that in order to get agreements, he gave ground in areas where he shouldn't have," remembers another committee staffer.

The deal the committee struck with North's canny lawyer, Brendan Sullivan, doomed Walsh's investigation and the hearings. The committee offered North "use immunity," which guaranteed that nothing he said could be used against him in future criminal proceedings. They also agreed to a series of other demands, including that they would not depose North prior to his testimony; that the duration of his testimony would be limited; that they would not have the option of recalling him later; and that he would be allowed to produce documents the committee requested less than a week before he was due to testify.

"I think [Iran-Contra] is radically different from Watergate," Cheney told a reporter on April 6, 1987, almost exactly a month before the hearings began. "I think there's a very real possibility that it's going to be at best a footnote in the history books."

The preconditions Cheney championed all but guaranteed that the substance of Iran-Contra would be forgotten.

To accommodate more than two dozen congressmen plus their staff, the joint committees built expensive two-tiered stages for the televised hearings. Director Steven Spielberg would later comment to Senate counsel Arthur Liman that the setup worked in favor of the witnesses, who would be shown on television "at the hero's angle, looking up as though from a pit at the committees, who resembled two rows of judges at the Spanish Inquisition." (When it came time to hold hearings for the Supreme Court confirmation of Judge Robert Bork later that year, Senate Democrats made sure they sat on level ground.)

Central Casting couldn't have chosen better characters to occupy the "villains' angle." In addition to the often bloviating congressmen, the two chief interrogators for the Senate and House were Liman and John Nields, the first a nasal-voiced New York ethnic with "spaghetti hair," and the second a balding lawyer with long locks down to his collar who couldn't keep his distaste for the witnesses from creeping into his voice. The two men would meet their match in Oliver North. And as Dick

Cheney would do throughout his career, he would be right behind his leading man, helping him along and reaping the benefits.

Cheney's opening statement explained his intentions for the hearings. At the time, Republicans were still playing defense. "Some will argue that these events justify the imposition of additional restrictions on presidents to prohibit the possibility of similar occurrences in the future," Cheney intoned. "In my opinion, that would be a mistake. In completing our task, we should seek above all to find ways to strengthen the capacity of future presidents and future Congresses to meet the often dangerous and difficult challenges that are bound to rise in the years ahead."

Through the first several witnesses, Cheney began to develop his themes, a counter-narrative to Iran-Contra that would have been absurd if not delivered in such a measured and matter-of-fact way by the congressman from Wyoming. Cheney's first point came as early as his opening statement, when he said, "One important question to be asked is to what extent did the lack of a clear-cut policy by the Congress contribute to the events we will be exploring in the weeks ahead?"

Cheney and the administration witnesses tried to make the case that because Congress had supported the Contras in the past, its refusal to do so later constituted a form of actionable negligence, which justified the administration's establishing a parallel support network as a "bridging" mechanism until Congress could be brought around to a sensible policy. Cheney's line of argument reached its most ridiculous extreme during his questioning of the notorious CIA agent Felix Rodriguez.

The agency had first recruited Rodriguez, a Cuban exile, in 1967, to train a team to hunt down Ernesto "Che" Guevara in Bolivia. Rodriguez caught the fatally naïve guerrilla leader in the Bolivian highlands in October of that year. After a brief interrogation, Rodriguez had Che executed. In Vietnam, Rodriguez flew helicopter missions and worked with the CIA. One of his superiors and a close friend from Vietnam was Donald Gregg, who would later become national security advisor for Vice President Bush. Gregg had helped place Rodriguez at the Ilopango Air Force Base in El Salvador, where, under the pseudonym Max Gomez, he managed the Contra resupply operation. It was this name that Eugene Hasenfus would tell his Sandinista interrogators was his point of contact. When Hasenfus was shot down, Rodriguez tried to phone Gregg at the

White House to report the news, but he couldn't get through to his former commander.

The extent of Bush's and Gregg's knowledge of the Iran-Contra affair was never fully clarified. But when Cheney questioned Rodriguez before the committee, his intent was not clarification. Instead he changed the subject, asking how folks in the Third World thought the United States measured up in the struggle against global communism. "Can you comment upon the difference in terms of the perception on the part of the people at the local level as to the long-term commitment of the United States versus, say, the long-term commitment of the Soviet Union?" Cheney asked. In courthouse terms, a fact witness was being turned into an expert witness.

Rodriguez was happy to oblige. When it came to consistency in foreign policy, the Soviet Union with its authoritarian government was the standard to beat. "The Soviet Union had a continuous policy no matter who changes in their hierarchy," answered Rodriguez.

Later in the hearings, when North once again blamed Congress and the American people for forcing the administration to lie to them, Senator Rudman had had enough. "The American people have the constitutional right to be wrong," he said. "And what Ronald Reagan thinks or what Oliver North thinks or what I think or what anybody else thinks makes not a whit if the American people say, 'Enough.' "

Rudman jokes today that the remark will probably be on his tombstone. "Yes, Congress voted for the Contras and then they voted against them, but it doesn't matter what the hell they did," he says. "The law changed, but it's still the law. That's just the way the country works."

But for Cheney and administration officials, the law was a secondary issue. Exhibit A was Elliott Abrams, who had denied the existence of third-country funding after himself flying to London to solicit a $10 million contribution from the Sultan of Brunei. He apparently had no qualms about misleading legislators and the American people if it furthered his ideological aims. Abrams would eventually plead guilty to two minor offenses, including withholding information from Congress. In 1992, President George H. W. Bush pardoned Abrams, who never felt it necessary to demonstrate any contrition. When Cheney got his chance to question Abrams—whose public deceptions included a cover-up of the 1981 massacre of almost a thousand civilians by the Salvadoran army at El Mozote—the congressman was effusive in his praise. "I, for one, want to thank you for your efforts over the years," Cheney said in closing. "I do personally believe you have an extremely bright future in the public arena in the United States."

Almost a decade later, Dick Cheney saw to it that Elliott Abrams was appointed deputy national security advisor in the Bush-Cheney White House.

While Cheney and the House Republicans had started the Iran-Contra hearings in a defensive posture, the appearance of Oliver North altered the terms of engagement. "Post-Ollie, their entire mood and goals changed," recalls a Democratic staffer. "It was 'Happy days are here again.' We are going to play this string. This is going nowhere."

On July 7, North first assumed the "hero's angle" in the marbled elegance of Room 325 in the Senate Office Building. He was costumed for the part, in his Marine dress uniform with rows of ribbons pinned to his chest. Over the next six days, he would put on a bravura performance, earnestly wrapping himself in the flag: just an obedient soldier following orders. As one writer would note, North exhibited a righteous glow that made him look "as if he were posing for an inspirational wall hanging." To question poor Ollie was one more injustice in a long history of political perfidy against the armed forces, dating back to Vietnam. "We didn't lose the war in Vietnam, we lost the war right here in this city," North said.

For two days, majority counsel Nields grilled North. During the interrogation, the colonel stated that Casey had directed him to create the clandestine Enterprise organization supporting the Contras, that Poindexter had authorized the transfer of money from the arms sales to the Contras, and that North believed the president was aware of the diversion. Once the operation came into public view, North confessed, he started destroying the evidence. On several occasions he had lied to Congress. North's admissions, delivered with exaggerated self-justification, came out in testy exchanges with a clearly frustrated Nields.

"I'd have offered the Iranians a free trip to Disneyland if we could have gotten Americans home for it," came one typical reply to a line of questioning on giving missiles to that Middle Eastern nation.

"He made all his illegal acts—the lying to the Congress, the diversion, the formation of the Enterprise, the cover-up—seem logical and patriotic," Liman would note with begrudging admiration in his autobiography, *Lawyer.*

It didn't help that Nields chose to target covert operations. The issue divided the Democratic caucus between those who wanted to use the hearings to pursue policy objectives like limiting covert action and those who wanted simply to get to the bottom of what had happened. A focus on covert operations united the House Republicans, as hampering the president's maneuvering room in this area was one of their greatest fears. "The issue for Cheney and Hyde as well as Colby was that [the hearings] would shut down the ability to conduct covert actions," recalls one GOP staffer.

At one point, Nields prodded North: "In certain communist countries, the government's activities are kept secret from the people, but that is not the way we do things in America, is it?"

The question was a slow, hanging ball right over home plate, and North hit it out of the park. His response mirrored Cheney's worldview perfectly: "I think it is very important for the American people to understand that this is a dangerous world, that we live at risk." Translation: Covert operations are essential to keep the nation, and yes, even dimwitted congressmen, safe.

At the end of the first day, Cheney enthused on PBS's *MacNeil/Lehrer NewsHour* that the colonel "probably was as effective as anybody we've had before the committee in coming forward very aggressively and stating what he did, saying why he did it, arguing that he was in fact authorized to take the activities that he did."

As if reading from the same playbook, North developed a theme oft repeated by Cheney and the House Republicans throughout the hearings: Because members of Congress leaked like an old faucet, the legislative branch could not be trusted with classified information that pertained to national security. For North, the argument extended to the hearings themselves: "I believe that these hearings, perhaps unintentionally so, have revealed matters of great secrecy in the operation of our government, and sources and methods of intelligence activities have clearly been revealed, to the detriment of our security."

Inouye forced North to admit that he had no evidence to support such a claim. "The greatest leaks came out of the White House," recalls Rudman. "North and company were the biggest leakers of all during that period." And today it's no different, he says. "Just look at the case now with that CIA agent [Valerie] Plame. God forbid anyone did that on the Hill, there would be hell to pay. The administration would be lining up howitzers on the White House lawn to fire at the Capitol."

On Friday, July 10, the fourth day of North's testimony, Cheney took his turn at questioning the witness. It was more like a duet than an interrogation. "Let me say at the outset that I have been tremendously impressed with the way you have handled yourself in front of the committee," Cheney told North. "And I know I speak for a great many people who have been watching the proceedings, because the Congress has been absolutely buried in the favorable public reaction to your testimony and phone calls and telegrams."

North had taken to putting stacks of supportive telegrams on his witness table, as if the increasingly cowed committee needed a reminder of the tens of thousands of messages of encouragement he had received. Although the telegenic colonel's public support was undeniable, not widely reported at the time was that Western Union offered a half-price special on pro-North telegrams sent to the committee.

Throughout the hearings, and in particular during the North testimony, it was as if the witnesses and the House Republicans were following a hidden script, complete with programmed queries and answers not available to everybody else. "It was apparent to me that there was coordination going on," says Rudman. Bruce Fein, who served as research director on the minority staff, confirms it. "Sure we talked with those folks," he says, and claims it wasn't unusual. "It's not that you lie but this is the way you can coordinate strategy."

As the ranking House Republican on the committee, Dick Cheney was the coordinator of the opposition. Through leading questions, Cheney helped North portray himself as just a guy guilty of wanting "to cut through red tape." Cheney, a man blessed with wonderful comedic timing, played an impeccable straight man. He fretted that North's eagerness to cut corners to help "the Resistance" could generate political opposition that would make it harder for Congress to renew aid.

North made the most out of this invitation to emote:

Hang whatever you want around the neck of Ollie North . . . but for the love of God and the love of this nation, don't hang around Ollie North's neck the cutoff of funds to the Nicaraguan Resistance again.

This country cannot stand that, not just because of Nicaragua, but because of all the other nations in the world who look at us and measure by what we do now in Nicaragua, the measure of our whole commitment to their cause. To things like NATO, to things like our commitment to peace and democracy elsewhere in the world.

The two men were now in the zone, a parallel radical-right fantasyland, blithely ignoring the damage to America's reputation caused by the administration's support for the Contras and its willingness to barter weapons for hostages with Iran and Hezbollah. Forgotten was the U.S. mining of Nicaraguan harbors that had killed innocent civilians and brought a swift condemnation by the World Court. Or the brutal Contra attacks on civilian infrastructure, including medical clinics, which provoked outrage in European capitals. Or even the ridicule to which now emboldened Iranian hard-liners had subjected U.S. overtures.

"And by way of closing, Mr. Chairman, let me again simply thank the witness," concluded Cheney. "Colonel North has been, I think, the most effective and impressive witness certainly this committee has heard, and I know I speak for a great many Americans when I thank him for his years of devoted service to the nation, both in the United States Marine Corps and as a member of the NSC staff. Thank you very much, Colonel North."

Cheney and Hyde had assembled a crackerjack staff that quickly responded to take advantage of the new dynamic of popular sentiment against the hearings that North had set in motion. From the beginning of the hearings, the two Republican congressmen had wanted to stake out a position on how they believed government should work, according to Fein.

Intense and energetic, Fein had worked at the Office of Legal Policy, President Reagan's legal strategy shop in the Justice Department. From there he had gone on to be general counsel of the Federal Communications Commission before answering the call to serve the committee. He wasn't the only Reagan loyalist on the team. Joining him on Cheney's staff was David Addington, a former assistant general counsel for the CIA. After 1984, Addington moved on to the House Committees on Intelligence and International Relations, where he continued to serve the interests of the agency while forging a lasting professional bond with Cheney. "It's on the [Iran-Contra] committee that he and Cheney seemed to really come together," remembers one Democratic staffer.

Working with their best witness, the minority team defined limits to the role of the Congress in conducting foreign policy. In command of the floor, and with the American public watching, North put forth complex constitutional arguments to justify his conduct. In particular, North mentioned a 1936 Supreme Court decision, *United States v. Curtiss-Wright Export Corp.* The case involved an executive order President Roosevelt issued at the behest of Congress, imposing an arms embargo on Bolivia and Paraguay, then at war with each other. Curtiss-Wright Export Corp., charged with violating the ban, argued that the embargo was illegal. The Court upheld the president's order. In his opinion, Justice George Sutherland declared the "exclusive power of the President as the sole organ of the federal government in the field of international relations." (In his opinion, Sutherland misquoted a speech by John Marshall from 1800. Marshall, a Virginia congressman at the time, was arguing not for expansive executive power but for the role of the president as the enforcer of treaties ratified by the Senate.)

"[Cheney and the House Republicans] were forced into the more theoretical arguments about the presidency because of the limitation of the evidence to support their positions [that nothing illegal had occurred]," Hamilton believes.

North's first attempt at referencing Curtiss-Wright occurred during questioning by Senator George Mitchell of Maine. "The Supreme Court held again that it was within the purview of the President of the United States to conduct secret activities and to conduct secret negotiations to further the foreign policy goals of the United States," North declared.

Senator Mitchell happened to be a very good lawyer.

"If I may just say, Colonel, the Curtiss-Wright case said no such thing," Mitchell responded. "I just think the record should reflect that Curtiss-Wright was on a completely different factual situation and there is no such statement in the Curtiss-Wright case."

But North wasn't finished trying to get it into the record. The next day, after careful prompting from another House supporter, New Jersey Republican Jim Courter, North read a quote from Sutherland's opinion.

Here was a career Marine Corps officer with no background in law explicating a Supreme Court case. When Louis Fisher heard North's use of Curtiss-Wright, he thought, "Someone is feeding him this." Fisher was the research director for the majority on the Iran-Contra Committee and a specialist on separation of powers. "This was one of the key arguments used by the Republicans and witnesses, and it was just a misuse of history," he recalls from his office at the Library of Congress, where he started working in March 2006. For thirty-five years the Congressional Research Service employed Fisher, until he wrote a report on whistle-blowers and commented in an online article that Congress and the courts were too deferential to the executive branch. This set off a series of rebukes from his superiors that led to his reassignment to the law office at the Library.

Fisher's job on the Iran-Contra Committee was to protect the legislative branch. In this he sometimes found himself at odds even with some of the committee Democrats who he believes misread Articles I and II of the Constitution, which respectively detail the powers of the Congress and the executive. "Some wanted to declare that the president was preeminent in foreign affairs," he says. "This was the institutional thing that I was supposed to watch."

Cheney had deferred twenty minutes of his allotted time for questioning North in case he had anything to say later. By the end of North's week of testimony, the House Republicans had been so successful that Cheney offered North his remaining time to deliver a slideshow on why funding the Contras was so important. The turnaround from defense to offense was complete.

After twelve weeks and more than two hundred fifty hours of testimony from thirty-two witnesses, all that was left to fight over were the conclusions. The Democratic leadership wanted a unanimous report. In order to placate Republicans, they agreed to leave out controversial aspects of the investigation such as accusations of an administration cover-up and evidence implicating Reagan. The committee produced dozens of drafts and revisions in an attempt to accommodate the minority. Once again, they underestimated Cheney and the House Republicans.

"From the get-go they wanted a minority report," says Fein of Cheney and Hyde.

Over the months of hearings, the minority developed its arguments to counter the mainstream impression of Iran-Contra. "Basically it was the brainchild of Cheney and Hyde, that was 99 percent of it," says Fein, who helped write the report. Fein says that Cheney and Hyde had made their positions so clear during the hearings that it was hardly necessary to consult them to write a report that would advance their arguments.

The official majority report was due to come out on Tuesday, November 17, 1987, but a printing problem delayed it by a day. On November 16, the House Republicans leaked a copy of the minority report to *The New York Times* in a successful attempt to upstage the majority. At a press conference the following day, all the Republicans on the committee save three—Senators Warren Rudman, Paul Trible, and William Cohen—attacked the majority for engaging in a "witch hunt" against Ronald Reagan and his administration. "There was no constitutional crisis, no systematic disrespect for 'the rule of law,' no grand conspiracy, and no administration-wide dishonesty or cover-up," the report read. "In our view the administration did proceed legally in pursuing both its contra policy and the Iran arms initiative."

Rudman called the minority report "pathetic." In a paraphrase of Adlai Stevenson, he said his Republican colleagues had "separated the wheat from the chaff and sowed the chaff."

The detailed minority report included three chapters of legal arguments dating back to the Constitutional Convention justifying why the executive branch had supremacy in foreign affairs. When the report was released, those arguments were largely ignored by the press, which focused instead on the conflict. The Democrats also dismissed the minority's position. "This was '87," remembers one Democratic staff member. "We had a substantial majority and the Republicans were trained to be what we thought was a permanent minority party. When they would yap and yell, we would let them yap. It just didn't matter."

The Democratic-led majority saw Iran-Contra differently, finding that the "clandestine financing operation undermined the powers of Congress as a coequal branch and subverted the Constitution." The administration had violated a key belief of the Framers that "the purse and the sword must never be in the same hands."

Within a week, Cheney's attention had already shifted to thwarting any attempt to use the hearings to enact reforms. On November 23, he held a press breakfast at which he threatened a "big fight" if Democrats tried to impose limits on covert action or the president's ability to conduct foreign policy. What worried Cheney was bipartisan legislation gaining support in the Senate that would require the president to notify Congress of covert actions within forty-eight hours, among other restrictions. In the end, no significant reforms came out of Iran-Contra, in no small part thanks to Cheney.

While Congress was finished, the special prosecutor was just getting started. Oliver North went on trial in February 1989. A jury convicted him on three counts and acquitted him on nine others. A judge gave North a three-year suspended sentence, two years' probation, $150,000 in fines, and twelve hundred hours of community service. A year later, a three-judge appeals court overturned the convictions because the congressional immunity grant had tainted the trial. The same appeals court also overturned a conviction of Admiral Poindexter on five felony charges.

Special Prosecutor Lawrence Walsh had one final big fish on the hook. In the course of his investigation, he discovered that then secretary of defense Caspar Weinberger had lied to investigators and Congress about whether he had kept notes of key meetings. Thus began an arduous attempt to bring Weinberger to trial. By this time, Cheney had already moved on to fill Weinberger's old job at the Pentagon. Yet Cheney's attempt to stymie the investigation of Iran-Contra continued.

At an arraignment of Weinberger on November 24, 1992, an attorney for the special prosecutor complained that Cheney had given Weinberger special access to government files to aid in his defense, as well as information about what investigators were looking at. This was contrary to Defense Department regulations, according to the lawyer. "One of our attorneys found that Weinberger's attorneys had documents that came from the Department of Defense," says a member of Walsh's team. "Cheney was passing them information that pertained to our prosecution. He was working on behalf of Weinberger's defense." At about the same time, Cheney went on *Meet the Press* and called Weinberger's indictment "a travesty."

On Christmas Eve 1992, after having failed in his reelection bid, President George H. W. Bush pardoned those who had been convicted in the special prosecutor's investigation, and threw in a preemptive pardon of Weinberger.

A few days before Christmas in 2005, Vice President Dick Cheney gave the press corps that travels with him a rare opportunity. On a trip to Muscat, Oman, he made himself available to answer questions from reporters on Air Force Two. *The New York Times* had just reported that the administration was involved in a program of warrantless wiretapping, and Cheney had something to say about it. In the course of the conversation, a questioner asked about the vice president's view on "executive power" in light of his experience under Ford. It would be the first time in years that Cheney would mention Iran-Contra.

> If you want reference to an obscure text, go look at the minority views that were filed with the Iran-Contra Committee. . . . Nobody has ever read them, but we—part of the argument in Iran-Contra was whether or not the president had the authority to do what was done in the Reagan years. And those of us in the minority wrote minority views, but they were actually authored by a guy working for me, for my staff, that I think are very good in laying out a robust view of the president's prerogatives with respect to the conduct of especially foreign policy and national security matters. It will give you a much broader perspective. I served in the Congress for ten years. I've got enormous regard for the other body, Title I [*sic*] of the Constitution, but I do believe that, especially in the day and age we live in, the nature of the threats we face, it was true during the Cold War, as well as I think what is true now, the president of the United States needs to have his constitutional powers unimpaired, if you will, in terms of the conduct of national security policy. That's my personal view.

As Cheney is finally in a position to turn his personal views into federal policy, Bruce Fein has parted ways with his old boss. He sees "a chasm of difference" between Iran-Contra and the current secrecy of Bush-Cheney. "Then it was part of the democratic process," he says. "The way you debate the process, it allows for self-correction. This is the essence, the lifeblood of democracy."

Whereas the Reagan administration was forced by a Democratic Congress to reveal its inner workings when it came to covert action, there is no disclosure today. "They think that democracy ends if you win elections," says Fein.

FIVE

Secretary of War

Although he stood just five foot six, John Goodwin Tower was a Texan larger than life.

The son of a Methodist minister, Tower was a World War II veteran who had done graduate work at Southern Methodist University and post-graduate work at the London School of Economics. In England, he had acquired an expansive worldview, an appreciation for tailored suits, and the notion that a public figure's sex life could remain private. The 1960 presidential election provided him a way out of a teaching position at an undistinguished state university in Texas. Tower ran for the Senate against LBJ, whose name appeared on the ballot twice in 1960—for the Senate seat he'd held since 1948 and for the vice presidency. When Johnson vacated his Senate seat in 1961, Tower was positioned to run again. He emerged from a pack of seventy-one candidates, and after a runoff, he became the first Texas Republican to win a statewide election since Reconstruction.

In Texas, John Tower worked to build a Republican Party where there was none, and helped the senior George Bush win a seat in the U.S. House. In Washington, he distinguished himself as a senator with a remarkable grasp of defense and banking policy. He left the Senate in 1985 and briefly campaigned to become Ronald Reagan's defense secretary. Reagan appointed him to lead the U.S. team in Geneva, negotiating nuclear arms reductions in formal bilateral talks with the Soviet Union. Along the way, Tower booked $750,000 in defense industry lobbying and consulting accounts. It was his experience in Geneva, his position on the Senate Armed Services Committee, and his generous political support that led President George H. W. Bush to nominate John Tower as secretary of defense in 1989. It was also Tower's experience in Geneva that ultimately made Dick Cheney secretary of defense.

John Tower was ideologically consistent—a fiscal conservative regarding domestic issues and a Cold War conservative when it came to foreign policy. He was equally consistent in what should have been his private life. The sort of Armed Services Committee chairman for whom "procurement" was a double entendre, Tower was a notorious drunk and a domestic and foreign ass-grabber with few peers in the United States Senate—a poor choice to send to arms negotiations in Geneva in 1985. The Soviet Union was a dangerous nuclear adversary. Tower was the custodian of his country's weapons intelligence. And Geneva was an international center of espionage, where attractive female Soviet agents known as "swallows" worked in bars, restaurants, and hotels.

Tower's colleagues on the Senate Armed Services Committee could not have been unaware of his drinking and the accounts of his pursuit of women. But a cabinet nomination entailed a level of scrutiny he couldn't withstand. An FBI background investigation of the former senator found a situation in Geneva so bad that the CIA had been called in to investigate American negotiators in 1985 and 1986. The agency's 120-page report confirmed that swallows from the KGB (Soviet intelligence) were assigned to U.S. negotiators. There were uncorroborated accounts of fourteen extramarital relationships in the U.S. delegation, some involving foreign women. Delegation members frequented bars that were known KGB hangouts. At one drunken bash, people drank from the shoe of a delegation member. Investigators even turned up a double-ended dildo.

The background report—and, of equal importance, concerns about Tower's close and possibly compromised relations with defense contractors—cost him the support of the Georgia Democrat who chaired the Senate Armed Services Committee. Senator Sam Nunn told reporters that the secretary of defense job required clarity of thought twenty-four hours a day, implying that Tower's drinking would present a problem. (Nunn also had concerns about Tower's defense industry contacts, but stories of sex and alcohol seize the public's attention and always make for a more marketable narrative than does corruption.) When his former colleagues on the Armed Services Committee rejected him by an 11–9 vote, it was over, even if the president refused to move on to a new candidate.

Dick Cheney has often had the good fortune or good sense to be in the right place at the right time. On the night of the committee vote, he was at the vice presidential residence with Dan Quayle, who was looking for someone to salvage the nomination. Cheney told the vice president it was over. "Tower's down the tubes. You've got to get someone to work with Congress," Cheney said, according to *Washington Post* editor Bob Woodward.

More than two weeks after Cheney's meeting with Quayle, the Senate rejected Tower's nomination by a 53–47 vote. George H. W. Bush became the first U.S. president to lose a first-round cabinet appointment. "There were Tower people moving into Pentagon offices and waiting for the secretary to be confirmed," says a former Defense Department employee. "Everything was on hold. We were going to go into May without a secretary." Bush had to find a nominee the Senate would confirm with no delay.

Cheney had warned the president that Tower's nomination was dead. He also suggested the president find someone "to work with Congress." Cheney himself fit the bill. His unopposed election as minority whip established his ability to work with Congress. He was a loyal lieutenant in the Republican Party. And he was the only member of the House to have served as a White House chief of staff. On the day the Senate voted to reject John Tower, Bush chief of staff John Sununu called Cheney over to the White House. Sununu and Bush national security advisor Brent Scowcroft were waiting in the office Cheney had occupied when he was Gerald Ford's chief of staff. Sununu asked Cheney whether he would accept the appointment if Bush offered it to him.

Cheney was Brent Scowcroft's choice. The two men had worked together in the Ford administration. "We needed a secretary of defense very badly," Scowcroft told James Mann, the *Los Angeles Times* reporter who wrote *Rise of the Vulcans*. "This was already March, and we just couldn't make policy with a big gap there. So we needed somebody fast. That meant it had to be somebody from the Congress because otherwise we'd go through long hearings. And then I automatically went to Cheney."

The FBI waved Cheney through. The only obstacle remaining was the questions that would be raised—as they are each time Dick Cheney makes a career move—about his heart. At forty-eight, he had already had three heart attacks. The previous August he had undergone quadruple by-pass surgery. It was an elective procedure, he told Sununu and Scowcroft. He did it because he wanted to continue downhill skiing. A cardiologist would, as always, provide medical records attesting that Cheney's heart was up to the job.

The nomination was announced the day after the Senate rejected Tower. And although confirmation looked like a formality, Cheney took no chances. He had watched the White House string John Tower's nomination along until the FBI provided his opponents with the information to destroy his career. He wasn't going to allow Bush's staff to handle his confirmation vote in the Senate. Cheney asked Alan Kranowitz to take charge of the process. Kranowitz was a friend who had worked as an aide for Democratic senator Thomas Dodd, for the Reagan White House, for House minority leader Bob Michel, and for Cheney.

Dick Cheney had never served in the military. He had received five deferments during the Vietnam War. He had never served on a House committee that dealt with military issues. But he was a proven leader in the House and had no skeletons (or dildos) in his closet. His confirmation vote would be a cinch in the Senate.

Sooner or later, it seems, someone always asks: What about Dick?

"The whole world we live in would be totally different if Dick Cheney had not been plucked from the House to take the place of John Tower," says Mickey Edwards, the former Republican House member from Oklahoma who served with Cheney. Edwards, a congressional scholar and author, recognizes the extraordinary influence Vice President Cheney exercises in the "war on terror." But he also emphasizes how Dick Cheney's departure from the Republican minority in the House changed the Congress and transformed American politics.

"Dick was in line to become the party's leader in the House and ultimately the majority leader and Speaker," Edwards says. "If that [had] happened, the whole Gingrich era wouldn't have happened." Newt Gingrich ushered in fifteen years of rancorous, polarized politics. He presided over the shutdown of the federal government when the House was unable to agree to a budget compromise with Bill Clinton. He drove the House to impeach Bill Clinton. Cheney had cultivated cordial relations with Michel, who was sixty-six when Cheney left and beginning to look toward retirement. He worked with Democratic Speaker Tom Foley.

It wasn't that Cheney was a nonpartisan Republican ingratiating himself with the Democratic leadership. He had, after all, called Democratic Speaker Jim Wright a "son of a bitch" and filed a questionable ethics complaint against Wright. But no one interviewed could envision Dick Cheney taking the House down the path that Gingrich followed when he became Speaker.

The Senate moved with breathtaking speed, racing through FBI investigations (agency background investigators were in Cheney's House office even as the president was announcing his appointment). A committee hearing and debate were all completed within a week of Tower's defeat in the Senate. On the floor of the Senate, the debate consisted of overblown encomia of the sort John Tower would not receive even after he died in a plane crash in Georgia in 1991.

Dick Cheney's tenure at the Department of Defense was, by most accounts, his finest hour. "I saw him for four years as SecDef," Colonel Lawrence Wilkerson says. "He was one of the best executives the Department of Defense had ever seen. He made decisions. Contrast that with the other one I saw [Clinton secretary of defense Les Aspin], who couldn't make a decision if it slapped him in the face."

Cheney had been in his Pentagon office for less than a week when he made a decision that established who was in charge. He publicly attacked Air Force chief of staff General Lawrence Welch. It was unprecedented that a defense secretary would openly criticize a four-star general. Cheney blindsided the general, complaining that he had been "freelancing" on Capitol Hill, where he was meeting with members of Congress to defend several options for the basing of ICBMs—without direction from the Pentagon.

Wilkerson, a lifetime soldier who ended his active military career on Colin Powell's staff, says Cheney instantly asserted his authority over the Pentagon's top brass. "There are two ways to take command of a military unit," Wilkerson says. "One is you come in and try to bribe, wheedle, and persuade everybody. The other is you come in and fire a couple of people and let everybody know who's boss, then back off. . . . If you've got to pick one, the best pick is to be a hardass."

Secretary of Defense Cheney picked the hardass management strategy. Air Force secretary James McGovern resigned, the chairman of the Joint Chiefs of Staff quietly disagreed, and some of the top brass in the building seethed. "Larry Welch wasn't doing anything that wasn't expected of him," says a retired officer who worked with Cheney at the Pentagon. "Policy had been in favor of smaller ICBMs. Larry was keeping the ball rolling on the Hill. That was the mantra: smaller ICBMs. He wasn't out there freelancing."

Welch had, in fact, cleared his congressional discussions with the secretary of the Air Force. "He was just an easy target for Cheney," says the retired officer. Cheney violated an unspoken code relating to civilian direction of high-ranking officials: no humiliating public reprimands of senior brass. And he didn't even slow down to look back.

On the Monday following his smackdown of Larry Welch, Cheney summoned the Pentagon's top civilian officials to his third-floor conference room. He told them the Welch affair was done with and that he wouldn't tolerate the four-stars getting "out ahead of civilian leadership—in particular the secretary of defense."

Cheney's dressing-down of the general bothered House Armed Services Committee chair Les Aspin. "It was unfair," Aspin said, because "it was a bum rap." When Aspin confronted Cheney and said Welch wasn't doing an end run, Cheney smiled. "It was useful to do that," he told Aspin.

It probably was. Three weeks earlier, Dick Cheney had been a minority congressman from Wyoming, hiring staff for the whip's office. Within a few days of moving into his third-floor office at the Pentagon, he was kicking ass and taking names. To underscore his point, and make sure his back was covered, he evicted a general from the office next to his. The new occupant would be Cheney's trusted assistant, David Addington.

It was an impressive beginning.

"He was a little slow to accept that the Cold War ended," says one of Sam Nunn's former staff defense policy analysts.

In fact, Cheney was fighting the Cold War even after German entrepreneurs were selling pieces of the Berlin Wall and Warsaw Pact leaders were openly discussing new relations with the West. Americans don't like to think of their country as militaristic, but no country in the world has ever proposed a military budget that would match what is spent by the United States. The increase in spending in the Reagan years was breathtaking. Total military spending in 1980, the last year Jimmy Carter was president, was $134.6 billion. By the time Reagan completed eight years of strategically outspending the Soviet Union, annual military expenditures in 1988 were $290.9 billion. (Bush-Cheney defense expenditures in 2005 were $493.6 billion.)

Before the Berlin Wall collapsed, Mikhail Gorbachev was discussing reductions in troops and military spending. When the Wall did come down, members of Congress began to clamor for substantial reductions in defense spending. Massachusetts senator Ted Kennedy talked about putting tens of billions in a "National Needs Trust Fund" to pay for social programs. Georgia senator Sam Nunn proposed cuts of $180 to $190 billion and an ambitious program to pay for the acquisition and dismantling of Soviet nuclear weapons (the Nunn-Lugar Comparative Threat Reduction Initiative). Military analysts from the Brookings Institution and policy intellectuals from Harvard proposed cuts as large as 10 percent in 1991, 20 percent in 2005, and 50 percent by 2000.

Cheney refused to get caught up in the euphoria. He believed an aggressive leader who would reverse the reforms in the Soviet Union would replace Gorbachev. Cheney proposed a budget request of $303 billion, $8 billion more than total military spending in the final year Bill Clinton was in office. *Business Week* described Cheney's reluctance to accept victory over the Soviet Union in the headline "Dick Cheney: The Loneliness of the Last Cold Warrior."

That hard-line position created budgetary problems for a president who faced declining revenues aggravated by his "read my lips" no-new-taxes pledge. Cheney was making final technical adjustments on his first budget as the Berlin Wall finally came down. Over the course of six quick rewrites, he grudgingly trimmed about $10 billion from the figure he had begun with. He went to Congress with a request of $295 billion, adjusted it upward, and got an appropriation of $297 billion. The following year, in 1991, he asked Congress for $291 billion and got only $270 billion. His final budget request to Congress in 1992 was for $261 billion, from which Congress cut another $10 billion. Cheney was a long way from the $180 billion in cuts the conservative and defense-oriented Sam Nunn had hoped for.

Cheney would later claim that he cut $300 billion from the defense budget. That claim doesn't measure up against the checks written for DOD spending. Defense Department budget requests are not the same as defense spending. Nor are appropriations bills, which do not account for "supplementals" added on to cover cost overruns and unanticipated expenses. The Congressional Budget Office calculates dollars actually spent on defense. Cheney did stop the huge annual leaps in spending that began when Ronald Reagan took office. But military spending was not "cut" until Bill Clinton submitted his first defense budget.

Total Defense Spending During Reagan's Presidency		Total Defense Spending While Cheney was Bush's Secretary of Defense		Total Defense Spending While Bill Clinton Was President	
FY	$ in billions	FY	$ in billions	FY	$ in billions
1981	158.0	1989	304.0	1993	292.4
1982	185.9	1990	300.1	1994	282.3
1983	209.9	1991	319.7	1995	273.6
1984	228.0	1992	302.6	1996	266.0
1985	253.1			1997	271.7
1986	273.8			1998	270.2
1987	282.5			1999	275.5
1988	290.9			2000	295.0

Cheney turned the inevitable reduction in troops garrisoned abroad over to his chair of the Joint Chiefs of Staff, Colin Powell. Cheney bypassed dozens of more senior officers to find the most talented candidate, even if he had misgivings about Powell's position on Iran-Contra. Powell designed a "base force" program that gradually brought home (and in some cases discharged) large numbers of American occupation forces in Europe, coordinating every reduction with individual commands. As personnel ac-

counted for almost 50 percent of the Pentagon budget, Powell's gradual reduction in force helped reduce defense spending.

The selection of Powell as chair of the Joint Chiefs, long assumed to
be Cheney's choice, was actually something of a shotgun wedding. At
fifty-two, Powell was younger than most others who were in line for the
job. But he had served as Reagan's national security advisor and was the
senior Bush's choice to lead the Joint Chiefs. Powell had doubts about
Cheney. He considered Cheney's uncompromising support of Ollie
North's rogue operations to be an endorsement of military officers going
out of channel and running unauthorized operations. The elder George
Bush, however, wanted Powell as chair of the Joint Chiefs.

Cheney did make one particularly bold move on the military budget.
While Ronald Reagan was president, spending on weapons had spiraled
completely out of control. Again, with one decision, Cheney took charge.
When he learned that the Navy's A-12 fighter jet was $1 billion over
budget and eighteen months behind schedule, he canceled the program
and fired the vice admiral in charge of naval aviation. He also ordered two
senior officers demoted for mismanagement. With three stars on his
epaulets, Vice Admiral Richard Gentz was the highest-ranking officer ever
dismissed for failure to manage costs and deadlines on a weapons system.
Cheney also curtailed production of the Air Force's B-2 Stealth bomber,
from 132 to 20—essentially killing a weapons system designed to penetrate
Soviet radar and conduct long-range bombing missions. He targeted the
Marines' V-22 Osprey, perhaps the most problematic American military
aircraft ever to make it off the drawing boards. But the tilt-rotor, vertical-
takeoff helicopter had powerful friends. Congress, led by the Texas and
Pennsylvania delegations, overrode the cut. When Cheney refused to
spend the money appropriated, Texas senator Lloyd Bentsen and Fort
Worth congressman Pete Geren filed suit—more over plant closings than
national security. To increase the pressure, Texans and Pennsylvanians on
the House Armed Services Committee passed a provision that would cut
5 percent per month from overall defense spending until funding for the
Osprey was released. "It wasn't exactly blackmail," says a general who
worked on Pentagon budgeting. "But they threatened to be a constant pain
in the ass for us until we gave in."

The Osprey proved to be a durable disaster. Midway through
George W. Bush's second term, the tilt-rotor helicopter Cheney had tried

to ground still wasn't exactly flying. Sixty helicopters had been produced. Five had crashed, which might have been predicted after the prototype crashed. The accidents killed twenty-six marines and four civilians. In March 2006, a year before the aircraft was to be deployed for combat in Iraq, another $71-million Osprey went down in the woods in Florida, though this time no one was injured.

In a 1992 speech, Cheney claimed he "terminated or canceled over 120 different weapons programs." He might have been using canceled software programs to pad his list. And he failed to ground the Osprey. But no secretary of defense since the beginning of the Cold War had taken as hard a look at weapons systems or gone head-to-head with the Pentagon brass and defense contractors. Cheney didn't deliver a peace dividend, but he did stop the exponential growth in the military budget that, along with tax cuts, had driven the deficit during the Reagan presidency.

Most of John Tower's hires at the Department of Defense moved on when the Senate rejected his nomination, but Cheney asked one high-ranking Tower appointee to stay. Paul Wolfowitz had begun his career as a Democrat, working for Washington senator Henry M. "Scoop" Jackson. He crossed party lines to work in the Nixon and Ford administrations, then took a midlevel position at the Pentagon when Jimmy Carter was elected president. Cheney's decision to keep Wolfowitz, though little noticed at the time, was a small first step toward the invasion and occupation of Iraq that consumed the Bush-Cheney administration fourteen years later.

While Wolfowitz was at the Defense Department during the Carter administration, Secretary of Defense Harold Brown asked him to look at Third World countries where the United States might face a threat. Wolfowitz's Limited Contingency Study, carefully tracked in James Mann's *Rise of the Vulcans*, shifted attention from the Soviet threat and considered the possibility of the seizing of Saudi Arabia's oilfields by a Persian Gulf nation. It focused specifically on Iraq, described in the study as the preeminent military power in the region. At the time, no one involved in preparing the report considered Iraq a threat. Saddam Hussein had not consolidated his power, engaged in any widespread repression, or acquired chemical weapons.

What concerned Wolfowitz was oil.

Brown wanted nothing to do with the report. He shelved it, fearing that were it leaked, the Iraqis would believe the United States was working on behalf of the Saudis. But Wolfowitz would not let it die, even if it would not be made policy during the Carter administration.

In a Pentagon where Dick Cheney was running the show, Wolfowitz was in a better position to again turn his attention to the Persian Gulf. In 1992 he was responsible for drafting the first biennial Defense Planning Guidance document that would not focus on the Soviet Union. Wolfowitz had assigned the project to his deputy, I. Lewis "Scooter" Libby, and Libby delegated the work to Zalmay Khalilzad. Both men would figure prominently in the administration of George W. Bush, Libby as Cheney's chief of staff and Khalilzad as the American ambassador to occupied Iraq, where he would exercise the plenipotentiary power of a viceroy.

The new planning guide, shaped by Khalilzad, Wolfowitz, and Libby, envisioned a superpower so dominant that it could intervene in and resolve any conflict: "Potential . . . competitors need not aspire to a greater role or pursue a more aggressive posture to protect their legitimate interests." The United States would "sufficiently account for the interests of the advanced industrial nations to discourage them from challenging our leadership or seeking to overturn the established political and economic order." A nuclear arsenal would "provide an important deterrent hedge against the possibility of a revitalized or unforeseen global threat, while at the same time helping to deter third party use of weapons of mass destruction through the threat of retaliation."

Among the threats the report anticipated were conflicts that threatened access to Persian Gulf oil, proliferation of weapons of mass destruction and ballistic missiles, and terrorist threats to U.S. citizens. The primary case studies that justified the use of the tactics described in the plan were Iraq and North Korea. The report made it clear that the United States would act unilaterally; there was no role for the United Nations.

A Defense Department employee who believed the policy Wolfowitz was promoting needed to be debated in public leaked the report to *The New York Times*. The report was immediately denounced by President Bush. The leaked document became a political issue in the 1992 campaign, attacked by Clinton. It angered foreign leaders, who saw it as a blueprint for American hegemony. After Bush distanced himself from it, Wolfowitz followed. Khalilzad was left hanging, the principal author of an orphaned report rejected by all of his superiors. Then Cheney read it. He told Khalilzad, "You've discovered a new rationale for our role in the world." He issued the report under his own name. "He wanted to show that he stood for the idea," Khalilzad said. "He took ownership in it."

The 1992 Defense Planning Guidance document would go back on the shelf while Bill Clinton was president. But like the Osprey tilt-rotor aircraft, it wouldn't go away. The original Iraq War thinking rejected by Harold Brown and George H. W. Bush had taken root and would be waiting eight years later when Dick Cheney returned yet again to the White House.

Cheney's canonization of the report marked an odd but important historical moment. George W. Bush was sitting in the owners' box seats of the Texas Rangers ballpark, where he was a managing partner and a 2 percent owner, while the men who would define his foreign policy ten years later were sitting in their Pentagon offices, where they were in charge, writing the foreign policy they would hand him after the 2000 election.

"He was the finest secretary of defense I've ever seen, from the standpoint of the military," says a general who was already at the Pentagon when Cheney arrived. It is a common response to the open-ended question: How would you describe Dick Cheney as secretary of defense? Like Colonel Lawrence Wilkerson, who would break with the Bush-Cheney administration because of its conduct of the war in Iraq, the general, a career officer who saw Cheney work at the Pentagon, describes him as a near-perfect administrator: "He was in control. Bill Clinton is the smartest man I've ever worked with. But Dick Cheney came close. In a briefing, he's so smart he's intimidating. He listens. He listens in a way that most people don't listen. And he gets everything. It is daunting, can be frightening. But when you walk out of his office, you know that he understands every detail you briefed and every implication of the decision he's going to make. No emotion. No anger. He's annoyed if you are not prepared. I have never seen him raise his voice."

Cheney's time at the Pentagon was a dress rehearsal for the vice presidency. He had no administrative experience, but he seemed to understand, almost instinctively, that the secret to success and control lies in staffing. David Gribben, the high school friend from Wyoming who served as Cheney's chief of staff in the House, was also his chief of staff at the Pentagon. Pete Williams, the former Wyoming television newscaster who worked as Cheney's House press person, was the Pentagon spokesman. And David Addington, who had been with Cheney since Congress, was now his special civilian assistant.

"Cheney always has the best staff," the Pentagon source says. "David Gribben was loyal, smart, and had no ego. And he understood legislative affairs. Pete Williams could take the most complex issue and dumb it down into a sound bite. And David Addington is one of the smartest people I ever knew. He was on top of things."

Addington, the Pentagon source added, could read the draft of an appropriations bill in one day and ferret out the one paragraph that wasn't supposed to be there: "He would fix that one paragraph, and he would know exactly which undersecretary had been over there on the Hill freelancing." After cleaning up the bill, Addington would "add a corrected provision that might adversely affect the undersecretary and send him a little message."

At the Pentagon, it sometimes seemed as if David Addington was training Dick Cheney to be vice president—or perhaps president. Almost every decision started in Addington's office, where he would meet with "the uniforms," civilians—even the Joint Chiefs. Then he would take his decisions in to Cheney, who would be briefed. When necessary, Addington would take the parties into Cheney's office. Addington, by intellect and force of personality, took charge and dealt with the details. "He allowed Cheney to be the chief."

"Addington was always deeply involved in issues," the Pentagon source says. "But he was always in the background. If you wanted to get something to Cheney, you did it through Addington. For three years it was the best-run operation you could imagine. It worked because Addington ran it on behalf of the Secretary of Defense."

Addington also worked on appropriations, which Cheney mastered by collaborating with Jack Murtha, the Pennsylvania Democrat who chaired the House Appropriations Subcommittee on Defense. Murtha is an institutional politician, always aware of and insinuating himself into positions of power in the House. When Cheney was appointed secretary of defense, Murtha hosted a dinner for Cheney and his wife and the Appropriations Subcommittee members—known as the cardinals—and their spouses. It was an invitation to collaborate—and a showcase of Murtha's influence on "Approps." Cheney, Murtha, Addington, and a few high-ranking officers from the Pentagon managed DOD appropriations and developed a working relationship between the Congress and the uniforms, to ensure that in a time of shrinking budgets, no vital weapons systems or bases were cut. Powell was intimately involved in appropriations. But difficult problems were resolved by discussions between Murtha and Cheney.

Murtha is a hawkish former marine and Vietnam veteran who has cultivated close ties to the military. Congressional staff traveling with him on congressional delegation trips ("codels") complain that he spends so much time listening to enlisted men that schedules are difficult to keep. Cheney and Murtha remained close friends when Cheney became Bush's vice president, which later made Murtha's harsh criticism of the Bush-Cheney White House so loaded. "I like guys who got five deferments and have never been there and send people to war, and then don't like to hear suggestions about what needs to be done," Murtha said in November 2005. One of Murtha's staff members insisted the Democratic congressman's statement didn't pertain to Cheney, but that was a hard sell. Cheney is the only high-profile member of the Bush administration who had five draft deferments and is making decisions that put American soldiers at risk.

Some of Cheney's critics claim the Pentagon brass was hostile to Cheney because he was a secretary of defense who had avoided service in Vietnam. (After all, during his confirmation Cheney had said, "I had other priorities in the sixties than military service.") A retired officer who was at the Pentagon while Cheney was there disagreed. "I never saw it," he says. "Everyone immediately saw he was a good administrator who had good relations with Congress. That's what matters. Rumsfeld came over as a former Navy pilot and within six months no one in the building wanted to talk to him because he is so arrogant. Cheney came over here aware that he knew nothing about defense issues. Cheney and David [Addington] listened."

Wilkerson, a career officer who worked for Colin Powell at the Pentagon and State Department, also says Cheney's deferments were not an issue. "There may have been a little grumbling," the retired officer says. But he added that Cheney was far too good at what he did, and far too protective of the interests of the armed forces, to engender much hostility. Wilkerson describes a moment at the end of the Gulf War at which the very officers who might have been expected to be Cheney's critics publicly embraced him. "It was at the National Military Command Center at Fort Leavenworth. Everyone got together, all the military types, and presented

Cheney with an honorary certificate of graduation from the Command General Staff College. The little speeches that accompanied that . . . were quite poignant."

While Dick Cheney's first big challenge as secretary of defense was the U.S. attack on Panama, his defining moment was the first Gulf War. The textbook success of both ventures perhaps convinced him that invading Iraq in 2003 would be quick work, followed by Iraqis tossing rose petals at American soldiers as they prepared to move east into Iran. Though he never wore a uniform, Cheney had been involved in every American military adventure since the Korean War: Vietnam, Grenada, Nicaragua, Panama, the Gulf War, and Afghanistan. If he missed Somalia and Bosnia, the company he directed had won big, lucrative contracts in both attempts at nation building.

The invasion of Panama was a textbook exercise in regime change. Initially a CIA asset, Panamanian president Manuel Noriega had become impossible for the American president to control. Noriega's thugs had beaten and bloodied their boss's opponent in the presidential race. Panamanian soldiers had shot one American serviceman and briefly detained an American lieutenant (and his wife, whom they threatened to sexually assault). They also arrested a CIA operative who was operating a clandestine radio station. It wasn't hostile warships in the Gulf of Tonkin, but for the first Bush administration, a sufficient casus belli to invade a country and remove a thuggish regime.

Cheney had been six months on the job at the Pentagon when the senior George Bush made the decision to attack Panama. It was a decision made in careful collaboration with Cheney, who was attentive to detail, aware of the larger foreign policy context of the invasion, and not hesitant to put overenthusiastic generals on short leashes. At one point he questioned plans to use the Stealth bomber, a high-tech radar-evading aircraft designed to penetrate Soviet defenses. (He reluctantly signed off on it, though he regretted it later.) He refused to allow the lieutenant's wife to do a TV interview in which she would have described the sexual taunts of Noriega's soldiers, arguing that it would only be inflammatory. He cut one target from the list of sites to bomb, complaining about a Stealth attack on a Noriega hangout. And he went after Congress for encroaching on the executive's authority to conduct foreign policy. Members of Congress, whom Cheney caustically referred to as "my former colleagues," were "literally calling [executive branch] agencies downtown, or even people in Panama," Cheney complained. "That creates all kinds of problems. [They] certainly complicate our lives when they run out and make public pronouncements in front of the press, knowing only half of what there is to know." Cheney also refused to provide New York congressman Charles Rangel copies of combat videos shot by Apache helicopters in Panama. Rangel was responding to numerous complaints that most of the civilians killed died in Apache attacks on civilian targets.

The assault on Panama bore all the signature marks for which Dick Cheney would become known. Willingness to exercise broad executive authority, low regard for the role of Congress in foreign policy, high tolerance for non-American civilian casualties, and near-absolute secrecy. The assault, in which fifteen Americans died, was a technical success, even if it involved the conquest of a small country already occupied by thirteen thousand American troops. Cheney allowed only reporters based in the United States to cover the war, so he could slow the credentialing process and thus slow the coverage, although there were fully credentialed bilingual American reporters on the ground in Panama. The result was sporadic coverage of the "war," in which hostilities lasted only a few days. Critics of the invasion, including the Catholic Church in Panama, insist that far more Panamanians died than the two hundred civilians listed in official American reports. The Catholic Church, no great friend of Noriega, said deaths numbered in the thousands. The use of the Stealth bomber in an attack in which the resistance was so feeble that only fifty Panamanian soldiers died was something of an embarrassment. More embarrassing was the fact that the 100-million-dollar bomber was far off target when it dropped its bombs. (Cheney was furious when he learned the Air Force had kept him in the dark about the Stealth's failure.) The operation took a while to achieve its objective, the capture of General Manuel Noriega. The Panamanian dictator eluded the army and took sanctuary in the offices of the papal nuncio. Rather than violate the sanctity of a church that was also a diplomatic mission, U.S. forces surrounded the nuncio's residence and played high-decibel rock music until Noriega and his host could endure it no longer and he surrendered to American forces.

"Operation Just Cause" in Panama was a dress rehearsal for the larger military adventure to follow, when Iraq's president Saddam Hussein invaded Kuwait in 1990. From the moment intelligence reports indicated that Saddam Hussein's troops appeared to be preparing to invade Kuwait, Cheney was at the center of the military campaign known as Desert Storm. The first Gulf War was Dick Cheney's war as much as it was George Bush's war. It began with yet another Iran-Contra connection. Saudi ambassador Prince Bandar had moved $25 million from the Saudis to the Contras, working with CIA director William Casey. He was also a friend of the Bush family. Powell had misgivings about Bandar; Cheney had none.

It was Bandar who initially informed Bush that Hussein's behavior had the Saudis worried. And it was Bandar with whom Bush negotiated, sending Cheney to Saudi Arabia on a critical diplomatic mission to persuade the Saudis to accept U.S. ground forces. Before the ground war in Iraq started in late February 1991, Cheney had flown to Riyadh four times. Yet on the road to the Gulf War, Cheney was cautious. Not as cautious as Powell, but not overeager to push the country into war. The story line for the American public was that Hussein had invaded a sovereign nation. The concern within the administration was that Hussein had designs on the oilfields of Saudi Arabia.

Cheney was practical. Given the alternatives of attacking Hussein or deploying a force to defend Saudi Arabian oil, he argued that it was better to avoid a direct confrontation with Hussein's million-man army. He was critical of Bush's personal attacks on Hussein, complaining to Brent Scowcroft that the overheated rhetoric was putting the lives of American soldiers at risk. And he cautioned Bush against ordering American sailors to board Iraqi tankers to signal the beginning of a blockade.

Cheney's August 1991 trip to Saudi Arabia to meet with King Fahd was critical to the success of a large mission to deter the Iraqis. Cheney, accompanied by Paul Wolfowitz and General Norman Schwarzkopf, imposed the American plan upon the reluctant and difficult king. There would be no caps on the size of the American force deployed in Saudi Arabia. Nor would there be any fixed date by which troops would depart. They would remain "until justice is achieved," Cheney told Fahd, adding that they would leave when the king asked them to leave. Cheney used classified satellite intelligence to convince the king of Hussein's intentions, and went to great lengths to emphasize the gravity of Iraqi troops amassed on his border and the impossibility of a U.S. mission to stop Hussein once he moved into Saudi Arabia. Fahd, the custodian of the two holiest sites of Islam, was being asked to accept the presence of troops from the country that was Israel's financial and military underwriter. Cheney wouldn't allow him time to think it over.

Once the decision was made to go to war, Cheney turned his attention to the generals who would do the fighting. "He looked at the war plan and was appalled by its lack of creativity and tore it to pieces," says a former defense aide on Sam Nunn's staff. Cheney spent days with Colin Powell, poring over war plans, pushing Powell, and leaning on the generals doing the planning. He personally got on the phone with, and in the faces of, the generals who were drawing up the war plans. "He wasn't a micromanager like McNamara," says one of the generals involved in the planning. "And he wasn't arrogant like Rumsfeld. He wanted this one done right." Cheney joined Powell in arguing for the "enhanced option"—adding a hundred thousand more troops to the American contingent in Saudi Arabia, bringing troop strength to half a million. It was his moment to end the country's Vietnam War syndrome. "The military is finished in this society if we screw this up," he told Prince Bandar.

Cheney and Powell agreed on most issues regarding the war. But they had one fundamental disagreement regarding weapons. As they were flying back from the Persian Gulf in the run-up to the war, Powell pulled out a report he had ordered his staff to complete. It was a proposal to retire the Army's tactical nuclear weapons arsenal. The copy of the report Powell handed Cheney as the two men flew home from Saudi Arabia was covered with critical marginalia, all in the hand of David Addington. Addington and Wolfowitz had strong objections to giving up nuclear weapons that Powell said were inaccurate, expensive to maintain, and irrelevant in a modern arsenal of sophisticated conventional weapons. Cheney dismissed Powell, saying "not one of my civilian advisers supports you." Powell would prevail—after a Gulf War in which the Army's tactical nuclear weapons were not necessary. In September 2002, President Bush overruled Cheney and implemented Powell's recommendations.

In the Gulf War, Cheney saw a limited role for Congress, just as he had in the Panama operation. Despite the fact that going to war with Iraq would be a larger undertaking than the D-Day invasion of Normandy,

Cheney argued that the president did not need the consent of Congress. He seemed more understanding of King Fahd's polling the royal family and calling Arab leaders than he was of Bush's willingness to go to Congress for consent. He told Bob Woodward that after meeting with his House colleagues, he remembered that four months before Pearl Harbor, the House had approved an extension of the Selective Service System by only one vote. Bush took his case to Congress. The Senate voted 52 to 47, the House 250 to 183, to approve the "all means necessary" resolution.

The Gulf War began with thirty-eight days of intense bombing of Iraqi positions in Kuwait—and strategic sites in Baghdad and across Iraq. In the first forty-eight hours of the war, 2,107 combat missions dropped more than five thousand tons of bombs on Baghdad, nearly twice the amount Allied forces dropped on Dresden in 1945. The bombing plan was similar to what was laid out for reporters four months earlier, by an Air Force chief of staff Cheney fired for his loose talk. "The cutting edge would be downtown Baghdad," Air Force general Michael Dugan said. Dugan also told a *Washington Post* reporter that he had been informed by Israeli intelligence that Hussein would be devastated by an attack on his family and his mistress. The September 16 *Post* story ran under the headline "U.S. to Rely on Air Power if War Erupts." The follow-up story on September 18 required a headline and a subhead. "Candor Cost Top Airman His Job; Dugan Discussed 'Things We Never Talk About,' Cheney Says." Cheney's firing of Dugan, who coincidentally had replaced General Larry Welch, was another demonstration of what Wilkerson described as Cheney's "real ability to administrate, to make a decision, to be an executive." No member of the Joint Chiefs had been fired since 1948. But Dugan had talked to the press, described a plan of attack, and revealed that Israeli intelligence was involved in a war his boss had just sold to King Fahd bin Abdul Aziz, Custodian of the Two Holy Mosques.

Cheney's firing of Dugan was bloodless and fast. He didn't even bother to interrupt President Bush's tennis game at Camp David to tell him the Air Force chief of staff was going to be canned.

News stories and various sources describe Secretary of Defense Dick Cheney and Joint Chiefs of Staff Chairman Colin Powell as a near-perfect tandem at the Pentagon. The SecDef who had avoided the draft and the general whose life had been defined by the Army set aside their differences over Iran-Contra and conducted the most successful U.S. military operation since World War II. After thirty-eight days of bombing, the ground campaign lasted four days and resulted in only 137 American fatalities.

The war that brought the two men together would also divide them. Cheney was already thinking about a run for the presidency in 1996. And while he was averse to the press, working to limit media coverage of the war and firing a four-star general for talking to reporters, he was not averse to hagiography when he could find it. The details he revealed to a *Time* magazine team read like a storyboard for a campaign video: never losing a night's sleep over a difficult decision; packing his own bag to fly to Saudi Arabia; bringing along his cowboy boots and lucky beige zippered jacket; and connecting with the troops once he was on the ground. David Hume Kennerly's campaign boudoir photography complemented what was probably the most glowing portrait of a cabinet minister done since newsweeklies went from black-and-white to color. Cheney was taking full advantage of the Gulf War success to write his campaign biography. But then, as now, he lacked Powell's charisma and telegenic qualities.

A general who worked at the Pentagon says he witnessed the public moment he believes caused the Cheney-Powell divorce: the "Salute to the Men and Women of the Desert Storm Campaign" at the Washington Hilton in April two months after hostilities in Iraq ended. Congressman Jack Murtha insisted on bringing in a large number of enlisted men. "There were E-1s to E-4s with their girlfriends dressed to the nines running all over the hotel. Everyone made speeches. The event broke up and those kids mobbed Powell. They couldn't get enough of him. Cheney was definitely not mobbed. The TV moved to Powell and left Cheney with a few people talking to him. Cheney looked over there and saw a rival he could not match."

There had been talk of a Cheney-Powell ticket in 1992. But as the pundits and the public sized up the two men, talk began to shift to a Powell-Cheney ticket. On the day Dick Cheney left the Pentagon to return to private life, he didn't even bother to stop by Powell's office to say goodbye, says Wilkerson. "There was no farewell. Powell never knew he departed and all of a sudden he's still the chairman and Cheney's gone."

SIX

Lawless CEO: The Halliburton Years

In the first and only vice presidential debate of the 2000 campaign, newly retired captain of industry Dick Cheney faced off against Connecticut Democratic senator Joe Lieberman. Astoundingly, there was not one mention of Halliburton in their debate. The closest they got to discussing the company Cheney had run from 1995 to just days before joining the Bush campaign in the summer of 2000 involved a question about partisanship. Cheney used his answer to burnish a myth that largely exists to this day. In it, he stars as the triumphant CEO, a self-reliant insider-turned-outsider who competently and ethically grew his company while increasing shareholder value.

While politically useful, it happens to be a lie.

"I've been out of Washington for the last eight years and spent the last five years running a company [*sic*] global concern. And I've been out in the private sector building a business, hiring people, creating jobs," said Cheney. "I've got a different perspective on Washington than I had when I was there in the past."

If the former executive had chosen Lieberman himself, he couldn't have picked a more clueless opponent to debate than the senator from Connecticut, who has proven himself an enemy of corporate reform and an ally of Lynne Cheney in the culture war. Lieberman not only failed to challenge the business bona fides of his rival for the vice presidency, he helped expand the myth. Attempting to make the case that America was better off after eight years of Clinton-Gore, Lieberman dryly noted that *Cheney* was certainly better off. In other words, he was the very picture of the successful CEO.

Cheney retorted: "I can tell you, Joe, the government had absolutely nothing to do with it."

It was a whopper of a falsehood—and one more that Lieberman failed to dispute.

The Gore-Lieberman campaign had tried to make an issue of Cheney's compensation from Halliburton. Despite retiring early, Cheney was reported by *The New York Times* to have received a severance package worth more than $20 million, and during his time at the company, total compensation of well over $10 million. In reality, he had received a total of $45 million. Not bad for a guy who was earning about $144,000 a year when he left the Defense Department in 1993. Before that, he had served in Congress making even less, calling his government service "a pauper's oath."

In 2006, Vice President Dick Cheney declared his net worth for the previous year could be as high as $94.6 million. Not all, but most, of that income came from Halliburton. Even deep into his second term in the Bush White House, as Halliburton raked in billion-dollar federal contracts, Cheney received compensation and held stock in the company. In his first five years in office, the vice president earned almost a million dollars in deferred salary from Halliburton. He promised to donate millions more in stock options to charity, but as late as the spring of 2006, Cheney still had fifty thousand Halliburton stock options worth almost $4 million. His staggering executive compensation cannot be fully appreciated without a full examination of his tenure at Halliburton, a company that has spent the years after his departure extricating itself from its former CEO's mismanagement and potentially actionable decisions. Even the pro-business *Fortune* magazine concluded in 2005 that Halliburton had suffered under Cheney's "poor leadership."

The true achievement of Dick Cheney, CEO—other than his personal enrichment—is that he somehow managed to keep a lid on an exceedingly messy Halliburton legacy long enough to get elected and re-elected to the White House. Some of it was just dumb luck. Some of it was his former company covering for him. Tellingly, a full six years after he left the company, at least one grand jury is still looking into Halliburton activities from that period.

Exactly how a man with no experience in running a multinational energy services company won the job leading Halliburton is itself shrouded in myth. The oft-told story involves a five-day fishing trip on the Miramichi River in New Brunswick in 1995. By then Cheney knew that his dreams of running for president were not to be. In 1994, he had gone so far as to set up an exploratory committee headed by his former Pentagon aide David Addington, but a nationwide speaking tour that year had failed to generate much interest. By year's end Cheney had more than likely seen the polling by his old Ford administration friend Bob Teeter showing that among Republican primary voters, Cheney trailed Bob Dole, Jack Kemp, Colin Powell, and, in all but one poll, Dan Quayle.

According to the New Brunswick fish tale, one night as Cheney slumbered back at the lodge, the corporate executives on the trip started to talk about the ongoing search for a Halliburton CEO. Among the executives was Halliburton chairman Tom Cruikshank, who had been leading the search. Cheney had wowed the chairman with stories of managing the Pentagon, and in July 1994, Cruikshank had donated a thousand dollars to the former defense secretary's presidential exploratory campaign. Out of the blue, someone suggested that Dick might make a good Halliburton CEO. And once again, with no discernible effort, Cheney, in the right place at the right time, had landed himself a new position of power.

Why a former secretary of defense would be attractive to the Halliburton board is fairly easy to see. Since the 1960s, Halliburton and its affiliate, now known as Kellogg Brown & Root, or KBR, have been a cornerstone of the military-industrial complex. Not only would a Cheney-led Halliburton benefit from government money, the company would depend on it. In just one example of many, in the five years prior to Cheney's arrival at Halliburton, the company received $100 million in government-backed loans from the Export-Import Bank of the United States, a federal credit agency that lends money to promote American exports. During Cheney's five-year tenure at the company, it would receive $1.5 billion.

Halliburton didn't begin life suckling at the public teat. Erle Halliburton had founded his company among the roughnecks in the Oklahoma oilfields back in 1919. He perfected a way to use concrete to secure wells and helped revolutionize oil production. By dint of hard work, self-sacrifice, and relentless promotion, the Tennessee native transformed his Halliburton Oil Well Cementing Company into a multi-million-dollar success story. While early financing from oil companies helped him grow, Erle avoided government money, after failure to win a public service contract soured him on Washington politicians and their pay-to-play lobbyists. The company branched into other oilpatch services and went public in 1948. In 1957 Erle died. Shortly thereafter, the company rechristened itself Halliburton. Faced with the imperative of constant growth in a cyclical industry of booms and busts, Halliburton found what looked like a solution in 1963. It proposed a merger with a Texas construction company then called Brown & Root.

Brothers Herman and George Brown had used seed money from brother-in-law Dan Root to found their company the same year Erle Halliburton founded his. But unlike Halliburton, Brown & Root thrived on federal contracts. After years of early struggles, the Brown brothers had lucked into a big public works project to build a dam on Texas's Colorado River near Austin. But they needed political muscle in order to see it to completion. The brothers turned to a young, ambitious Texas Hill Country congressman named Lyndon Baines Johnson. After LBJ proved himself able to deliver, the Browns paid to help the Texas pol steal a U.S. Senate race against Coke Stevenson in 1948. (After a campaign fueled by illegal contributions, Johnson won the primary election by eighty-seven votes when an extra ballot box in anything-goes South Texas mysteriously appeared several days later. LBJ's primary victory assured his election in then-solidly Democratic Texas.) For the next thirty years, LBJ and George and Herman Root would work so closely together that Johnson would become known as the senator from Brown & Root. The relationship floated along on a river of campaign cash—sometimes delivered in suitcases—and in exchange, the politician ensured an endless supply of big public works projects.

As LBJ's fortunes grew, so did those of his patron. In 1947, Brown & Root had barely made a list of the top fifty construction companies in the country. By 1965 it was number two, and by 1969 number one, with sales of $1.6 billion. As noted in Dan Briody's book, *The Halliburton Agenda*, most of the momentum took place while Johnson was president. The escalation of the Vietnam War proved a boon to the company. In wartime, when quick results are demanded, few quibbled over massive cost overruns. So ubiquitous were the company's government projects in Vietnam that war protesters dubbed it "Burn and Loot."

The two firms, which merged in 1963, had much in common. Both were based in Texas. Both were vehemently antiunion and anticommunist. And both of their strong-minded founders, Erle Halliburton and Herman Brown, each of whom would likely have objected to the merger, had died in the previous decade.

The period that followed the Brown & Root / Halliburton merger has been called Halliburton's Golden Age. By 1981, revenues had shot up to $8.5 billion, profits were $674 million, and Halliburton employed more than 110,000 workers. But the company had lost its political rainmakers. The oil bust of the 1980s hit Halliburton hard, and profits sank. More than half the employees were laid off. Painful downsizing and consolidation continued into the early 1990s. By 1992 the financial chemotherapy had started to work. It also didn't hurt Halliburton's prospects when government contracts started to flow again, including a very important Army logistics plan commissioned by Secretary of Defense Dick Cheney, which promised a revenue stream that could save the company from the economic roller coaster of oil and gas. Over the three and a half years before Cheney took the reins of Halliburton on October 1, 1995, the company's stock rose 82 percent.

Cheney had lucked into an ideal situation. He was inheriting a company on the upswing, recruited by a board with relatively low expectations of his management prowess. "When we brought Cheney in, it really wasn't to run operations, it was to make the proper strategic decisions, and to establish relationships," Chairman Tom Cruikshank subsequently told *The New York Times*. Halliburton wanted Cheney's Rolodex, and in particular, his contacts in the Middle East.

Unfortunately for the company, Cheney was not content to be a door opener or a celebrity CEO.

By now the world is aware of the dangers of collateral damage when Dick Cheney goes hunting. Certainly, Austin lawyer Harry Whittington, whom the vice president inadvertently shot in the face, knows. In 2004, the Sierra Club also got a taste. It petitioned U.S. Supreme Court justice Antonin Scalia—to no avail—to recuse himself after he and his pal the vice president went duck hunting just before the court ruled on whether Cheney's energy task force logs could remain secret. The environmental group lost that one, as did the interest of open government.

Halliburton stockholders and employees can also count themselves among those who have suffered when Cheney shouldered his shotgun. In January 1998, Dick Cheney, Halliburton CEO, went quail hunting in South Texas with Bill Bradford, the chairman of Dresser Industries. In a glimpse of how small Cheney's circle of loyalty can be, the two men had three ranches in the area from which to choose: his old friend James Baker's ancestral spread, the hunting camp of George Brown's daughter Nancy Negley, and the almost fifty-thousand-acre ranch of Halliburton board member and former Ford administration ambassador Anne Armstrong. (Years later Negley would be present when Cheney peppered Whittington nearly to death with buckshot on Armstrong's ranch.) Neither Cheney nor Bradford have said where their hunt took place.

Prior to Cheney's joining Halliburton, the two rival Dallas-based oil service companies had discussed merging, but not much had come of the talks. When Cheney arrived at Halliburton, merger mania gripped corporate America. The 1990s would see massive consolidations in the oilpatch, including the pairing of Exxon and Mobil, BP and Amoco, and Chevron and Texaco. By 1998, Cheney had already successfully absorbed several smaller companies. In particular, analysts cheered his acquisition of Landmark Graphics, a software company that produces computer models of hydrocarbon reserves. After joining Halliburton, Landmark posted its highest quarterly revenues since it was founded in 1982.

Dresser was a company of another magnitude altogether. A merger with Dresser would create the largest oil services and construction firm in the world. Cheney believed that Halliburton needed to become the Wal-Mart of oil service companies in order to survive. He envisioned a corporation that would do everything from locate the oil reserves to build the offshore platforms to extract the crude from the ground. As part of his vision, he centralized control within Halliburton, leading one former executive quoted in *Fortune* magazine to compare the company's bureaucracy to "the Soviet navy."

During the quail hunt, Cheney suggested to Bradford that Dresser and Halliburton renew their merger talks. Over the next two months, the men met secretly at the Crescent Court, a Dallas hotel, to work out the details. In February 1998, the two sides agreed that Halliburton would purchase Dresser for $7.7 billion. On paper it made sense. Other than oilfield and engineering departments, most of their divisions did not overlap. Cheney said that he and Bradford did not expect the kinds of devastating layoffs then employed by merger kings like Al "Chainsaw" Dunlap of Sunbeam Corp. But his timing proved disastrous. By the time the two companies finished the last of the paperwork in September 1998, the price of oil had plummeted. Halliburton purchased Dresser at the top of the market at a 16 percent premium. To help compensate, Cheney immediately slashed ten thousand jobs.

The worst was yet to come. Hunting buddies Cheney and Bradford were so comfortable with each other that they had decided to forgo much of the standard investigation that constitutes normal due diligence in such a merger. This may be why a thorough detailing of Dresser's asbestos liability was not included in the prospectus explaining the deal that was sent to the shareholders of both companies. Cheney would be safely in the White House by the time it became clear that he had saddled Halliburton with $4 billion worth of asbestos liability.

Cheney's failure to take the asbestos threat more seriously may have derived from a false sense of security. He believed that Halliburton had already escaped Brown & Root's liability for the cancer-causing fiber through a clever corporate shell game. In 1996, not long after Cheney joined the company, Halliburton spun off a wholly owned subsidiary called Highland Insurance Group. Once Highland was separated from its corporate parent, Halliburton asserted that thirty thousand asbestos claims against Brown & Root belonged to Highland. This came as a shock to Highland investors, as a letter signed by Cheney explaining the spin-off to stockholders failed to mention the liability. It wouldn't be until 2002, two years after Cheney's departure, that the Delaware Supreme Court closed the door on Halliburton's scheme to avoid liability, forcing the company to spend $80 million to settle the asbestos cases.

Cheney apologists assert that there is no way he could have known just how bad Dresser's asbestos claims would be. Yet even by 1998, litigation frenzy over worker exposure to asbestos had bankrupted dozens of companies. And it wasn't as if Dresser had a tangential relationship to the workplace carcinogen. A Pittsburgh division of the company called Harbison-Walker had used asbestos until 1970 in insulating bricks and coatings it sold. Most of the 66,000 asbestos claims aimed at the company could be traced to Harbison-Walker, which Dresser had spun off several years before the merger with Halliburton. While the new owner of Harbison-Walker had promised to cover claims filed after 1992, in mid-1998, prior to completion of the merger, it demanded that Dresser take on more of the burden. Halliburton later claimed ignorance of the pre-merger demand.

The real bleeding started in December 2001 when Halliburton revealed that it would have to pay three large asbestos awards. Its stock fell 42.5 percent in a day, to $12 a share. Claims swelled to 274,000 by the end of 2001. In the beginning of 2002, Harbison-Walker filed for bankruptcy, leaving its liability to Halliburton, whose stock tumbled to $9 a share. As Cheney sat in his West Wing office and contemplated taking out Saddam Hussein, Halliburton found its salvation in a "prepackaged Chapter 11 proceeding." The bankruptcy deal allowed Halliburton to jettison its liability and save the company. In exchange, it paid $5.1 billion in cash and stock, of which insurers paid $1.4 billion, to be held in trust for current and future asbestos victims.

Dick Cheney didn't just avoid any consequences, political or otherwise, from the ill effects of buying Dresser. His company lavishly rewarded him for his folly. In December 1998, Halliburton gave Cheney a $1.5 million bonus for "bringing the Dresser merger to a successful conclusion."

Asbestos would not be the only problem Halliburton would inherit from Dresser. It also acquired an emerging corruption scandal in Nigeria involving secret bank accounts and a shady lawyer doling out government bribes. Consistently ranked among the most corrupt in the global community, the West African nation is just one of many dysfunctional and authoritarian places where a Cheney-led Halliburton did business. Halliburton's rogues' gallery of pariah-state clients also included Iraq, Iran, Burma, Libya, Indonesia, and Azerbaijan. Cheney has defended Halliburton's operations in countries that regularly abused the human rights of their citizens, and even some that exported terrorism, by simply stating, "We go where the business is."

In a speech to the Cato Institute in 1998, CEO Cheney made the case that his company could ill afford the luxury of factoring ethics into where it operated. "The good Lord didn't see fit to put oil and gas only where there are democratically elected regimes friendly to the United States," he noted. "Occasionally we have to operate in places where, all things considered, one would not normally choose to go."

It's not surprising that bottom-line-oriented businessmen would rationalize dealing with despots or even paying off foreign officials. Government authority exists to restrain such corrosive behavior. Cheney has seen it from both sides and is nothing if not consistent: oil and gas trump government authority, and they certainly supersede human rights considerations. Cheney put this attitude on display in a tour of former Soviet bloc countries in the spring of 2006. During a stop in Lithuania, he castigated Russian president Vladimir Putin for "unfairly and improperly" restricting the rights of his people and using oil and gas as "tools of intimidation." The next day, in Kazakhstan, which has an abysmal human rights record but extensive gas and oil fields, Cheney said hardly a word about one of the most repressive regimes on the planet. A month later, Putin fired back on the *Today* show. "I think your vice president's expression there is like his bad shot on his hunting trip," the Russian president said. "I believe that his concerns do not look sincere and therefore they are not convincing."

Whether Dick Cheney put his business above the law in Nigeria is the subject of a seemingly stalled Department of Justice and Securities and Exchange Commission investigation. The reason we even know about the case is that France, Italy, Switzerland, and Nigeria have also investigated. All of these countries as well as the United States have statutes making it illegal to bribe a foreign official to obtain business. The U.S. bribery inquiry has dragged on for at least three years without a definitive answer to a simple question: Did Halliburton, under Dick Cheney, violate the Foreign Corrupt Practices Act (FCPA) in Nigeria?

Somebody broke the law, by Halliburton's own admission. "We have reason to believe, based on the ongoing investigations, that payments may have been made to Nigerian officials," the company has stated. Considering what's already on the public record, the company position seems understated.

When Cheney bought Dresser, its subsidiary M. W. Kellogg had likely been involved in illegal activities in Nigeria since at least the early 1990s, about the time it joined the international business consortium TSKJ to bid on a contract to build a gas liquefaction complex at Bonny Island in Rivers State, Nigeria. According to documents Halliburton provided to foreign investigators, the consortium agreed to pay London-based lawyer Jeffrey Tesler $180 million to smooth the way for the Nigerian contracts. In a French deposition, Teslar claimed the $180 million was used to obtain Nigerian currency for the project. He has denied the money went for bribes. In 1995, TSKJ won the $2.2 billion contract.

Tesler reportedly was a financial adviser to Nigerian dictator General Sani Abacha. He also had a longtime relationship with A. Jack Stanley, the head of Kellogg's operations in Nigeria. When Halliburton took over Dresser, Cheney named Stanley chairman of the newly formed Kellogg Brown & Root subsidiary. Cheney told an industry newsletter that before the merger went through, what worried him the most was integrating Kellogg with Brown & Root. He happily reported that it had gone more smoothly than he had thought it would, in part because of Stanley. In March 1999, TSKJ won another Nigerian contract, worth $1.4 billion, to build more facilities on Bonny Island. French media would later report that Tesler deposited as much as a million dollars in a Swiss bank account controlled by Stanley. How the money was disbursed and to whom is still unclear.

In 2003, while Cheney enjoyed unprecedented power in the White House, an executive with one of the companies in the consortium revealed to French investigators the existence of the $180-million slush fund. A year after the involvement of the French, the SEC and DOJ joined the investigation. The U.S. Attorney for the Southern District of Texas in Houston convened a grand jury and issued subpoenas for documents from both Halliburton and Stanley. Investigators have interviewed Stanley at least three times. Stanley's lawyer refuses to comment. Halliburton has said that it is cooperating with all of the investigations.

Halliburton has communicated to shareholders that its internal investigation uncovered plans for payments to Nigerian officials beginning as early as 1995, as well as bid rigging by Stanley and other employees dating possibly as far back as the mid-1980s. In June 2004, well after the investigation had begun, the company ended its relationship with Stanley. "The termination occurred because of violations of Halliburton's Code of

Business Conduct that allegedly involved the receipt of improper personal benefits in connection with TSKJ's construction of the natural gas lique-faction facility in Nigeria," reported Halliburton.

Around the same time, the SEC broadened its investigation to include Halliburton's conduct abroad over the past twenty years. If the agency ever finishes its exhaustive review and determines that the company vio-lated the Foreign Corrupt Practices Act, Halliburton could be barred from receiving government money. At stake would be $6.6 billion in fed-eral contracts. The company has already indicated that if charged, it would ask for "administrative agreements or waivers from the DoD and other agencies to avoid suspension or disbarment." With its former CEO as vice president and Halliburton an essential cog in the War on Terror, it's doubtful the company would be denied a waiver.

Evidence has yet to surface that Cheney knew of any illegal activities undertaken in the company's name, and the degree to which Dick Cheney had a permissive approach to the Federal Corrupt Practices Act may well take subpoenas to pry out. There is plenty of evidence that the vice presi-dent is willing to disregard legislation with which he differs. One need look no further than his chief of staff David Addington and the more than eight hundred signing statements he has helped inspire, in which Presi-dent Bush declares he will interpret the law as he sees fit. Such legal flex-ibility is harder to conjure when you're just the executive of a corporation rather than a country. Nonetheless, one can imagine Cheney taking a dim view of the Foreign Corrupt Practices Act. Passed in 1977 as part of Con-gress's Watergate-era reforms, the law emboldens federal regulators and represents government intrusion into the activities of corporations.

With a few exceptions, Cheney has been outspoken in his opposition to the use of the government's economic power to impose unilateral inter-national sanctions. "I think it is a false dichotomy to be told that we have to choose between commercial interests and other interests that the United States might have in a particular country or region around the world," he declared to the Cato Institute crowd, before making a case for constructive engagement.

As a congressman in 1986, Cheney was one of only eighty-three rep-resentatives to vote against overriding President Ronald Reagan's veto of a South African sanctions bill. At the Cato conference, he even extended his argument to Cuba, the third rail of presidential politics. A better approach to Cuba would be to create a West Berlin–type enclave of Cuban democracy and free enterprise out at the U.S. Navy base in Guantánamo Bay, Cheney reportedly said. Less than a decade later, as vice president, he did help transform Guantánamo—into a place of torture and indefinite detention. Yet as CEO, Cheney's defiance of sanctions while at Halliburton put the company in legal jeopardy. As with the Nigeria bribery allegations, federal investigations into Halliburton's possible violations of U.S. sanctions are ongoing.

Cheney's political opposition to sanctions didn't stop at speeches. Human rights activists in the 1990s, encouraged by the role of sanctions in South Africa's transformation and Democratic control of the White House, hoped to use U.S. economic power to force change on some of the world's worst regimes. In their sights were countries such as Burma, Haiti, Nigeria, and Uzbekistan. Responding to their efforts, in 1997 Halliburton helped found a lobby group called USA Engage to fight the growing sanctions movement. Cheney and USA Engage argued that unilateral sanctions didn't work and only hurt U.S. companies. The new association successfully fought off a bill that would have imposed sanctions on foreign governments that persecute religious groups. It opposed but failed to halt bipartisan bills that impose sanctions on financial transactions with governments that support terrorist activities, and one to bar American investment in Iran and Libya.

The lobby association had some of its most notable successes at the state level. It stopped a 1998 effort by the Maryland legislature to impose sanctions against firms doing business in Nigeria. Perhaps its greatest victory came in a Supreme Court case on the constitutionality of a Massachusetts law that restricted state purchases from companies doing business with Burma, also known as Myanmar. Cheney signed an amicus brief calling for the court to overturn the law. In June 2000, in a unanimous decision, the justices ruled that the Massachusetts law interfered with the federal government's ability to conduct foreign policy. Not coincidentally, a Halliburton affiliate, European Marine Contractors, helped build an environmentally damaging oil pipeline in Burma—through villages the Burmese military had brutally "pacified" to make way for the project.

It appears that each member of USA Engage picked a particular region or country about which to lobby. Cheney focused on Iran, where he had a history with industrial commerce. As members of the Ford administration, he and Donald Rumsfeld proposed selling Tehran Westinghouse technology that would have allowed Iran to reprocess plutonium and obtain uranium for a nuclear energy program. The agreement, which Ford reluctantly accepted, fell apart in 1979 under the Carter administration, when the Shah was overthrown as the current Islamist government seized power. The CEO wanted Iran's oil service and construction business, and he didn't appreciate his government's telling him Halliburton had to stay out. Iran boasts 10 percent of the world's confirmed oil reserves and the second largest reserve of natural gas. Nonetheless, in 1995 President Clinton signed an Executive Order prohibiting U.S. companies from doing business there. The sanctions were further expanded in 1996, over Cheney's objections, with the passage of the Iran Libya Sanctions Act (ILSA).

Once ILSA became law, Cheney lobbied a friend, Texas senator Phil Gramm, for a waiver for Halliburton so it could work in Iran, even as the federal government investigated the company. In October 1997, Halliburton Energy Services reached a $15,000 settlement with the Department of Commerce over charges that it had violated the U.S. Export Administration Act fifteen times between 1993 and 1994 involving transactions with Iran. As part of the agreement, the company admitted to no wrongdoing. While the violations had occurred prior to Cheney's tenure at the company, he wanted to avoid such settlements in the future.

At the 1998 Cato Institute conference, Cheney devoted much of his speech to Iran. "American firms are prohibited from dealing with Iran and find themselves cut out of the action, both in terms of opportunities that develop with respect to Iran itself, and also with respect to our ability to gain access to Caspian resources," he complained. "Iran is not punished by this decision. There are numerous oil and gas development companies from other countries that are now aggressively pursuing opportunities to develop those resources."

Having failed to change the Iran sanctions, Halliburton decided to work around them. The U.S. prohibition included a loophole that allowed foreign subsidiaries of U.S. companies to work in Iran as long as they were completely independent of their parent in America. In early 2000, while Cheney was CEO, a Halliburton subsidiary registered in the Cayman Islands opened an office in Tehran. In 2001, the Treasury Department began an investigation into more than $40 million worth of Halliburton projects in Iran. The investigation foundered. In 2004, a *60 Minutes* report revealed that the Cayman office was nothing but a letter drop without employees. The subsidiary's actual address in Dubai shared offices and staff with Halliburton. Several months before, citing new leads, a federal grand jury subpoenaed Halliburton for more information about its dealings with Iran. Two years later, the investigation has yet to reach a conclusion—but with Cheney's special interest in Iran dating back to his work with USA Engage, it is unlikely that he wasn't fully aware of Halliburton's work in the country.

One of the few occasions when Cheney said that he agreed with sanctions was in connection with Iraq after the Gulf War. "I had a firm policy [at Halliburton] that we wouldn't do anything in Iraq, even arrangements that were supposedly legal," he told ABC News during the 2000 campaign.

Well, that wasn't entirely true. While Cheney was CEO of Halliburton, the company's subsidiaries signed $73 million worth of contracts with Iraq. And ironically, the Iraq sanctions regime, codified by the United Nation's Oil for Food program, was a textbook case of how not to do an embargo. Halliburton subsidiaries Dresser-Rand and Ingersol Dresser Pump Company sold spare parts and equipment to Saddam Hussein from 1997 to the summer of 2000 to help rebuild Iraq's oil infrastructure—which Secretary of Defense Dick Cheney had helped destroy. Since Halliburton went through France and complied with Oil for Food, the transactions were technically legal. But by the late nineties it was clear that the U.N. program was thoroughly corrupted. Saddam and his officials skimmed billions from profits destined to pay for medicine and food for ordinary Iraqis. When Cheney was pressed again as vice president about his former company's dealings with Iraq, a spokesperson explained it involved joint ventures in which he had no knowledge.

A year after joining Halliburton, Cheney did a cameo in a promotional video for the firm that handled his company's accounting work. "I get good advice from their people based upon how we're doing business and how we're operating—over and above just sort of the normal by-the-books auditing arrangement," he pitched gamely to the camera.

The promotional video was for Arthur Andersen. It would take another five years before the irony of Cheney's words would be fully evident. By then Enron had imploded, and Andersen, its handmaiden in fraud, was under federal indictment for shredding documents. (The Supreme Court would later overturn Andersen's conviction for obstruction of justice on a technicality, but the decision came too late to save the venerable firm.) Halliburton was Andersen's third biggest client, right behind Enron. Both Andersen and Enron were among the top campaign donors to the Bush-Cheney effort in 2000. By the time evidence of Halliburton's own accounting irregularities from that period surfaced, Cheney was already in the White House.

The trouble in this case began in 1997, when Halliburton simultaneously embarked upon several larger-than-usual construction projects throughout the world. The company took on many of these projects on a fixed-price basis, arranging to complete the job based on a set, agreed-upon fee that would cover all costs. The profit from such an arrangement comes from the margin by which the fee exceeds the contractor's expenses. A fixed-price contract can potentially be more lucrative for a contractor, if it can keep expenses down or somehow persuade its customer to pay more. In the past, Halliburton had mainly worked under safer "cost-plus" contracts, under which the company was guaranteed a certain profit regardless of the cost of the job.

Halliburton's fixed-price projects didn't work out as planned, and by 1998 the company was looking at more than $100 million in cost overruns. The extra expense couldn't have come at a worse time for Cheney and Halliburton. A recession in the oil industry had depressed an already volatile company stock. Investors had not been as excited about Cheney's deal with Dresser as he had. A one-time $1 billion charge against earnings for costs related to the merger didn't help.

Arthur Andersen offered a quick way to enhance Halliburton's bottom line. Historically, Halliburton would count payment for cost overruns in its financial statements only after the client paid them. Beginning in the second quarter of 1998, the company began to book revenue for cost overruns under the assumption that clients would pay at least some of it in the future. With the stroke of a pen, losses became gains. With the accounting change, for just 1998, Halliburton's pretax income was 46 percent greater than it would have been without the unapproved claims. But shareholders didn't know that. Halliburton didn't disclose this new accounting procedure to investors, even as the revenue it reported from un-collected claims grew from $98 million to $106 million in 2000, numbers first revealed in the March 2000 company report.

After a 2002 *New York Times* story raised questions about Halliburton's accounting, the Securities and Exchange Commission launched an investigation. Cheney's handpicked replacement as CEO, David Lesar, who had worked for Arthur Andersen before coming to Halliburton, blamed politics and the media for the SEC investigation. Because the vice president was the company's former CEO, the media were covering Halliburton like a political story, not a business story, Lesar complained in a phone conference with analysts. The SEC disagreed, fining Halliburton $7.5 million and imposing minor fines on two company officials. The agency took no action against Cheney, who cooperated with the investigation.

Cheney's and Lesar's gamblers' affinity for fixed-price projects would lead to one of the future vice president's greatest debacles at Halliburton. Before leaving the company in 2000, Cheney signed a contract for a $2.5 billion fixed-price job for Halliburton to build the infrastructure for the Barracuda and Caratinga oilfields beneath about three thousand feet of water off the coast of Brazil. Costs for the project quickly spiraled out of control. By the project's completion in 2004, overruns had cost Halliburton $762 million.

On the presidential campaign trail in 2000, the Brazil disaster, like most of Cheney's Halliburton legacy, remained hidden. When he left the company, its stock price was at a five-year high, having increased 157 percent during his tenure at the company. Its $44 plunge was still two years off. The peak in the stock allowed Cheney to pocket $18.5 million when he exercised his stock options in 2000.

Still, without doubt Cheney had achieved one of the key objectives of his hiring: positioning Halliburton to win federal contracts. He did most of the work before even joining the company, as defense secretary in the late eighties, when the Pentagon awarded Halliburton a five-year contract to study how a private company could supply logistical support for troops in various deployment scenarios. Not surprisingly, because Halliburton designed it, Brown & Root won the first LOGCAP (Logistics Civil Augmentation Program) contract in the Balkans. And while it earned high marks for its work there, questions of cost overruns and poor supervision later surfaced.

Cheney's grand dream of transforming Halliburton into *the* one-stop-shopping place for oil services had proved unattainable. Rather than building on the Dresser merger, Halliburton entered a period of retraction, selling off some of its newly acquired subsidiaries almost immediately. In 2005, Halliburton put its construction division, Kellogg Brown & Root, on the block. Thanks to Cheney, the company had achieved a level of federal contracts that would have been the envy of the Brown brothers. But with it had come death, political liability, and small profit margins.

SEVEN

Lady MacCheney

If the premier power couple in Washington, D.C., are Bill and Hillary Clinton, Dick and Lynne Cheney come a close second. For more than forty years they've been a team, even serving together in the first Bush administration. Lynne is just as much a partner and counselor to Dick as Hillary was to Bill. Long before the media dubbed David Addington "Cheney's Cheney," Lynne had that role. Those who know her say she is as ideological as her husband, if not more so, but while Dick has cultivated a gravitas that seductively whispers "calm and ready to govern," Lynne is all about the fight. It's the difference between the solemn pronouncements on *Meet the Press* and the rapid-fire slap-down of CNN's now defunct *Crossfire*, where Lynne was a host for four years. Yet unlike Hillary's effortless slide into public office, it's an open question whether Lynne, who has privately expressed interest in a political run, can escape her husband's shadow.

Lynne didn't always play second fiddle. In the beginning, she was the dazzling standout with the promising future, and Dick, the quiet but eager suitor who wasn't quite worthy. Back in Casper, many still believe that Dick would never have made it to the White House without Lynne's ambition fueling his ascent. They met for the first time shortly after the Cheney family moved to Casper from Nebraska. Lynne recalls seeing a fourteen-year-old Dick sweeping out the Ben Franklin five-and-dime where he worked after school. Nearly half a century later, on the presidential hustings, Dick Cheney would recall those early years. "Lynne talks about knowing me since she was fourteen years old, that's true, but she wouldn't go out with me until she was seventeen," he cracked.

Dick would credit their match to the 1952 victory of Dwight Eisenhower. When Ike reorganized the Agriculture Department, Cheney's father, an engineer who worked for the Soil Conservation Service, was transferred to Casper. The Cheney family's move and its consequences for Dick and Lynne's future would become a well-worn campaign joke, with more than a bit of truth. "If it hadn't been for Eisenhower's election victory, Lynne would have married someone else," Cheney would tell the audience, "and then *he'd* be Vice President of the United States."

As teenagers, the two seemed remarkably compatible. They shared similar backgrounds. Both came from north European frontier stock. Civil War veterans and Indian fighters numbered among their ancestors. Lynne's father, Wayne, also worked for the government as an engineer. Both of their mothers were strong, independent women in the western mode. Lynne's mother, Edna, was a deputy sheriff (she had a badge, but had clerical, not law enforcement, responsibilities). They loved to read, and logged countless hours at the Carnegie-built public library in Casper. Dick favored military histories. Lynne's scholarly appetites, even then, were more wide-ranging.

"There is nobody else like Dick Cheney, except for Lynne," says John Perry Barlow, who knew the couple years later in Wyoming. "She's like Dick, wicked smart, highly motivated, and, as with Dick, without much empathy."

Natrona County High School yearbook pictures of Lynne show a plain and petite blonde, her hair coiffed in Sandra Dee waves. Her face is too asymmetrical to be called pretty, but what sets her apart is a strong chin and full lips fixed in a determined half-smile. It's the face of someone who hungers for something beyond what a small and insular 1950s town in Wyoming can offer.

Lynne was a straight-A student, and in her senior year was elected Mustang Queen, a position chosen by, among others, the football team, of which Cheney was co-captain. He was also senior class president and a desirable catch for any girl—only they were both already attached to others. That abruptly changed when, with the prom only months away, Lynne's beau ended their relationship. At the time, her friend Joan Frandsen had been seeing Dick for three and a half years. "She has a real competitive edge, our girl does," Frandsen told the *San Francisco Chronicle* in 2004. "She had to get a boyfriend real quick."

Despite a friendship with Frandsen that dated from the first grade, Lynne made a play for Dick, the boy who seems to have pined for her for years. Cheney promptly dumped Frandsen. The very next day he took Lynne home to his parents for his birthday dinner.

Lynne dominates Casper memories of the couple. An oft-repeated story involves Lynne's victory at the state championship in baton twirling, one of the few competitive sports available to women at the time. The winning routine featured flaming batons. Dick stood in the wings with a coffee can filled with water, ready to douse the ends when Lynne completed her performance.

After high school, the couple maintained a long-distance relationship as college pulled them in opposite directions. Lynne had introduced Dick to Thomas Stroock, a Casper oilman and Yale alumnus. Impressed by the young football player, Stroock made a few calls and obtained a scholarship to Yale for Dick. While Lynne had demonstrated more intellectual promise, she had to settle for Colorado College. When Dick flunked out of Yale and returned to Wyoming to work as a lineman for the power company, Lynne was none too pleased. The blue-collar life was not the one she had envisioned for herself. It probably didn't help that Dick had started to drink heavily. She refused to marry him unless he sobered up and returned to school. Lynne's prodding—combined with the Vietnam draft—focused Dick and helped persuade him to enroll at the University of Wyoming in Laramie. The couple married on August 29, 1964. Lynne was already on her way to a master's degree in English at the University of Colorado. They both moved on to the University of Wisconsin to pursue advanced degrees. While Dick opted to shelve his doctorate in political science for the real thing, Lynne finished a weighty dissertation on the influence of Immanuel Kant's philosophy on the Victorian poet Matthew Arnold.

By the time the couple moved to Washington, D.C., they had a young daughter and another on the way. Dick soon fortuitously found a patron in Donald Rumsfeld. As her husband's career began its meteoric rise, Lynne was stuck as a housebound mother. Homemaker was not a role for which Lynne was suited by either temperament or skill. Dick would later joke that for the first year of their marriage, they would pretend that she could cook, and that he liked it. Once they got over that fiction, he handled all the serious cooking. Lynne had hoped to find work as a college professor, but the opportunity wasn't there. "I got my Ph.D. in 1970 and discovered that I was unemployable," she told Fox News in 2002. "There was a glut on the market that year. And this was before people were enlightened about women, and married women in particular."

Lynne turned to writing in part to escape the boredom of domesticity. To date she has written or co-authored eight books. In many ways, her three forays into fiction are the most interesting, for what they unintentionally reveal about the author. Lynne's first effort, *Executive Privilege*, published in 1979, is perhaps her most remarkable work, not for the writing, which is pedestrian at best, nor the convoluted plot, which some reviewers described in an excess of enthusiasm as "a political thriller." What makes *Executive Privilege* a page-turner in 2006 is how nakedly autobiographical it is. It's obvious that Dick's pillow talk and Lynne's life and fears as a White House widow provided the fodder for her tale.

The tortuous narrative begins with one of Dick Cheney's all-consuming passions: a White House leak. In this case—reminiscent of the tactics of Ford's senior staff—a fictional vice president leaks a week's worth of the daily presidential schedule, hoping that the leak will incite his supporters. The log shows that the president has cut him out of decision-making, in much the same way that Ford, with Cheney's help, marginalized Vice President Nelson Rockefeller. Instead, the media seize on details in the log involving the president's daily meetings with an adviser who is a psychiatrist. Is President Zern Jenner scheduling therapy sessions in the Oval Office? He refuses to comment. It turns out the psychiatrist is really a secret envoy to Filipino guerrillas seeking to overthrow Ferdinand Marcos. To reveal the true topic of the meetings would spike the revolution.

The central thesis of the book—that the president needs more latitude to keep affairs of state secret—is vintage Dick Cheney. Lynne is channeling Dick when she has President Jenner muse, "It seems to me that the history of the presidency in the twentieth century is the history of a gradually weakening institution." But the true meat of the book is found in the subplots. They center on the relationship of two couples—and both resemble the Cheneys.

First there are presidential assistant Dale Basinger and his needy wife Marie. Basinger—like Cheney under Ford—is the very picture of a behind-the-scenes faithful presidential counselor. Basinger would never write a "kiss-and-tell" book when his White House days are over. Lynne's fictional Basinger, like her husband, works to keep his outward demeanor "calm and positive," even if it's just a pose in the face of disaster. "So many staffers took their cues from him, and if their spirits were low, the press was sure to pick it up, and it wasn't long then before the stories started about how demoralized the Jenner staff was," Lynne writes.

But while obsessing about his job, Basinger suffers momentary pangs of guilt over abandoning his family for the grind of the White House. If it bothered Basinger, it was a workload under which Dick Cheney thrived. He described a typical day as Ford's chief of staff as beginning with his arrival at the office at 6:30 A.M. and ending with his departure sometime around 10 P.M. During one six-month period in the midst of the presidential campaign, he took off a single Sunday. Cheney didn't find this a problem, as he loved his job. But in an interview at the time he did allow that it could take a toll on a family. "It does apparently affect their personal lives—plus the strain on marriages and so forth," he said. It would be just one of many sacrifices Lynne would make for her husband's career.

Next to secrecy, the strongest plot thread in *Executive Privilege* is infidelity. Marie wonders if Basinger is bedding the First Lady's press secretary. He tries to reassure her, but to no avail. "He knew that his being home so little was part of the problem. And part of it was jealousy. She resented the women he saw at work. She saw them usurping her place in his life, and no amount of arguing could convince her that was not the case."

While Basinger truthfully tells a disbelieving Marie that he's too busy to have an affair, this is not the case for the other workaholic Cheney-like husband in the book, Rudy Dodman. White House correspondent for *Newstime* magazine, Dodman leaves the care of their two-year-old son to his stay-at-home wife, Nancy. She, as Lynne once did, spends her days working on a thesis involving Immanuel Kant. Throughout the book, Rudy is on the verge of straying into the bed of a flirtatious fellow reporter. Nancy, sensing his temptation, muses about how Washington is a place where the power that men amass attracts women. She had already decided that if he slept with another woman, she'd leave him. "There was a basic standard of honesty that had to be met in a relationship, if it was to have any meaning at all."

When queried by a reporter in Rawlins, Wyoming, about whether her husband supported the idea of her writing *Executive Privilege*, Lynne responded that it wasn't a question of asking permission; it was more like a consultation.

The most notorious of Lynne's fictional books is the 1981 novel *Sisters*. Written in prose that manages to be both stilted and overwrought, *Sisters* follows its heroine through a gritty frontier west. During the 2004 campaign, much was made of the breathy and positive treatment of lesbianism in the book. In an attempt to capitalize on the attention, New American Library, which owns the rights, wanted to reissue the now out-of-print novel. Cheney family lawyer and literary agent Robert Bennett called the publisher to request that it reconsider. It seems Lynne didn't think it was her best work. New American Library shelved the reprint. Nonetheless, several websites have made it available online. By excerpting the racier passages, they save the curious from the drudgery of having to read the entire book. In truth, the sex scenes in the novel are fairly tame. But the acceptance of homosexuality they evince contrasts sharply with the way, in public, Lynne handled the lesbianism of her youngest daughter, Mary.

Mary says that when she came out in junior high, her parents accepted her unconditionally. (This didn't stop Congressman Cheney from compiling an anti-gay voting record during this period.) As an adult, Mary was not only living openly as a lesbian, but also using her homosexuality as a professional selling point. She took a job with the Coors Brewing Company to help one of the radical right's deepest pockets market itself to homosexuals and other niche markets. A year before the 2000 campaign, she told the lesbian magazine *Girlfriends* that she went to work at Coors "because I knew other lesbians who were very happy there."

Yet in Lynne's first major interview of the 2000 presidential campaign, when ABC's Cokie Roberts addressed Mary's open lesbian life, Mary's mother took umbrage. Embracing a gay family member, instead of trying to convert her to heterosexuality, Family-Research-Council-style, would have offended a conservative Christian Republican base that was unaware of her daughter's sexual orientation. "Mary has never declared such a thing," Cheney snapped. "And I'm surprised, Cokie, that you even would want to bring that up."

The outburst served its purpose, cowing most of the media into avoiding the topic for the rest of the campaign. Not surprisingly, Mary's homosexuality returned as an issue in 2004. This time Mary was earning a six-figure salary running her father's reelection campaign. Despite her active campaign role, Mary seldom appeared with her longtime partner, Heather Poe, at events that involved the GOP base. Gay and lesbian activists, incensed by the Republican Party's use of same-sex marriage as a wedge issue, tried to force Mary out of her stealth lesbianism. They started a website, dearmary.com, where more than twenty thousand visitors wrote her letters, most imploring her to use her position to make a statement. The site featured Mary's likeness on a milk carton, to underscore her disappearing act. But Mary remained silent, and so did her parents. There was no public outrage from the Cheneys, even when members of their own party, like Alan Keyes, attacked Mary as "a selfish hedonist" or offered to pray for her soul.

Then, in the final presidential debate in mid-October, Senator John Kerry clumsily mentioned Mary in response to a question about whether lesbians and gay men are born or choose to be homosexuals. "We're all God's children," Kerry said. "And I think if you were to talk to Dick Cheney's daughter, who is a lesbian, she would tell you that she's being who she was, she's being who she was born as."

The next day Dick and Lynne went on the offensive. Lynne called Kerry's comment "a cheap and tawdry political trick. . . . The only thing I can conclude is he's not a good man. I'm speaking as a mom." Dick derided Kerry as "a man who will do and say anything to get elected." The mainstream media failed to note the hypocrisy. Mary Cheney sold her sexual orientation to build a professional career in marketing with Coors, yet her family was offended when a Democrat mentioned it.

Her father safely reelected, in 2005 Mary decided it was time to use the privacy her parents had guarded so zealously to cash in. A new publishing imprint of Simon & Schuster, run by Dick Cheney's longtime political adviser Mary Matalin, paid Mary a reported one million dollars to write a memoir. The book, *Now It's My Turn*, covers her time on the campaign trail and what it's like to be a lesbian in the Cheney family. Despite a huge publicity campaign in the spring of 2006, by mid-August, Mary's book had sold fewer than 8,000 copies, according to Nielsen's BookScan, which tracks retail book sales. By contrast, John Dean's book, *Conservatives Without Conscience*, released that summer, sold close to 48,000 copies in its first six weeks, also according to BookScan. Simon & Schuster, according to a source who knows the Cheney family, brought Matalin on with the understanding that she would get Mary Cheney under contract. The book, poorly reviewed in most places, was Matalin's first effort.

In 1986, Lynne, at that point an undistinguished writer with limited teaching experience, won a presidential appointment to head the National Endowment for the Humanities (NEH). Lynne's lack of a record proved advantageous in this case. She was a compromise nominee after the Senate rejected President Ronald Reagan's first choice, Edward Curran. (It was eerily similar to how Dick Cheney would win his job as secretary of defense.) For six years, from 1986 to 1992, she would run the NEH, the largest funder of humanities programs in the nation.

Lynne managed the NEH with an eye toward the future, both for herself and for the GOP. She worked hard to insulate herself from controversy to avoid being tagged by it later. Proposals that failed to meet her ideological criteria died before they arrived at her desk. If a proposal could remotely offend the right wing of the Republican Party, it received no NEH funding.

When it came to literature, says John Hammer, director of the National Humanities Alliance during this period, "she seemed to have the view that the canon was frozen around 1957." Anything that suggested multiculturalism or deviated from a certain right-wing romantic view of American history fell into the unwelcome category. Chicano art was too subversive to support. She overruled her staff and refused to fund a proposal for a documentary on the Pilgrim myth in American history as part of a larger exploration of the role of myth in society. "I learned from one of her close staff that she feared the American public would misunderstand the term 'myth'—they might think it meant something that is simply false," recalls Don Gibson, who worked under her at the agency.

The agency's multilayered review process allowed her to exert her influence discreetly. In what came to be known as "the chairman's list," names of acceptable candidates for review panels circulated among the staff. If an undesirable proposal slipped through the first stage of peer review, Cheney or one of her loyalists would subtly lobby at the next level, the National Council on the Humanities. After a while, many academics simply stopped applying for NEH support.

During her tenure, Cheney nearly doubled the NEH's public relations department, from ten under her predecessor Bill Bennett to eighteen. She surrounded herself with a tightly knit group of lieutenants, whom agency staffers labeled the "fifth-floor mafia." Few of them had serious education experience. Lynne, like her husband, valued loyalty above all. Day-to-day operation fell to Celeste Colgan. A Ph.D. in English literature, Colgan served as NEH deputy director, but she had spent most of her career as chief operating officer for a Wyoming lumber company. After Lynne left the NEH, Colgan went to work for Dick Cheney at Halliburton. As part of her responsibilities, she served as a liaison to the Halliburton board's executive compensation committee, which in 2000, despite his lackluster job performance, awarded Dick Cheney a pay and severance package worth $33.7 million.

Even as Lynne earned a reputation as one of the most feared agency heads in the federal government, she scored some notable successes, particularly at streamlining the grant process. She also belatedly embraced the agency's program for the preservation of historical documents, which went on to earn considerable praise. Under her tenure, overall grants for women's studies programs quietly increased as well. Those who regularly worked with Lynne characterized her as not only a brilliant debater but also a gifted conversationalist. "When she was not performing for people around her, she was a lot easier to talk with," says Hammer.

Toward the end of her tenure, Lynne Cheney increasingly spoke out against what she saw as "political correctness" in academia. Less than a month after the Clintons moved into the White House, Cheney announced she was quitting the NEH, despite the fact that nearly sixteen months remained in her term. (Terms are staggered to make it easier to keep the agency bipartisan.) She left the government and moved to the conservative American Enterprise Institute. Republicans, rallying behind Newt Gingrich, were preparing for revolution, and one of the strategies for victory would be to exaggerate cultural conflict to demonize their opponents. Lynne would play a significant part in the well-financed effort.

Sheldon Hackney, the chairman of the NEH who replaced Cheney, would later describe the Culture War as "a theater in which the players plot scenes and follow scripts designed to convince an audience that their side is the hero and the other side is the villain"—or, as Cheney described the villains, the "cultural elites."

Less than three weeks before the 1994 midterm elections, which would end forty years of Democratic majorities in Congress, *The Wall Street Journal* published an op-ed by Lynne. In it, she singled out new history teaching standards as an example of the evil in academia. With the standards, Cheney and the culture warriors had found the perfect scapegoat. On their face, the standards seemed innocuous. They served as a voluntary curriculum guide to American and world history for teachers of elementary and secondary students. The standards were not offered as course content, but rather as historical themes and areas of study. Along with the standards came a thousand classroom activities to encourage teachers to look at what their peers were doing.

Cheney and her allies conflated the standards with the classroom activities and then judged them by what wasn't included. No mention of Thomas Edison! No mention of Robert E. Lee! No mention of George Washington! Clearly, Academics Who Hated White Men wanted to hide the Founding Fathers from the nation's impressionable school children. It mattered little that by design, the standards didn't focus on names, but were guidelines to spark discussion and evaluate a student's knowledge. For instance, a suggested activity might read, "Analyze the character and roles of the military, political, and diplomatic leaders who helped forge the American victory" in the Revolution, or, regarding the Civil War, "Compare the civilian and military leadership of the Union and the Confederacy." Under the standards, if a student didn't mention Washington and Lee when answering the questions, he would fail the exercise. But try to explain that in a sound bite.

The media lavished attention on the controversy. Gary Nash, who with two other colleagues at UCLA had supervised the creation of the standards, recalls that in one twenty-four-hour period beginning on October 26, he opposed Cheney on PBS's *MacNeil/Lehrer NewsHour*, ABC's *World News Tonight with Peter Jennings*, the Pat Buchanan radio show, and the *Today* show. Put on the defensive against shrill and scurrilous attacks, Nash and his colleagues lost the battle. Every Cheney zinger required a detailed, audience-losing explanation to rebut.

In January, after the Republicans took the House, Cheney helped secure a 99-to-1 vote for a nonbinding U.S. Senate resolution condemning the standards. "They blitzed the Senate," the NEH's Hackney remembers. "This was like the war resolution on Iraq. It came down to a notion of whether you were patriotic or not."

Ironically, Lynne had originally championed the creation of these same standards. She had picked the majority of the council members who reviewed them. An NEH project officer followed the process on her behalf, providing reports every step of the way. When the National Center for History in the Schools at UCLA (whose creation Lynne funded) released the first draft of the standards in October 1992, Cheney wrote one of Nash's colleagues a two-line memo: "What nice work you do! I've been saying lately that the best grant I've ever given is to your standards-setting project." Cheney wrote the note before she recognized the political capital she could earn by attacking the standards.

"We were dumbfounded [by her attacks]," remembers Nash. "She had seen the drafts. She had made it clear she was pleased with the process as well as the product."

In order to explain her prior support, Cheney created a narrative that only insiders could dispute, whereby the standards radically changed after she left the agency. "I was flimflammed," she said.

Her opponents felt the same way. In talking with those who battled Lynne Cheney during the Culture War that raged in the 1990s, a common attitude toward her emerges: begrudging respect. It's not her intellect, mastery of the facts, or scholarship that impresses them. They do not describe her as an admirable or particularly principled foe. What confounded her adversaries were Lynne Cheney's political abilities, her mastery of media manipulation, and her talent at bending institutions to her will.

"It was as if we all had pop shooters and she had a howitzer," recalls Stanley Katz, chairman emeritus of the American Council of Learned Societies. "I have to say, Lynne Cheney is a minor genius at public relations, at operationalizing her ideology."

The academics and bureaucrats who stood in her way never really had a chance.

Just how far she would go was on display on January 24, 1995. That morning the opinion page of *The Wall Street Journal* featured another op-ed written by Cheney, this one under the provocative title "Kill My Old Agency, Please." In it, the former chairman of the National Endowment for the Humanities excoriated the agency she had once run. "In a time when we are looking at general cutbacks in funding for many groups, including welfare mothers and farmers, it is time to cut funding for cultural elites," wrote Cheney.

Cheney knew that eliminating the NEH's paltry $177 million budget would have little impact on the federal deficit, then at $180 billion. (Just a month earlier, Senators had doled out billions of dollars in pork that the Pentagon hadn't even requested, one commentator noted.) As a former chairman of the NEH, she also knew that the endowment leveraged its budget to attract other funding sources many times greater than the grants it distributed. One advocacy group had even calculated that combined, the NEH, the National Endowment for the Arts, and the federal Institute for Museum Services generated more than $36 billion annually and supported 1.3 million jobs.

But the focus on facts missed the point. This was political theater. Back at her old agency, those who had once worked with Cheney greeted this drama with anger and astonishment. "It was shocking to those of us who were left behind," recalls one current NEH staffer.

They remembered the memorandum Lynne had written to all NEH personnel when she left in December 1992. The one in which she described her "main accomplishment" as "actively expanding the mandate of the Endowment." She ended the letter by saying, "It has been an honor for me to be a part of this agency's work. . . . I have valued my time here and my association with the fine men and women of the National Endowment for the Humanities."

Now, the "fine men and women" were worried about the future of their agency, if its former director succeeded. "There was real fear that the agency would be abolished," remembers Don Gibson.

The *Journal* editorial served to soften up the terrain for the day's main event, when Cheney repeated her message before the House Interior Appropriations Subcommittee. The new Republican House leadership had arranged for a showy hearing on eliminating the NEH and the National Endowment for the Arts. "The American people deserve to understand why their money supports artists who submerge a crucifix in urine," Cheney testified. It was the kind of statement that made her critics joke that Cheney could teach a class on how to turn anecdotes into evidence. The image of a crucifix in a jar of urine was offensive, and clearly a questionable use of government funding. But Andres Serrano, the artist behind the "Piss Christ" piece, had received support not directly from the NEA, but from a museum that had obtained an NEA grant. The agency was being punished for the decision of an errant curator. Cheney's attacks on ideological intolerance in academia created a similarly false impression. "Political correctness was real, but it was not limited to the left, which was her view," says John Hammer.

At the hearing, Cheney described a humanities endowment bent on brainwashing children to despise their country. The NEH could not be trusted because even benign-sounding grant proposals would be transformed into hate-America screeds. "Many academics and artists now see their purpose not as revealing truth or beauty, but as achieving social and political transformation," Cheney said, rehearsing an argument she would expand in a book published later that year, *Telling the Truth*. "It's easy enough for grant recipients to toss objectivity to the winds since the postmodern view is that objectivity is an illusion—one that the white male power structure uses to advance its interests."

Cheney's testimony, along with that of former NEH chairman Bill Bennett, failed to carry the day, in part because right-wing actor Charlton Heston testified against them. Moses argued that the endowments were essential, and the Republicans parted. Constituents whose communities had received NEH funding also lobbied their congressmen not to eliminate the agency.

With Republicans dominating Congress, Lynne bided her time in the late 1990s, writing books and arguing politics on *Crossfire*. She had confided to the National Alliance's Hammer while at the NEH that she coveted the position of Secretary of Education. Yet there was no way that she would be appointed to the cabinet while her husband was Secretary of Defense. When the Clintons came into power, the prospect of her working in the federal government evaporated. Then in 2000, with her husband about to take office as vice president, his career smothered Lynne's ambition. As Dick pondered joining the Bush ticket, Lynne was unenthusiastic about the move since she knew it would sideline her career. At the time of the election, Lynne was working on a book on elementary and secondary education reform, but she shelved it to avoid creating controversy for the new administration. She has kept her position at the American Enterprise Institute, but instead of ginning out hard-hitting polemics, today she writes children's books and styles herself "the first grandmother."

The sense of sacrifice could be heard in her words to *NewsHour's* Jim Lehrer when he asked her about the change. "I'm not sure it would have occurred to me to do the children's books if I had just gone on the course I was on. I'm at the American Enterprise Institute, where typically scholars aren't writing children's books."

But Lynne's legacy lives on. Two months after the September 11 attacks, a self-styled academic watchdog group called the American Council of Trustees and Alumni (ACTA) issued a report under the modest title "Defending Civilization: How Our Universities Are Failing America and What Can Be Done About It." It purported to make the case that "college and university faculty have been the weak link" in the nation's response to the al-Qaeda attack. The authors painted a dire picture of America's system of education. They described a "pervasive moral relativism," which endorsed the notion that Western civilization is "the primary source of the world's ills." Insufficiently patriotic professors were traitors. "We learn from history that when a nation's intellectuals are unwilling to defend its civilization, they give comfort to its adversaries." To prove its point, the report included 117 alleged instances of unpatriotic statements that occurred after the attacks, with the names of the perpetrators listed.

In the weeks that followed, the report came under heavy criticism. Many of the unpatriotic statements didn't hold up or proved so mild as to be ridiculously inoffensive. Former U.S. ambassador Strobe Talbott, then at Yale, was quoted as saying, "It is from the desperate, angry and bereaved that these suicide pilots came." One of the co-founders of ACTA, Senate Democrat Joe Lieberman, asked that his name be removed from the organization's website. Not Lynne. She lauded the group in a speech at Princeton for speaking "out forcefully in favor of well-rounded general education." Editorialists decried the report as a blacklist. Under the barrage of criticism, ACTA took the report off its website a week after its release. When the report reappeared, the names were gone. Today, not even the report is available online.

To Lynne Cheney watchers, all of this came as no surprise. She had helped start ACTA, originally called the National Alumni Foundation, as a vehicle to attack the national history standards. She was still chairman emeritus of the group. ACTA's two leaders, Jerry Martin and Anne Neal, had been part of Cheney's "fifth-floor mafia" at the NEH. According to the Media Transparency project, the right-wing Bradley and Olin foundations had provided the seed money to launch the organization. It appeared that Cheney the culture warrior was back, only behind the scenes.

Rumors began to circulate that Cheney was surreptitiously running the NEH. The Bush administration had nominated art history professor Bruce Cole to chair the endowment. Cheney had placed Cole on the National Council on the Humanities during her tenure. Cole picked Lynne Munson, one of Lynne Cheney's confidantes, as his top deputy. Flagging grant proposals for ideological purity, which had ended under the Clinton administration, resumed.

Evidence mounted that Cheney was operating behind the scenes in at least one other agency as well. A month before the 2004 election, the *Los Angeles Times* ran a front-page story reporting that the Department of Education had destroyed more than three hundred thousand copies of a history study guide printed to help parents who were homeschooling their children, a key GOP constituency. The *Times* revealed that department officials destroyed the booklets after the office of the vice president's wife had contacted them. The copywriters who produced the pamphlets had committed the unpardonable sin of mentioning the national history standards. Secretary of Education Rod Paige's chief of staff at the time was Anne-Imelda Radice, another former Cheney mafia member at the NEH, with no education experience. A Democratic congresswoman from California, Zoe Lofgren, sent a letter to Paige asking how much it cost taxpayers to destroy and reprint the booklets. Paige never responded. Luckily for Cheney, no other media picked up the story and it didn't become an election issue.

Publicly, Lynne Cheney is seldom seen. In recent years, she has given few public speeches. She spends her time with her daughter Mary's partner Heather at Restoration Hardware buying things for the new house they are building with Mary's advance, or playing with the grandkids. "She's bored," says a friend. "She wants to run for office."

When her husband is scheduled to leave the White House in January 2009, Lynne will be almost sixty-eight years old. Her controversial past makes any future appointment requiring Senate confirmation doubtful. And although some who know her say she would like a Senate seat, a run for higher office remains a long shot. Still, those who have felt her wrath are loath to count her out.

EIGHT

Back to the White House

I t starts with a trip to the governor's mansion. Located in downtown Austin, the mansion is a commanding Greek Revival with six imposing Ionic columns across the front. But the grandeur of the building does not reflect the stature of the office. Texans decided early on that they didn't want a powerful governor. They created a weak executive and a strong legislature.

It's December 1998. The occupant of the mansion is a Republican of modest accomplishments, a politician who has learned to work with the Democratic statehouse across the street and won high approval ratings in the process. At the beginning of his second term, the governor is already looking beyond his Lone Star state. He wants the biggest political prize of all. Yet while he has mastered his current elected office, and despite a sterling pedigree, he's not knowledgeable enough to be the president. Thus begins the education of George W. Bush.

Bush had always liked and respected Dick Cheney, a rare departure from his tendency to reject his father's advisers and associates. In 1992, as the senior Bush's presidency degenerated into crisis and recrimination—

often played out as leaks in the press—the eldest son put aside a difficult filial relationship to move into the White House and lend a sharp elbow. Bush helped his father oust chief of staff John Sununu, who was replaced by Samuel Skinner. But the former secretary of transportation couldn't make the executive office run. The son and his father's advisers cast about for a competent manager to substitute for Skinner, someone with organizational abilities and loyalty—a quality prized above all others by the younger Bush. Reportedly the man the son favored was Dick Cheney, but the secretary of defense resisted this draft. He wasn't going to give up what he told congressional colleagues was "the best job you could ever have." Instead, the elder Bush turned to the family's trusty handyman, James Baker III—like Cheney, a former chief of staff.

While George W. was in the governor's mansion, Cheney was just a short drive up I-35, in Dallas, running Halliburton and getting his first taste of the plutocracy. Throughout the mid-1990s, the governor and the CEO would see each other at events, keeping open the lines of communication. When it came time for Bush to receive tutoring to fill the biggest blank spot on his résumé—foreign policy—Cheney was an obvious choice for instructor. Bush had also developed a rapport with Condoleezza Rice, his father's special assistant for national security affairs. As early as the summer of '98, the two met at the family vacation compound in Kennebunkport. Rice was then a tenured provost at Stanford, but she wanted out of academia and back into government. The campaign signed her up as foreign policy "coordinator."

In mid-December, Rice took fellow Stanford professor and former secretary of state George Shultz to the mansion for a seminar with the prospective candidate. Cheney also attended that mid-December policy session. He brought along a guest, too: Paul Wolfowitz, who would become a regular tutor at Bush's home school. Wolfowitz would not be the only member of the Project for the New American Century whom Cheney introduced to the governor, but he was one of the more popular ones. The absence of Bush père loyalists such as Brent Scowcroft suggested Bush the younger would follow his PNAC advisers and chart a more aggressive and unilateral foreign policy distinct from his father's soft internationalism. Wolfowitz believed in the neoconservative ideal of muscular moralism, the notion that the world could be remade in America's image—as that was what people everywhere really wanted anyway—if necessary at the tip of a spear. With Wolfowitz and Cheney in Austin, the future war cabinet had started to form almost two years before the election.

When Cheney came back for another session in February 1999, Bush responded to a reporter's query about the visit. "It's not the first time he's been down here," said Bush. "It won't be the last time he'll be down here. He's a person whose judgment I rely on a lot."

Throughout the summer and into the fall, the foreign policy team expanded to include Donald Rumsfeld and Richard Perle, both PNAC cofounders. Bush even mixed in a few token realists, Colin Powell and Richard Armitage, among the ideologues. (His advisers were smart enough to at least feint toward the more pragmatic side of the Republican Party to try and keep everybody happy.) But the tutoring wasn't enough to help the governor when he opened his mouth. Repeated gaffes fed a perception that he was out of his depth. Bush would counter by pointing to the experience of those he had gathered around him. But what the governor knew didn't really matter. He had enough money to clear the Republican field, and an agile and ruthless campaign team headed by Karl Rove, soon to be dubbed "Bush's Brain." By Super Tuesday on March 7, Bush had effectively put away his only real rival, John McCain—when necessary, with the dirty campaigning that is a Rove trademark. It was time to think about choosing a vice president.

Back at the mansion in Austin, Bush invited his first choice for the job to dinner. After the meal, the two men retired to the library. Surrounded by portraits of Stephen F. Austin and Davy Crockett, Bush asked Dick Cheney to join him on the ticket.

At that moment, there were plenty of reasons for Cheney not to accept the offer. For starters, he was sitting on hundreds of thousands of Halliburton shares and options worth tens of millions of dollars. By joining the ticket, he would deny himself the opportunity to sell his shares and exercise his options when the market dictated the maximum price. Also, he had signed an employment contract that stipulated he would lose some compensation if he retired before the age of sixty-two. There was a loophole—the board could waive the deal—but a mutually acceptable agreement would take time. An early vice presidential pick wouldn't do Bush any favors either, as Rove surely knew. Vice President Al Gore would be pitching policy proposals from here to the convention in August. The Bush campaign had to give the media something to report. If they named someone now, the press would spend months dissecting the ticket. Yet if they conducted an elaborate search, one that would stroke the GOP's strongest candidates, it might help unite the party behind Bush, and provide the easy horse-race stories reporters adore. During dinner they decided not to announce that Cheney had turned down the job.

The Bush campaign waited until April 19 to start leaking that Dick Cheney would manage the vice presidential search team. As word spread, the Halliburton CEO conveniently couldn't be reached for comment, as he was traveling in Australia, where apparently there are no telephones. In almost a week of free media, the news dribbled out as campaign officials fed favored reporters the scoop. The articles cited unnamed sources, usually identified as "close to Bush" or "from the GOP." The campaign officially remained silent. This debut would set the tone for the artful media manipulation to come.

On Tuesday, April 25, Bush formally made the announcement in Austin that "he couldn't think of a better person" than Dick Cheney to lead the hunt. "Fortunately, there are many good candidates to choose from in our party," read a prepared statement from Cheney. "We will look at them all. And we will make sure we have the best possible ticket this fall."

Three weeks later, at a Halliburton board meeting, Cheney denied he would serve in another Bush administration. He had "made a long-term commitment to the company." There was nothing left for him in Washington. "I have no plan, intention, desire under any circumstances to return to government," he said.

Then Halliburton stock rose slightly. On May 31, Cheney filed an intent to sell nearly half his Halliburton holdings, about a hundred thousand shares, for an estimated payoff of $5.1 million. If there were a futures market on the vice presidency, this stock sale would have grabbed the attention of Wall Street analysts.

One of those "many good candidates" to whom Cheney referred was Oklahoma governor Frank Keating. He made everybody's short list. Keating had all the qualities the campaign wanted. The former FBI agent had served in a number of posts in the Reagan and Bush administrations. He was widely praised for his response to the Oklahoma City bombing. A devout Catholic, he was a favorite of the GOP base because of his pro-life stance. Granted, Oklahoma was a lock for Republicans, but Clinton's choice of Gore had disproved the conventional wisdom that a ticket needed regional diversity or a state with a large number of electoral votes. Above all, Keating's self-effacing style wouldn't upstage Bush. That was one of the overarching concerns regarding the VP pick. Cheney had a budget for polling, and campaign advisers went so far as to present focus groups with pictures of Bush in different pairings, to check the height ratio.

So it was not a surprise that the governor received a phone call from his old friend Dick Cheney. After the Oklahoma City bombing, Keating had successfully recruited Cheney to chair the fundraising committee for the memorial to the victims. Cheney wanted to send Keating a background questionnaire that was being given to all the potential nominees. Would he fill it out? Keating had been through this before, having worked in three separate government agencies: Justice, Treasury, and Housing and Urban Development. He had been confirmed by the Senate four times and gone through six FBI background checks. He had even been a nominee for the U.S. Court of Appeals for the Tenth Circuit, and had been awaiting confirmation when George H. W. Bush lost to Bill Clinton. How bad could Dick Cheney's questionnaire be? Keating readily assented. Others got the call as well: Pennsylvania governor Tom Ridge, Nebraska senator Chuck Hagel, Tennessee senator Bill Frist, and former Tennessee governor Lamar Alexander, to name a few on a "short list" of about eleven.

The questionnaire was extensive. Lamar Alexander received the eighty-three-question document in early June, during what was supposed to be his holiday month in Nantucket. It asked for the address of every residence in which he had lived from the age of nine, every political contribution he had made since the age of eighteen, every taped interview he'd given, and every article written about him. The last item was laughable. All the prospective candidates had lived in the public spotlight, many for decades. "I have been governor of Tennessee twice, run for president twice, I've been through a Senate confirmation [when appointed secretary of education], and I've never seen anything like it," Alexander would tell *The Washington Post*.

"These [forms] are not easy to do," says a Republican who has participated in a vice presidential search. "It's a long, complicated process. It's everything: personal history, family health; but it's real heavy on financial. You can spend thousands on this with your CPA and lawyers."

"Dick Cheney knows more about me than my mother, father, and wife," Tennessee senator Bill Frist told the *Post* after filling out the questionnaire.

Keating gave Cheney three big indexed binders with an offer of boxes of supporting background material. While the search meandered on, the governor basked in the media exposure that the consideration brought him. As the candidates complied with Cheney's interrogatories, a steady drumbeat of newspaper stories and television chatter hashed and rehashed who was up and why that person would be best or not. Campaign officials shrugged and told reporters that the only two people in the know were Bush and Cheney. Communication Director Karen Hughes said Bush "leaves the room" when Cheney calls to report on how the search is progressing.

On July 3, Cheney visited Bush's ranch in Crawford, Texas, to give what campaign spokesman Ari Fleischer termed "an update." Bush and Cheney participated in the obligatory press conference before their meeting. The all-business Halliburton CEO carried a battered briefcase in which he had brought information from the questionnaires. "I'm running the process in advance to make sure we've done the kind of thorough scrub on these individuals in terms of their backgrounds both public and private that you would expect these days of a vice president," said Cheney.

After he accepted the nomination, he would subsequently describe to CNN's Larry King what happened later that day. "After lunch, [Bush] walked me out on the back porch and reiterated once again his desire to consider me as a potential candidate for the post," he related. "And I told him at that point that—in light of his desires and an obligation I felt, that I'd take a look at it; that I'd talk to my family about it, and see whether or not it was something that I could agree to."

It was official—at least between Bush and Cheney. They were still not ready to tell the public. Within a week, Cheney went to Washington, D.C, for a thorough medical exam by his doctors. He had to answer the same nagging question Bush's father had asked before choosing Cheney as secretary of defense. The man had survived three heart attacks and quadruple bypass surgery. He suffered from high cholesterol and gout and had been treated for skin cancer. Could he endure the rigors of a presidential campaign? Would he be able to serve? His doctors once again pronounced him ready to go.

On July 15, Bush and Cheney met with the "iron triangle" of Rove,

Hughes, and Joe Allbaugh. Hughes would claim that it was the first time the group had talked through the ramifications of naming Cheney VP. The Halliburton CEO would manage to escape the scrubbing he required for the nominees under his review. According to Hughes, Allbaugh would vet Cheney's public record and, implausibly, Bush, a man notoriously averse to details, would look into Cheney's finances and personal life. (At one point, Hughes also claimed that Cheney had investigated himself.)

The most serious consideration was still Cheney's health. Before they announced, Bush and his father, who approved of the choice, wanted a second opinion. Bush family friend and cardiac surgeon Denton Cooley spoke with Cheney's doctors. Cooley, a heart transplant pioneer, agreed that Dick Cheney's heart was up to the task. Still, the search charade continued. During this period, Bush and Cheney had high-profile meetings with potential candidates, even flying a clueless Senator John Danforth to a private meeting in Chicago.

On Thursday, July 20, Bush publicly ruled out Florida senator Connie Mack and Colin Powell, who had long made it clear he wanted the State Department. When asked about Cheney, Bush paused, smiled, and then said: "I'm not going there." The next day Cheney boarded a Halliburton jet and flew to Wyoming to change his voter registration from Dallas to Jackson. (The Constitution precludes the Electoral College from voting for a vice president and president from the same state.) The same day, NBC's Lisa Myers broke the Wyoming news, thanks to a tip from her colleague Pete Williams, who had returned to the media after a stint as SecDef Cheney's spokesman. The story helped beat back a growing draft-McCain movement among influential Republicans that threatened the Bush-Cheney plans.

According to the campaign narrative, Bush called Cheney in Dallas at 6:22 A.M. on Monday morning with a formal offer. Lynne Cheney answered the phone, as the nominee (the one with the health problems) was exercising on his treadmill. Then the future president started to call the other candidates to break the news.

By the time Keating received Bush's call, he wasn't surprised or entirely disappointed. The Oklahoman still believed in Bush and believed in his ability to win. Keating had been the first governor to endorse his colleague from Texas. If the GOP took the White House, there would be cabinet posts to fill. He had served as Attorney General Meese's second in command at Justice during the Reagan administration and hoped to be appointed to the top job. Keating publicly praised Cheney and volunteered to serve in any way he could. "Whatever he wants me to do, I'll do it," he told *The Washington Times*, even if it was just "to serve iced tea at a reception somewhere."

For Keating, the other shoe didn't drop until December. By that time, the Bush-Cheney transition team needed an attorney general. Governor Keating planned to spend Christmas giving out presents to the members of the Oklahoma National Guard stationed in Kosovo. Before leaving, he called Cheney to say that while he was happy to continue as governor, he was available for attorney general. Cheney asked Keating for a refresher on something the Oklahoma governor had disclosed about money he had accepted from retired New York banker Jack Dreyfus. Keating proceeded to retell the story of how Dreyfus had contacted him while he was at the U.S. Justice Department in 1988 with an idea to use the widely prescribed anticonvulsant Dilantin to medicate federal prisoners. Keating had hooked up Dreyfus with a prison official. Nothing had come of the idea, but Keating and Dreyfus became friends. Two years later, Dreyfus started writing checks to the Keating family to help pay education costs for the children. Keating would describe the gifts as simply a friendly gesture from an incredibly wealthy man. The gifts eventually totaled $250,000, all publicly disclosed when legally required. Keating offered to send the filings from the various ethics offices that had cleared the gifts, but the terse vice president–elect didn't want them. Keating sent a note to Cheney explaining it all again anyway. On the way back from Kosovo, as his plane refueled in Iceland, Keating learned that Bush had picked John Ashcroft for AG.

In early January, Keating took a call from *Newsweek*'s Michael Isikoff while in Florida for the college football national championship between the Oklahoma Sooners and Florida State. The reporter wanted to talk about Dreyfus. Isikoff's story of the compromising gifts spread quickly to newspapers in Oklahoma and Washington, as the governor tried in vain to defend himself. As the controversy grew, a furious Keating called to complain to White House chief of staff Andy Card, eliciting an apologetic return call from Bush, who confirmed that someone from the campaign had leaked the information. Keating never learned why. In his article, Isikoff focused on Keating's comments from 1999, when drug use allegations in-

volving George W. Bush first surfaced. Keating, responding to a hypo-
thetical question, said all candidates should "address issues about private
conduct. . . . In today's world, every one of us who serves in public office
needs to answer questions about conduct that is arguably criminal." The
statements had apparently upset Bush. It was, Isikoff asserted, seen as an
example of disloyalty.

One Republican political friend of Keating sees another motive.
Karen Hughes had described Keating as the best surrogate the Bush campaign had. Keating was a star, a legitimate threat to Cheney in four years.
Cheney had moved Nelson Rockefeller off Gerald Ford's ticket and
watched the dump-Quayle movement in the last year of the presidency of
Bush's father. "Thinking ahead to 2004, now Frank Keating would never
be a threat to [Cheney]," says the longtime GOP consultant. "It's too bad
that they had to ruin his career to do it." Oklahoma Democrats savaged
Keating, and ultimately he would exhaust his savings to repay Dreyfus in
order to put the issue to rest. After serving out his term, he left public life,
accepting a position as the head of a Washington trade association. But he
had been in the game long enough to know who was responsible for
sidelining his political career. When he wrote his requisite check to the
Bush-Cheney campaign in 2004, Frank Keating omitted Dick Cheney's
name.

Dick Cheney had at least six months to contemplate what it would be like
to be George W. Bush's vice president before he publicly accepted the
nomination. But he'd had years to observe the younger George Bush and
understand his limitations. Cheney knew in a way few others do what it is
like to work inside the Oval Office and what could be accomplished with
that power. Plans across decades, spoken and unspoken, percolated in his
brain. Maybe he had even sketched some of those ideas out previously
with Bush. In his first media appearance as the nominee, on *Larry King
Live*, the former Ford chief of staff articulated the importance of "that
personal relationship you develop with the president."

"In recent administrations," said Cheney, "the vice president's role has
taken on new meaning and new significance, but that's primarily because
the job of the man on top is big enough that there's plenty of work to go
around. And recent presidents have been willing to share that."

When he accepted the invitation to join the ticket, Cheney could indulge in thoughts of how he would redefine the vice presidency. According to some polls, Gore trailed Bush by as much as 16 percentage points. That would change with a Bush nosedive that started with the selection of Dick Cheney. The failure to properly vet and prepare for the announcement became apparent immediately. George, Laura, Lynne, and Dick flew to Casper for a formal announcement. It was supposed to be a victory lap of sorts, but at a pre-event press conference, George and Dick faced a barrage of questions about Cheney's congressional record, helpfully provided to reporters by Democratic operatives. "I am generally proud of my record in the House," Cheney hedged. "I'm sure, if I were to go back and look at the individual votes, I could probably find some that I might tweak and do a bit differently."

There were already plenty of people who were doing the looking for him. Within days, the Democratic National Committee had aired a television commercial defining Cheney as a right-wing extremist. "Cheney was one of only eight members of Congress to oppose the Clean Water Act; one of the few to vote against Head Start. He even voted against the school lunch program, against health insurance for people who lost their jobs," detailed the ad.

In fact, his congressional voting record was so far from the mainstream it might as well have been in another river valley. In a body of 435 members, Cheney often aligned himself on the losing side of landslides. His mind wasn't focused on individual votes as much as on control of the House. Cheney voted against a ban on armor-piercing bullets (one of only twenty-one to do so), against a ban on plastic guns that could escape detection by X-ray machines (one of four), against the Federal Employees Medical Leave Act (one of nine), and against the reauthorization of the Endangered Species Act (one of sixteen).

In those early days of the campaign, when Cheney was confronted with these and other similar votes on television talk shows, he seemed flustered and defensive. After pointed questioning by Sam Donaldson, Cheney tartly replied, "Well, Sam, I'm sorry but I explained my vote. . . . I think the key question, again, if we come back to the trivial aspects of the debates that rage in Washington, is what we're going to do in the future."

In a campaign environment of sound bites and absolute positions, he couldn't explain the context of those votes satisfactorily. How could he make it understood that they occurred during a procedural war that he was waging against Tip O'Neill and Jim Wright? While most, if not all, of those votes stemmed from his actual beliefs, they were more than anything tactical statements of noncooperation with a leadership he despised. Since the truth wasn't an option, Cheney fell back on his calm and measured persona to draw a contrast between how he had voted a decade earlier and what viewers saw on television.

But the bad press continued. His tenure as a freewheeling CEO at Halliburton quickly became an issue as journalists wondered whose interests he really represented. Cheney had once advocated reducing the world's oil supplies so gasoline prices would rise, which in turn would spur exploration and result in more business for Halliburton. Under questioning from Tim Russert, Cheney allowed that $2-a-gallon gasoline might be too expensive for the average consumer. (By 2006, gas topped $3 a gallon in many places, and oil company profits soared.) CEO Cheney's penchant for badmouthing and otherwise trying to undermine international sanctions generated media clucking as well. While Cheney made halfhearted attempts to stay true to his belief that sanctions had failed in places like Cuba and Iran, he insisted that the policy he'd follow would be Bush's. His record raised additional issues. It came out that in the past five years, while living in Dallas, he had voted only twice in sixteen elections. Questions arose about conflicts of interest involving his executive compensation.

It was not until the 2000 Republican convention in Philadelphia that Cheney finally found his campaign métier: attack dog. Nobody could say nasty things and make them sound measured and matter-of-fact like Dick. In the coming weeks, the Bush campaign would have to go negative to recoup the lead it had lost after Cheney joined the ticket. They would imprison Gore inside a distorted caricature from which he could not escape. Cheney would take the lead in putting him there. It comes down to credibility, he would say. Gore "simply makes some things up out of whole cloth and repeats them over and over again until he's called on it." GOP campaign consultant Stuart Stevens explained it best: "We couldn't control whether or not Gore might suddenly wake up and latch onto a powerful, coherent message. But we could remind people why they didn't like Gore."

Cheney's convention speech on August 2 was a tour de force. Democrats counted twenty-two separate attacks. The speech included a rousing refrain of "It's time for them to go." The biggest applause line came after

Cheney accused Clinton and Gore of "extend[ing] our military commitments while depleting our military power." He had led the troops as secretary of defense in the first Bush administration. He vowed they would soon have a commander in chief they could respect. "I can promise them now, help is on the way," Cheney said to the cheers of delegates.

On election night, the Bush ticket and campaign advisers assembled at the governor's mansion in Austin to watch the returns. Bush senior's old confidant James Baker III joined them. For Bush it was an olive branch extended to a man he didn't particularly like. For Cheney it was déjà vu. Baker had been Ford's campaign manager in the other national election Cheney had quarterbacked, Ford v. Carter. That vote had been close enough to contemplate what to do if it came down to a contested election. With an even closer vote looming in 2000, this time the campaign would take no chances. They had a team of lawyers on standby, ready to contest the election if necessary. This one wasn't going to slip away. The evening dragged into the morning without a result. As Baker drove back to Houston, Bush called him and asked him to go to Florida to bring home their victory.

The day after the election, it was Cheney more than Bush who struck the tone and made a bold tactical move. He declared the Republican ticket the winner. They had won, and it behooved Gore to recognize that and move on. "I would simply add to what the governor says," Cheney told reporters at a press conference. "We look forward to getting this matter resolved as quickly as possible so we can get on with the important business of transition."

By that Friday, November 10, Cheney was planning the transition even as a recount proceeded in Florida and Bush hid at the ranch in Crawford. As the process dragged on, the soon-to-be-vice-president-elect took the lead in morning conference calls with Baker and Bush, demanding they give no quarter to the Gore team. Two days before Thanksgiving, with a victor still not proclaimed, Cheney woke up at 3:30 A.M. with a familiar sensation on the left side of his chest. He rousted Lynne, and with his Secret Service agents in tow, headed for the emergency room at George Washington University Hospital while medical staff received phone calls telling them to come in to work immediately.

Heart attack number four would come for the fifty-nine-year-old on the cusp of unprecedented power. Doctors found 90 percent of one of his arteries blocked and surgically installed a wire mesh stent to open up the passage. During his campaign checkup four months earlier—the one to determine whether he was healthy enough to withstand a presidential campaign and the rigors of the Oval Office—doctors had performed a stress test, but it appears they had failed to do an angiogram, a more invasive procedure that can detect blockages in the arteries.

When Cheney left the hospital just two days after the attack, he was determined to make one thing clear: This setback would not deal him out of a return to the White House. Cheney's will and ambition were too strong for that, just as they had been back in Wyoming with the first heart attack during the first congressional campaign. But Cheney's heart attack this time was more severe than has previously been reported, according to a source knowledgeable about his case. The immediate care he received at the hospital—care not available to most Americans—probably saved his life.

He told reporters outside George Washington University Hospital that Bush had vetted his health before he joined the ticket. "Nothing has happened subsequent to that that changes their judgment with respect to my ability to be able to perform the responsibilities of that office," he insisted.

Yet Cheney was not a healthy man. In March, the same artery clogged again, requiring yet another procedure to reopen it. Then in late June, doctors implanted under the skin near Cheney's collarbone the latest in heart technology. The Medtronic GEM III DR monitors the heart and can both speed or slow down its rhythm when necessary. Described as having "an emergency room in your chest," the device is implanted only in patients who are at risk of sudden death from heart failure.

There is one school of thought in Washington that holds that Cheney's health problems have contributed to a change in his personality. Those who ascribe to this theory point to Al Haig. James Cannon helped prepare Haig for his Senate confirmation hearing for secretary of state in the Reagan administration. Cannon had known Haig before he received his triple bypass surgery prior to the confirmation. "Haig was a different person," he recalls. "He was messianic and had completely blotted out Watergate."

Haig himself has always denied that his health problems altered his personality, as would Cheney, no doubt. But as Cannon observes, "We don't see change in ourselves."

It is unknown if Cheney suffered any brain damage from his numerous heart attacks. A heart attack occurs when a clot forms in any of the coronary arteries. When this happens, a portion of the heart no longer receives oxygen and vital nutrients and stops functioning properly. End organs such as the brain and kidneys may have decreased blood flow from this reduction in heart function, especially during the acute phase of the heart attack or during subsequent episodes. Since the blood is responsible for transporting oxygen to all the tissues, cells may begin to die in the brain and other organs. Cheney has long suffered from high cholesterol and hardening of the arteries, which has the potential to create areas of plaque around the body, restricting the flow of blood in the circulatory system, including to the brain. The possibility that Cheney's health problems and the medications his doctors prescribe for them affect his mental state is real. Yet the vice president has never released his full medical records for public review. Nor will he give the media the precise list of medications he takes. And when *Nightline*'s Ted Koppel pressed him in 2001, Cheney bristled at the idea that he has not been forthcoming. He cited at least three press conferences given by his doctors. "I'm probably the best known heart patient in America," he said. "I think we've provided a vast amount of information."

On November 24, the day Cheney left the hospital, the U.S. Supreme Court agreed to hear *Bush v. Gore*.

Doctors had suggested that Cheney could return to work in a few weeks, but he didn't have that kind of time. A long absence would feed speculation that he was unfit for the job. And he was doing much of the thinking for the campaign. Not only did he have to plan for a transition, he needed to do it with private funding, as public money would not be available until the election was conclusively decided. He was back at work in three days. He opened the Bush-Cheney Presidential Transition Foundation, Inc., in a suite of an office in McLean, Virginia, not far from his house.

The Transition Foundation existed in the kind of pre-Watergate legal gray area tailor-made for Cheney's needs. The law permitting such a foundation dated to a legislative fix passed after the contested election of 1960 between John F. Kennedy and Richard Nixon. Donors were not subject to the Freedom of Information Act or any other disclosure or oversight requirements. By mid-December the Bush-Cheney foundation had raised $3 million. Funding was assumed to come from corporate executives, including energy industry stalwarts. A number of the Bush-Cheney campaign's top corporate donors called "pioneers" sat on the transition teams that handled the various agencies that regulated their businesses. Company executives picked lobbyists to fill regulatory positions. Long after the election was decided, the foundation continued. Its new function was funding policy groups managed by Michigan governor John Engler and former New York representative Bill Paxon, at the time a high-powered K Street lobbyist. Engler and Paxon would push the Bush-Cheney agenda in Congress.

To staff his transition team, Cheney did what he had done throughout his career. He turned to people he could trust. His first appointment was David Gribben, the high school friend from Wyoming who had worked for Cheney in Congress, at the Department of Defense, and then at Halliburton. David Addington, Cheney's staffer from the House Intelligence Committee and the Iran-Contra Committee, was also brought on to the transition team, as was fellow Pentagon alum Scooter Libby.

On December 12, the U.S. Supreme Court ruled in favor of Bush and Cheney by a 5–4 vote. In the weeks and months to come, Cheney would assemble Bush's cabinet. The vice president–elect understood that Bush didn't want briefing books or excessive detail. Cheney would provide Bush what he needed to know in digestible nuggets. The president-elect would learn of the progress of his administration's transition from his number two man. The filter was in place, and Cheney was finally about to arrive back in the Oval Office, if not in the top position, in the closest second place in American history.

NINE

Soldiers of Fortune

Since George Bush and Dick Cheney replaced Bill Clinton and Al Gore, congressional oversight of the executive branch occurs only when there is a crisis so outrageous that Congress can't ignore it—such as CBS's release of harrowing images of U.S. soldiers torturing prisoners at Abu Ghraib or *The New York Times* report that the administration is engaged in illegal wiretapping. Even in those instances, the response of Congress has proven tepid at best, and the surprises were revealed by the media rather than by congressional investigators.

Michael Mobbs's June 18, 2004, briefing of a House committee staff included a surprising moment of testimony that should have been repeated before a full committee hearing. Yet only House staffers in a Rayburn Building committee room would ever hear what the lawyer from the Defense Department had to say. Mobbs was on the Hill to discuss what the vice president's staff might have known of the multibillion-dollar government contracts awarded to Halliburton and its subsidiary Kellogg Brown & Root. It was one of the smaller questions at the edge of a potential scandal involving Vice President Dick Cheney. The larger and more direct question—Did Dick Cheney help steer $7 billion in Iraq construction con-tracts to Halliburton?—was discreetly avoided. In a Congress that took its oversight responsibility seriously, Mobbs's visit to the Hill would have been a prelude to testimony before a full committee. In a republic with a healthy system of public ethics, a no-bid government contract awarded to a company that was mailing deferred compensation checks to the vice president would itself be a full-blown ethics scandal.

This is no longer that republic.

At the time Mobbs went up to the Hill to testify, Kellogg Brown & Root (KBR) was the nation's biggest single recipient of government fund-ing for military logistics and reconstruction. Two years into the Bush-Cheney administration, the company was the Army's number one contractor, up from the number 19 spot it had held in 2002. Not only had Dick Cheney been Halliburton's CEO for five years before he was elected vice president, the no-bid process by which Halliburton got the contracts had been put in place ten years earlier by Cheney when he was secretary of defense. Democratic members of the House Committee on Govern-ment Reform, led by Los Angeles congressman Henry Waxman, wanted to know if anyone on the vice president's staff had been involved in award-ing the contracts. Considering what was known, Waxman believed his re-quest was within the reasonable scope of congressional oversight, so his committee staff members were among those questioning Mobbs.

The vice president didn't find it reasonable. He had already addressed the questions being asked of Mobbs on NBC's *Meet the Press* nine months before the June 2004 hearing, when Tim Russert asked Cheney if he was in any way involved in the awarding of Halliburton's Iraq contracts:

> Of course not, Tim. Tim, I had, when I was secretary of defense, I was
> not involved in awarding contracts. That's done at a far lower level.
> Secondly, when I ran Halliburton for five years and they were doing
> work for the Defense Department, which frankly they've been doing
> for sixty or seventy years, I never went near the Defense Department.
> I never lobbied the Defense Department on behalf of Halliburton.
> The only time I went back to the department during those eight years
> was to have my portrait hung, which is a traditional service rendered
> for former secretaries of defense. And since I left Halliburton to be-

come George Bush's vice president, I've severed all my ties with the company, gotten rid of all my financial interests. I have no financial interest in Halliburton of any kind and haven't had now for over three years. And as vice president, I have absolutely no influence of, involvement of, knowledge of in any way, shape or form of contracts let by the Corps of Engineers or anybody else in the federal government.

Defense Department officials stayed on message for the vice president, telling Waxman that Cheney's office had nothing to do with the contracts. Then Judicial Watch filed a Freedom of Information Act request for the information. When the DOD refused to comply with the request, the conservative public-interest law firm sued and obtained files that included an e-mail contradicting what Waxman had been told. In the e-mail, Defense Department contract officer Stephen Browning wrote that Halliburton contracts were "coordinated through the Vice President's office."

The staff meeting at which Mobbs testified was closed to the public. He wasn't sworn in, as this was not a full committee hearing with members of the House present. But as lying to Congress is a violation of federal law, staff members at the briefing expected the truth. They got more than they expected.

"We didn't know anything about Michael Mobbs at that time," says a staff member who sat in on the committee briefing. "Someone even asked if he was the same guy who wrote the Mobbs Declaration that was filed in the Hamdi case, saying Hamdi was a high-profile prisoner and had to be detained. We just knew he was a DOD employee coming up to address the issue of the Browning e-mail."

This was indeed the same Michael Mobbs who had appeared in court with a two-page memo written to strip Yaser Esam Hamdi of all his constitutional rights and justify his indefinite detention at Guantánamo Bay. He was more than an employee. Michael Mobbs was a high-level political appointee at the Defense Department. "We asked Mobbs who, outside the Pentagon, he had spoken to regarding the KBR contracts. He said he met with the deputies. . . . He began to name one deputy after another [including Cheney's deputy national security director Stephen Hadley, who chaired the meeting]. Then we asked him, what about Cheney's office? And he said, yeah, Scooter Libby."

"Yeah, Scooter Libby"?

That was a surprise.

"I don't think anybody in the room expected to hear that," says the House staff member.

Until he was indicted for perjury and obstruction of justice, I. Lewis "Scooter" Libby rode to work with Dick Cheney. As the vice president's chief of staff, he met with Cheney every day. They worked together. They were friends. Their families dined together. If Libby had been briefed on the Halliburton contracts, it was all but impossible that Dick Cheney was out of the loop. What Cheney had told Russert about the distance between his office and the Halliburton contracts was false. (It is not a crime to lie to a reporter.) In fact, much of what the vice president said on *Meet the Press* was not true. Dick Cheney received deferred compensation from Halliburton through 2003 and held more than $3 million in Halliburton stock options until some time in 2005, according to his IRS filings. But not according to what he told Russert. In the same year that Dick Cheney told the NBC news anchor "I have no financial interest in Halliburton of any kind and haven't had now for over three years," Halliburton paid the vice president $178,438 in deferred compensation.

The focus on Halliburton and KBR put the White House in a bind. If deferred compensation and stock holdings in a corporation doing business with the federal government weren't enough to trigger the public's gag reflex, stacking the deck in a $7-billion poker game was. The idea that the public would get wind of the Vice President's Office's involvement with Halliburton's war contracts was a problem. The administration could have opened its books to the public, or at least to Congress, to demonstrate that there was no impropriety. Instead, they shut down. The administration— and the Army Corps of Engineers—took great care to control any paper or anecdotal trail that might taint them. Documents were tightly guarded. Members of Congress were denied access to contracts. Responses to reporters' questions were circumspect at best. Or awkward at worst, as White House spokesperson Scott McClellan demonstrated when confronted at a press conference: "It's not something that, as a contracting matter, the White House decides; it's something the Pentagon decides."

Pentagon e-mails and Michael Mobbs's statement to the House committee staff contradicted McClellan's clumsy denial and the vice president's artful, self-assured dismissal of the same question. As information was pieced together by the minority staff on the House Government Reform Committee, it became evident that Vice President Cheney was misinformed.

Or he was lying.

Halliburton has a history of outrageous costs, huge unexpected billings, and unexplained charges that extend back to the Clinton administration and into Bosnia. But the company's incestuous relationship with the Bush-Cheney administration is a case study in political cronyism, out-of-control outsourcing, and absence of oversight—much of it related to Halliburton's vast logistical undertaking in Iraq. Some of the issues have been covered by the press, some exposed by Halliburton Watch and other advocacy groups, some ignored.

Responding to requests from Congress, the Army Corps of Engineers reported that Halliburton billed $2.64 per gallon on seventy-five million gallons of gasoline it transported from Kuwait into Iraq for civilian use. At the same time, the Iraqi national fuel company was paying only 97 cents a gallon to purchase fuel in Kuwait and other nations bordering Iraq. Also at the same time, the U.S. Defense Energy Support Center, which supplied fuel for the military, was importing gas from Kuwait at $1.32 per gallon. No one in the region was charging Halliburton's rates. Halliburton subcontracted with Altanmia Commercial Marketing Company, which had no experience in transporting fuel, much less doing it in a war zone. Altanmia was the preferred provider of the U.S. ambassador in Kuwait, so Halliburton wasn't exclusively at fault. At least that's what is suggested in an e-mail that Ambassador Richard Jones wrote to his staff: "Tell KBR to get off their butts and conclude deals with Kuwait now! Tell them we want a deal done with al-Tanmia within 24 hours and don't take any excuses." In the end, the $61 million that KBR paid above market price was passed on to taxpayers. The gasoline contracts were bid, according to Waxman, by telephone in one day. Evidently, not much effort was put into finding the best price.

In another gasoline deal, a Halliburton procurement officer took a $1 million kickback for transportation subcontractors, according to the company's own admission and an indictment handed down in Illinois. Halliburton cooperated with a government investigation and repaid the $6.3 million that the kickback scheme had cost taxpayers.

On another occasion, Halliburton billed the government for forty-two thousand meals per day when it was serving only fourteen thousand. Halliburton did not reimburse the government, because the language in their contract for meals didn't specify how many meals per day they had committed to serve.

There were other accounts found in embassy e-mails of subcontractors delivering bribes or kickback money to Halliburton executives staying at the Kuwait Hilton. In most cases, Halliburton has denied any impropriety.

The Kuwait Hilton was also the scene of a quintessential "ugly American" story involving KBR's Middle East Division chief Tom Crum and his wife's wristwatch. According to an embassy e-mail, Crum's wife lost a diamond-encrusted watch on the hotel grounds and insisted that the Hilton management find it or replace it. When the hotel manager couldn't turn up the watch, valued at $2,600, Mr. Crum called and ordered him "get off your fucking ass, put my wife in a car, and go get her a watch." With Halliburton (more precisely, U.S. taxpayers) spending about $1.5 million a month at the Hilton, Mrs. Crum's watch looked like a bargain. The hotel manager accommodated the Crums, opening up a hotel jewelry store in the middle of the night to make nice. The e-mail, one of four hundred documents obtained by the House Committee on Government Reform, suggests that KBR will make demands of local contractors if the stakes are high enough. While a small incident, it says a great deal about how the Army's private ministry of public works conducts itself in Iraq.

Some of these transgressions can be attributed to the hasty, nasty, and hugely expensive nature of a war in which logistical services are contracted out to companies whose managers are required to increase earnings. Call it the fiscal fog of war. And the fiscal fog of war is more dense when the war and occupation are as badly planned as the Bush-Cheney-Rumsfeld invasion of Iraq. Some transgressions can be attributed to cost-plus contracts that encourage big spending because company profits are based on a percentage of total costs. "A billion here, a billion there, and pretty soon you're talking real money," Illinois senator Everett Dirksen said more than forty years ago. Today, real money is more than $10 billion in Halliburton Iraq War contracts that don't pass the standard ethical smell test. The vice president created the process that started money flowing from the federal treasury into the accounts of Halliburton and its subsidiaries. The vice president's staff, if not the vice president himself, was involved in directing the flow of some of that money. And despite his public statements, or his odd parsing of the term "financial interests," the vice president had a financial interest in Halliburton when the deals were being done.

Halliburton's Iraq War revenue stream can be followed back to the military outsourcing that began in 1992, while Dick Cheney was secretary of defense. At Cheney's bidding, the Defense Department paid Halliburton $3.9 million to prepare a classified report on privatizing the logistics of war: housing, feeding, refueling, and clothing troops. Halliburton went through the $3.9 million, secured an additional $5 million for a follow-up, then landed a five-year Corps of Engineers contract to provide logistical support for the Army. That process became the template for Halliburton-KBR Iraq War contracts ten years later. It was an extraordinary deal for Halliburton. On the DOD's dime—or millions—the company wrote a classified marketing plan for its own product. Then—because it owned the proprietary information, which was classified—it effortlessly moved into the market. As Halliburton followed the Army into Somalia and Bosnia, it became the Wal-Mart of the defense service economy. Halliburton even used Wal-Mart's big-box pricing plan: Accept low margins, squeeze competitors, and make it up on volume. The cost-plus pricing model the company devised guaranteed one percent profit on contracts—with the possibility of bonuses that would push the profit margin up to almost eight percent. It wasn't a win-win proposition, it was win-and-win-bigger, with an incentive to increase expenditures in order to increase the company's return. It was particularly lucrative when buying and shipping commodities, which entailed little work but was subject to the same one-percent-plus billing.

In the run-up to the Iraq War, the Bush-Cheney administration also turned to Halliburton. KBR was paid $1.9 million to draw up a contingency plan to extinguish the oil well fires Saddam Hussein's troops were expected to ignite. The proposed Restore Iraqi Oil (RIO) plan was worth as much as $2 billion to the company that would win the contract. The Defense Department was inviting Halliburton to follow the course it charted ten years earlier: Draw up a contingency plan on which contractors would bid, then join the competition in bidding on the contract. The process put Halliburton squarely in conflict with procurement guidelines at the U.S. Army Corps of Engineers, which was issuing the big Iraq contracts. USACE (and most other) procurement protocols do not allow a company that drafts a contingency plan to bid on the contracts the plan creates. It's a logical prohibition: knowledge of the scope and budget of a plan provides a competitive advantage. Yet Pentagon officials waived the rule. Halliburton drafted the contingency plan, then bid on the contract.

That odd arrangement caught the attention of Bunnatine Greenhouse, the PARC, or Principal Assistant Responsible for Contracting, at the Corps of Engineers. It was not only that KBR was bidding on a proposal it had drafted; "Bunny" Greenhouse sensed something more was afoot when a large contingent of Halliburton contractors filed into a meeting at which the contract was to be discussed. The date was February 26, 2003. The United States was very close to invading Iraq. And the Pentagon secure room where the bid was to be discussed was crammed full of Halliburton executives. Greenhouse was so disturbed by the presence of KBR executives that she discreetly asked the lieutenant general chairing the meeting to order them to leave the room.

Greenhouse agreed to accept the "compelling emergency" logic, which would permit awarding the contract to the contractor that had prepared the contingency plan. The compelling emergency was evident. Two days earlier, the United States, Spain, and Britain had submitted a resolution to the U.N. Security Council asking for authorization to use military force in Iraq. But Halliburton was being awarded a five-year sole-source contract worth $7 billion. Greenhouse wasn't buying into a five-year emergency with a guaranteed 2 to 5 percent profit margin. She insisted the contract be limited to one year, which would allow the government to evaluate Halliburton's performance and possibly reopen the contract for competition at the end of the year.

She was the lone dissenter in the room and knew she couldn't stop the contract. But the five-year term bothered her enough that she included an addendum to her signature, as she had done on other contracts about which she had reservations. "I caution that extending this sole source effort beyond a one-year period could convey an invalid perception that there is not strong intent for a limited competition." The one-line protest, squeezed in between her signature and that of Lieutenant General Robert Flowers, would ultimately, it is alleged, cost Greenhouse her management position. After she added that cautionary note to the KBR contract, Greenhouse received the first negative evaluation in her tenure at the

Corps of Engineers, where she had climbed from a lowly G-5 to the apex of the management pyramid. Following the poor evaluation, she was demoted, stripped of her oversight responsibilities, and moved into a small office. Rather than dismiss her for challenging the contract, her supervisors claimed Greenhouse was not doing her job.

Bunny Greenhouse didn't know just how compromised the procurement process was—even if her instincts were right. And she was no match for Michael Mobbs, who was moving the contract through the bureaucracy. Mobbs is an example of the hybrid vigor that results from the Bush-Cheney administration's inbreeding. In the late eighties, Mobbs was at the Feith & Zell law firm, where Bush's future undersecretary of state Douglas Feith was a name partner. Mobbs left Feith & Zell to work as a transactional lawyer in Moscow in 1990, when Western business interests saw Russia as a perpetual boom economy. When the inevitable bust came at the end of the 1990s, Mobbs was part of the great American business-class flight from Moscow. He got back to the United States as George Bush and Dick Cheney were staffing up for war and got a DOD gig because his former colleague from Feith & Zell brought him in. At the time Halliburton's deal with the Army Corps of Engineers was consummated, Mobbs was a special assistant to Undersecretary of Defense Feith.

Unlike some of the administration's other crony hires, Mobbs was not without qualifications. He is an accomplished international trade lawyer with experience in arms control negotiations in the Reagan administration. He is fluent in Russian, and by all accounts a genuinely decent guy. If he was ill suited to the Iraq civil administration director's position Feith eventually slid him into—a failed performance in a hopeless situation—at least he was adept at negotiating contracts, such as Halliburton's deal with the Corps of Engineers. His pedigree and CV—undergraduate degree at Yale, University of Chicago Law School, undersecretary of state during the Reagan administration, partner at Feith & Zell, high-profile positions at several other law firms—made him a formidable adversary for Bunny Greenhouse. Greenhouse grew up in a rigidly segregated Louisiana cotton town and worked her way through the bureaucracy to become the first African American to have the final say on procurement at the Army Corps of Engineers— a civil servant earning $137,000 a year. Mobbs is part of the permanent government, men who move effortlessly from the public to the private sector and are always at ease with their authority. (Greenhouse's story, however, might hold considerable appeal for the jury hearing her whistleblower lawsuit in Washington, D.C.—where even the most skillful practitioners of voir dire can't purge juries of African Americans and bureaucrats.)

Bunny Greenhouse had no idea that the Halliburton contract was a done deal when she sat down in that Pentagon secure room on February 26. An e-mail written by a Corps of Engineers official discloses that the process had already been completed by February 5. The names of the correspondents are redacted, though it was later established that one of them was Stephen Browning, director of the South Pacific Division of the Army Corps of Engineers. The language indicates that the contracting decisions had been run through Cheney's staff, with the president standing in line to sign off on whatever was acceptable to the Office of the Vice President.

> Accompanied OHRA [Office of Reconstruction and Humanitarian Aid] leader to get release of declass and authority to execute RIO [the Restore Iraq Oil program]. DepSecDef sent us to UnderSecPolicy Feith and gave him authority to approve both. Douglas Feith approved, contingent on informing the WH [White House] tomorrow. We expect no issue, since action has been coordinated with VPs office.

To keep pace with the administration's relentless war schedule, Mobbs had folded the Iraq contract into something known as the Logistics Civil Augmentation Program. LOGCAP is based on the system Halliburton devised in 1992, when Cheney was in charge at Defense. It is an open-ended monopoly contract through which a private company becomes the government quartermaster, providing services to the U.S. military. The Pentagon had rebid it again in 2001, and Halliburton/KBR had won a ten-year LOGCAP contract to supply meals, mail, and laundry service to troops in the field. Using the contract for Iraq oil infrastructure work and extinguishing oil well fires was a stretch. The career staff counsel at the Army Materiel Command objected, as did the deputy counsel to the Army. The Defense Department's general counsel, who answered to Doug Feith, overruled both lawyers. Feith was orchestrating the entire deal from the top.

There was even a backstory to the backstory. At a "Deputies' Committee" meeting of top level administrators in October 2002, Mobbs told the vice president's chief of staff, Scooter Libby, that Halliburton was getting the sole source contract. Mobbs had already contacted three companies—Halliburton, Bechtel, and Fluor—and determined that all three were capa-

ble of completing work in Iraq. He decided that Halliburton was better positioned because it was familiar with the military's operational plans. The
entire Restore Iraq Oil deal was done before it was announced. The February 26, 2003, meeting Bunny Greenhouse had attended in a secure room
at the Pentagon was a sham. The decision had been made at least four
months earlier—with the assent of the vice president's chief of staff.

There was even a role for Paul Wolfowitz, the deputy secretary of defense and the principal architect of the Iraq War and the larger plan to re-
make the Middle East. Wolfowitz, who first handed Secretary of Defense
Cheney the Iraq smackdown plan in 1992, wrote a December 2003 order
eliminating competitive bidding for $18 billion in Iraq reconstruction proj-
ects, essentially shutting out Halliburton's foreign competitors by restricting contracts to members of Bush's "Coalition of the Willing." With
Libby, Wolfowitz, and Feith's former law partner Michael Mobbs connected to the Halliburton deal, contract talks might as well have been
done at a neocon poker night.

The Corps of Engineers made one attempt to create a bidding
process—or at least the illusion of a bidding process. The agency was responding to prodding by Henry Waxman and embarrassing accounts of
Halliburton's cost overruns under the existing contract. Five months after
the February meeting that allegedly cost Bunny Greenhouse her position,
the Corps of Engineers reopened some of the Iraq oil contract work for
competitive bidding, informing contractors that $2 billion in work would
be made available. The bidders' conference was held in Dallas on July 14,
2003, and 184 contractors signed in. "It was a farce," says Sheryl Elam
Tappan, who prepared Bechtel's proposal. "The Iraq work plan was posted
on the Internet on a Friday afternoon. I read it Saturday morning and it
was crystal clear to me that it was all signed by U.S. government and Iraqi
Ministry of Oil people who had agreed to commit to Halliburton." Tappan, a consultant who had written contract proposals for Bechtel for
twelve years, was so offended by the process that she wrote a self-
published (and career-ending) book entitled *Shock and Awe in Fort Worth*.
In her book, and in an interview, Tappan makes a good case that the game
was over before it began. Her title itself poses an interesting question.
Why was such a big contracting process run out of the Corps's regional
offices in Fort Worth instead of Washington?

As bidders gathered in Dallas, Halliburton was already on the ground in Iraq, with more work in the pipeline—as a result of the contract that Bunny Greenhouse had protested. Tappan ran the numbers on a ten-page spreadsheet and concluded that 82 percent of the $1.144 billion for which Bechtel executives believed they were competing was already assigned to Halliburton by default. The work in Iraq was scheduled to be completed by December 2004. The Corps of Engineers wouldn't announce "the two winners" to emerge from the Dallas conference until October 15. In the end, it didn't wrap up the process until January. Many of the projects that bidders believed they were bidding on were already under way or even completed.

Tappan wasn't the only skeptic. As the Dallas meeting concluded, Sandy Davis from Fluor Engineering stood up and raised the question most in the room wouldn't touch:

> Just for the record, the last question. One of our worthy competitors you already have under contract over there and have had for a number of months. It happens that they've already performed all of the tasks that you ask for in the sample projects and can pull that information obviously off the shelf. So the direct question is, has the government performed a conflict-of-interest determination and convinced yourself that there's no competitive advantage to the incumbent?

The Corps of Engineers' lawyer responded that Team RIO, representatives of the agencies working on the Iraq oil projects, had written the contract in Baghdad and vetted it for conflicts. He didn't mention that Halliburton had participated in the Team RIO planning. Tappan, however, figured that out. She followed a paper trail to a Baghdad meeting held July 6, a week before the Dallas bidders' conference. Of the 184 competitors in the room in Dallas, only one had been in the room in Baghdad. Halliburton's RIO contract director had flown in from Baghdad to attend the Dallas meeting. "Nobody in that room believed the process was fair," Tappan says. "But contractors are like a big dysfunctional family. They keep quiet and take the abuse. If they get a reputation for speaking out in public, they fear they will lose work later."

Tappan called the head of the sales division at Bechtel and suggested they withdraw because the game was rigged. Bechtel withdrew its bid, though it competed for other work in Iraq. Bechtel's withdrawal from a bidding process in which they already had a substantial investment is an indictment of the system the Corps of Engineers was using. An executive at another company involved in the bidding agrees. "It was evident that we were competing for far less than what the Corps of Engineers said was available," he says. Tappan says the public blames the contractors, adding that "the government is supposed to manage and oversee the process."

In the three years since Bechtel and the others got shut out in Dallas, KBR emerges as the biggest and perhaps the only winner in the disastrous war in Iraq. The victory might be short-lived, not unlike the vice president's approval ratings. The war has obviously been better to KBR than it has to the vice president, whose public support is somewhere under 20 percent. But because the war didn't go quite as Cheney intended, when he predicted Iraqis would be greeting Americans with flowers, KBR's revenue stream is drying up. American and Iraqi money intended for rebuilding Iraq has been siphoned off to provide security in a civil war precipitated by the American invasion. KBR's declining fortunes are spelled out in its 2006 prospectus:

> Our government services revenue related to Iraq totaled approximately $5.4 billion in 2005, $7.1 billion in 2004 and $3.5 billion in 2003. We expect the volume of work under our LogCAP III contract to continue to decline in 2006 as our customer scales back the amount of services we provide under this contract. Moreover, the DoD can terminate, reduce the amount of work under, or replace our LogCAP contract with a new competitively bid contract at any time during the term of the contract. We expect the DoD will soon solicit competitive bids for a new multiple provider LogCAP IV contract to replace the current LogCAP III contract, under which we are the sole provider. Revenue from United States government agencies represented approximately 65% of our revenue in 2005 and 67% in 2004. The loss of the United States government as a customer, or a significant reduction in our work for it, would have a material adverse effect on our business and results of operations.

Corporations face legal sanctions, fines, and civil liability for lying to prospective shareholders. So the government's contractor has little choice but to admit that things aren't going so well in Iraq. After the 2006 prospectus was released, the Pentagon announced that the next LOGCAP contract will be split into three parts. The Army had decided that the old process of sole source, long-term contracts discouraged accountability, competitive pricing, and a broader range of services for the troops. The Pentagon's decision, if a little late, vindicates Bunny Greenhouse—and will certainly be included in the case her attorneys are compiling.

Did Dick Cheney know that Halliburton was being lined up for most of the work in Iraq? "Of course he knew," says a congressional staffer who has been working on Halliburton issues. "Of course the vice president knew what was going on. How does Cheney not know who is going to run all the Iraq infrastructure? Cheney had to know."

The vice president's office did not respond to questions regarding his possible involvement in the Halliburton contract. Yet an answer to the question—Did the vice president personally steer business to the company he had left two years earlier?—is not unobtainable. The House Committee on Government Reform could subpoena Scooter Libby and ask him. Or use its subpoena power to bring in Halliburton executives and ask them. That, however, is not going to happen—unless the Democrats win a majority of House seats in November 2006. The House Committee on Government Reform routinely overrules Henry Waxman's subpoena motions—on a straight party-line vote. (Waxman's enthusiasm for robust congressional oversight lies at the heart of Republican fears of a Democratic takeover of the House in 2006.)

So the story continues to evolve. Halliburton is at $16 billion and counting on its Iraq totals, even as profits decline. Bunny Greenhouse is awaiting her day in court, which might provide answers to some questions related to Halliburton. Mike Mobbs won't be back to tell his story to a congressional committee hearing open to the press and public unless and until Democrats control Congress. And as the country looks toward the 2006 midterm elections, the vice president has had little to say about Halliburton. He brushes off the few reporters' questions on the topic. He has largely ignored Waxman's inquiries. When Vermont senator Patrick Leahy approached him on the Senate floor on the eve of the 2004 elections and mentioned the sole source contracting that Bunny Greenhouse had challenged, Cheney's response was straightforward.

"Go fuck yourself," said the vice president of the United States.

TEN

Dick Cheney's War

I think he saw those towers come down, saw what terrorists were capable of, and at that moment he became a strategic hysteric," says a defense policy analyst who learned the trade while working for Georgia senator Sam Nunn.

It's an interesting theory:

A man known for almost unnerving calm and the ability to set aside emotion and make rational decisions even when dealing with angina so intense he is gasping for breath sees what al-Qaeda visited on two U.S. cities on a clear September morning and becomes Dr. Strangelove.

It's more convincing after discussing the September 11 attacks with Pentagon staffers who were caught in the inferno. Or with women who were told to remove their high heels and run—from the Pentagon, the Capitol, or the White House. Or with a seasoned military officer who ran head-on into Defense Secretary Donald Rumsfeld desperately searching for members of his staff in a smoke-filled corridor in the E Ring of the Pentagon.

Living that moment as Dick Cheney did, knowing that the one passenger jetliner unaccounted for was "ten minutes out" from Washington, must have had enormous transformational power.

There's another theory:

The al-Qaeda attack on September 11, 2001, was Dick Cheney's rendezvous with destiny. The moment he had been waiting for since he watched the nation's last imperial presidency collapse under the burden Richard Nixon imposed on it, then threw himself into Gerald Ford's effort to put the pieces of the shattered institution back together again. This is not to suggest that Dick Cheney wanted a violent, transformative event; but rather, that he was searching for the unifying principle that would define the U.S. role in the world in the absence of the threat of nuclear conflict with the Soviet Union.

Cheney's groping for that central purpose is evident in the digressive answer he gave Nicholas Lemann when interviewed for a May 2001 *New Yorker* article. Lemann wanted to know if there was an organizing principle that could be compared to the Cold War. In the interview, which was probably recorded six months before the 9/11 attack, Cheney responded:

> Well that's—I think it's much more difficult to say. Back at the time when I was at the Pentagon, ten years ago, the world had been arranged in a certain way throughout the postwar period, into the eighties. And because the Soviets represented a strategic threat to the United States—they could potentially threaten our very existence—we were organized from a military standpoint, and to some extent from an economic standpoint, to deal with that. When the Soviet threat went away, it was clearly a world-shaking event. The reunification of Europe, the end of the Cold War—it was fairly easily identified.
>
> It's much more difficult now. Whatever the arrangement is going to be in the twenty-first century is most assuredly being shaped right now.

Lemann asked if it still made sense to talk about "the threat," as we used to during the Cold War. Cheney said the threat is much different today:

> There are still regions of the world that are strategically vital to the U.S. . . . And anything that would threaten their independence or their relationships with the United States would be a threat to us. Also, you've still got to worry a bit about North Korea. You've got to

worry about the Iraqis, what ultimately develops in Iran. . . . I think we have to be more concerned than we ever have about so-called homeland defense, the vulnerability of our system to different kinds of attacks. Some of it homegrown, like Oklahoma City. Some inspired by terrorists external to the United States. . . . The threat of terrorist attack against the U.S., eventually, potentially, with weapons of mass destruction—bugs or gas, biological, or chemical agents, potentially even, someday, nuclear weapons. . . .

Cheney was holding his cards close to his vest. At the time, he was already involved in discussions about regime change in Iraq. And if he wasn't being evasive, he was way off the mark ("got to worry a bit") on North Korea.

Asked the question six months later, he would have answered with greater clarity. But like the American defense policy principles he struggled to describe at that moment, the Bush-Cheney administration lacked focus. In fact, it appeared that the team whose focus, discipline, and sense of purpose had carried it from the Florida recount to the White House was coming apart in those initial months in power.

Shortly before the September 11 attack, word from the Pentagon and Congress was that Cheney's confidant, colleague, and friend Don Rumsfeld was finished at Defense. While most agreed that Rummy had the right program for reform of the military, according to one retired general, Rumsfeld—"SecDef" for the second time in twenty-six years—was so arrogant and abusive that he alienated everyone he would need to make his reform agenda happen. Another source who served on a House committee at the time says Sean O'Keefe's name was floated as Rummy's replacement. O'Keefe had been comptroller at the Defense Department and secretary of the Navy during the first Bush Administration.

"Within six months Rumsfeld wrecked the DOD," says the general. "He refused to talk to the military. The opposite of what Cheney had done. He was worse than Les Aspin. He asked for a $37 billion appropriations increase. But he was out of sync with his own administration. All they were talking about over there was tax cuts. Nobody on the Hill took him seriously. No one in the Pentagon took him seriously.

"By September 8, they were talking about his replacement. [Senator Richard] Lugar, I would guess. O'Keefe would have been his deputy, not secretary. On September 7 there was a function at Walter Reed. [Senator Daniel] Inouye was there, [Senator Ted] Stevens, [Congressman Jack] Murtha. The talk then was that it was over for Rumsfeld."

The problems extended beyond the Pentagon. Six months into their first term, Bush and Cheney were adrift. Dick Cheney and Karl Rove treated Senator Jim Jeffords so shabbily that he left the Republican Party, returning Democrats to the majority. Secretary of State Colin Powell had to clean up after George Bush and negotiate a public apology when the president's hostile comments inflamed a crisis that began with an American EP-3 spy plane colliding with a Chinese fighter jet. The budget surplus was disappearing. The president was incapable of making a decision on stem cell research. And the vice president was back in the coronary unit at George Washington University Hospital, his third trip since the election. This visit required implanting a pacemaker/defibrillator in Cheney's chest, reviving late-night talk show jokes about George W. Bush being a "heartbeat away from the presidency."

The man who was a heartbeat away from the presidency was reading to second-graders in the Emma E. Booker Elementary School in Sarasota, Florida, when two passenger planes struck the World Trade Center towers on September 11. Dick Cheney was in his White House office with then national security advisor Condi Rice. As eight Secret Service agents escorted Cheney to the PEOC (the Presidential Emergency Operations Center bunker) in the East Wing, White House antiterrorism director Richard Clarke thought he saw "a reflection of horror" on Cheney's face. Among the others in the bunker were Lynne Cheney, political operative Mary Matalin, Cheney's chief of staff, Scooter Libby, deputy White House chief of staff Josh Bolten, and Bush's communications director, Karen Hughes. From the emergency command center in the bunker, Cheney directed Air Force One and the president to a secure site at Offutt Air Force Base in Nebraska—the vice president calling the shots from Washington while a seemingly confused president flew from Florida to Louisiana to Nebraska.

Looking back on that morning in the White House bunker, Clarke writes that he knew that the vice president had been one of the "five most radical conservatives in the Congress," whose views would seem "out of place if aired more broadly." But in his book *Against All Enemies,* Clarke also seemed to find Cheney's presence in the PEOC bunker reassuring. While he had no sense of the president, he knew Dick Cheney. At the time, Bush hadn't been briefed on terrorism threats, although Clarke had briefed Cheney, Rice, and Secretary of State Colin Powell. And while Cheney, Rice, and Powell had been briefed on Clinton's National Security Presidential Directive to "eliminate al-Qaeda" by arming the Northern Alliance and pushing the CIA to use lethal force, Bush was unaware of that plan as well. Eight months into his presidency, the president was the only principal out of the loop on his predecessor's plan for dealing with al-Qaeda.

Despite the contrasting images—the president and First Lady in a room full of schoolchildren, the vice president and his wife in the communications bunker at the White House—the right guy, Dick Cheney, was in Washington and in charge. It's unlikely that what Cheney experienced that day rendered him in any way incapable of making policy decisions. For the vice president, September 11, 2001, was the day when all the variables in the national security/presidential power equations fell into place. The country's need for a strong leader who could make snap decisions unencumbered by the deliberative inefficiency of a Congress provided an opportunity to restore an imperial presidency undone by Watergate. Constitutional impediments to intelligence gathering and arrest, detention, and prosecution of individuals who threatened "homeland security" could henceforth be selectively observed.

And the terrorist attacks of 9/11 could be used to move the country beyond the "Vietnam syndrome." From the White House, Cheney had watched an earlier moment of national humiliation on April 29, 1975, when the fall of Saigon became America's first military defeat broadcast on the evening news. The night the president ordered the evacuation of the U.S. embassy in Saigon, Cheney had stood silently in a West Wing corridor, with a dejected Ford and Rumsfeld, each man alone in his thoughts. Cheney would later say the war was lost because "America didn't do enough." Use of force in the Middle East would serve to end the executive's reluctance to use force that followed defeat in Vietnam.

Yet as deliberations regarding a response to the 9/11 attacks got under way, the vice president was cautious to an extent that recalled reporters' comments about adult supervision when Bush announced that

Dick Cheney would be his running mate. Cheney and Powell had scripted and executed the near-perfect Gulf War ten years earlier. This time around, if Cheney wasn't as cautious and thoughtful as Powell regarding invading Afghanistan, he was close. He seemed determined to remind Bush of the unintended consequences of any decision he might make regarding war.

Cheney warned about the collapse of Pakistan. He was concerned about the rugged terrain of a country that had swallowed up the British Army when it was a colonial power. He asked whether Pakistan's decision to support the United States would galvanize enough Islamist radicals to overthrow Pakistani president Pervez Musharraf. When Deputy Secretary of Defense Paul Wolfowitz, at an August 4, 2001, meeting documented in Bob Woodward's *Bush at War*, advanced the preposterous argument that there was a 10 to 50 percent chance that Saddam Hussein had been involved in the 9/11 attacks, Cheney refused to take the bait.

Cheney maintained that the overarching goal of any campaign must be to ensure the "homeland" was never again attacked. If the best route to achieve that was through Kabul, he was willing to go there. He also refused to support Rumsfeld's argument, early in the deliberations that followed September 11, that Iraq was the country to attack because there were "not enough good targets" in Afghanistan. And after American pilots encountered no defenses of any consequence while bombing Afghanistan, Cheney also rejected Rumsfeld's proposal to take the war to other countries where there were large numbers of Islamic terrorist organizations. The focus of the military campaign should remain the capture or killing of Osama bin Laden.

Yet as the Afghan War wound down, concluding with the failure to capture Osama bin Laden, Cheney became the administration's leading proponent of war in Iraq. Cheney bears his share of responsibility for bin Laden's escape from the cave complex at Tora Bora. In December 2001, when CIA operatives were perched in the remote mountains of Afghanistan monitoring bin Laden's shortwave radio and pleading for American special forces to encircle the area, Bush, Cheney, and Rumsfeld decided to honor an agreement with Pakistani president Musharraf to let the Pakistani Army close off its side of the border and grab bin Laden if he tried to escape into Pakistan's tribal lands.

Perhaps Cheney had already shifted his focus to Iraq.

Six years into the Bush administration, it seems clear that when historians look at its legacy, that legacy will be Iraq—which more and more appears to be a colossal foreign policy blunder. And while the buck might stop on George Bush's desk, Dick Cheney was the man who made the war happen.

Cheney wasn't always obsessed with overthrowing Saddam Hussein. His belief that the United States had achieved its objectives in the first Gulf War is evident in his response to a question following a speech he made at the Discovery Institute in Seattle after the Gulf War ended:

> Well, the question often comes up about Saddam.
>
> My own personal view continues to be one that he is not likely to survive as the leader of Iraq. I emphasize that's a personal view. You can get all kinds of opinions. That's based on the fact that he's got a shrinking political base inside Iraq. He doesn't control the northern part of his country. He doesn't control the southern part of his country. His economy is a shambles. The U.N. sanctions continue to place great pressure on him. We've had these reports of an attempted coup at the end of June, early July, against him. I think he—I think his days are numbered. . . .
>
> The question that is usually asked is why didn't we go on to Baghdad and get rid of him? And let me take just a moment and address that if I can, because it is an important issue. Now, as you think about watching him operate over there every day, it's tempting to think it would be nice if he weren't there, and clearly we'd prefer to have somebody else in power in Baghdad. But we made the decision not to go on to Baghdad because that was never part of our objective. It wasn't what the country signed up for, it wasn't what the Congress signed up for, it wasn't what the coalition was put together to do. We stopped our military operations when we'd achieved our objective—when we'd liberated Kuwait and we'd destroyed most of his offensive capability—his capacity to threaten his neighbors. And no matter what he may say today, he knows full well that he lost two-thirds of his army, about half of his air force, most of his weapons of mass destruction, a lot of his productive capability. His military forces were decimated, and while he can try to regroup and reorganize now, he does not at present constitute a threat to his neighbors.

If we'd gone on to Baghdad, we would have wanted to send a lot of force. One of the lessons we learned was don't do anything in a halfhearted fashion. When we committed the forces to Kuwait, we sent a lot of forces to make certain they could do the job. We would have moved from fighting in a desert environment, where you had clear areas where we knew who the enemy was. Everybody there was, in fact, an adversary—military, and there was no intermingling of any significant civilian population. If you go into the streets of Baghdad, that changes dramatically. All of a sudden you've got a battle you're fighting in a major built-up city, a lot of civilians are around, significant limitations on our ability to use our most effective technologies and techniques. You probably would have had to run him to ground; I don't think he would have surrendered and gone quietly to the slammer. Once we had rounded him up and gotten rid of his government, then the question is what do you put in its place? You know, you then have accepted the responsibility for governing Iraq.

Now what kind of government are you going to establish? Is it going to be a Kurdish government, or a Shia government, or a Sunni government, or maybe a government based on the old Baathist Party, or some mixture thereof? You will have, I think by that time, lost the support of the Arab coalition that was so crucial to our operations over there because none of them signed on for the United States to go occupy Iraq. I would guess if we had gone in there, I would still have forces in Baghdad today, we'd be running the country. We would not have been able to get everybody out and bring everybody home.

And the final point that I think needs to be made is this question of casualties. I don't think you could have done all of that without significant additional U.S. casualties. And while everybody was tremendously impressed with the low cost of the conflict, for the 146 Americans who were killed in action and for their families, it wasn't a cheap war. And the question in my mind is how many additional American casualties is Saddam worth? And the answer is not very damned many. So I think we got it right, both when we decided to expel him from Kuwait, but also when the president made the decision that we'd achieved our objectives and we were not going to go get bogged down in the problems of trying to take over and govern Iraq.

There, in Dick Cheney's reasoned and measured monotone, is the logical argument against a war that has overextended and undermined the most powerful military machine ever created—to a point that general officers now hold press conferences as they retire from the Army, denouncing U.S. military policy in Iraq.

Yet it was Dick Cheney who pushed a hesitant George W. Bush into that war. Early in 2002, as the war in Afghanistan looked like a success with a relatively low loss of American life, the vice president sat down for a serious talk with his boss.

Cheney's persistent defense of the senior Bush's decision to end the Gulf War without overthrowing Saddam Hussein served to strengthen Cheney's hand as he changed his position and made the case for war. In *The New Republic*, Franklin Foer and Spencer Ackerman capture the moment early in 2002: Cheney's heart-to-heart with Bush, in which the vice president explained that he had been part of a team that planned and executed what he had come to realize was a flawed war policy. Leaving Saddam Hussein in power had been a mistake, Afghanistan an unqualified success that silenced Bush's critics, and conditions were right to go into Iraq. "The reason Cheney was able to sell Bush the policy is that he was able to say 'I've changed,' " a former member of the Bush-Cheney administration told *The New Republic*. " 'I used to have the same positions as [James] Baker, [Brent] Scowcroft, and your father. And here's why it's wrong.' "

Wolfowitz immediately went to work as Cheney's drummer. On March 17, 2002, Wolfowitz was at the British embassy in Washington for Sunday lunch. According to one of the "Downing Street Memos" obtained by reporter Mike Smith of the London *Sunday Times*, Wolfowitz wasn't focused on the weapons of mass destruction Bush and Cheney would use to justify attacking Iraq. "Wolfowitz thought it was indispensable to spell out in detail Saddam's barbarism," reads the March 18 memo to Tony Blair's political adviser. There was a second justification. "Wolfowitz said that it was absurd to deny the link between terrorism and Saddam." There might be doubt about the alleged meeting in Prague between

Mohammed Atta, the lead hijacker on 9/11, and Iraqi intelligence (the same meeting Cheney would later use to justify the war, which, in fact, never occurred). But there were other substantial cases of Saddam giving comfort to terrorists. This was a full year before the start of hostilities in Iraq. Yet shortly after Cheney sold Bush on Iraq, Wolfowitz was out working the Brits—prior to a trip that Prime Minister Tony Blair would make to Bush's Texas ranch to discuss Iraq. "There's no way he would have done that without the approval of Rumsfeld," says a State Department source who was disturbed to see the DOD doing diplomacy. "And Rumsfeld would never have approved it without Cheney's okay."

The vice president might have been ready to take Saddam out. But polls indicated the public wasn't with him. Nor was Secretary of State Powell, who was trying to persuade Bush to work through the United Nations. In August, while Bush was on his ranch in Texas, riding his mountain bike, cutting brush, and preparing for a speech he was scheduled to deliver to the United Nations on September 12, *The Wall Street Journal* published an op-ed piece written by Brent Scowcroft. Under the headline "Don't Attack Saddam," the national security advisor from the George H. W. Bush administration made a convincing argument for diplomacy and challenged Cheney's justification for war: the unproven allegation that Saddam Hussein was connected to the al-Qaeda attacks on the United States on September 11. Scowcroft's argument seemed to carry the imprimatur of Bush Sr., and in fact gave voice to an argument many conservative Republicans, such as Senator Chuck Hagel, were making at the time.

Beyond dismissing the Iraq-9/11 connection, Scowcroft presciently warned that invading Iraq "would not be a cakewalk. On the contrary, it would be very expensive—with serious consequences for the U.S. and the global economy—and could as well be bloody." Published on the American conservative movement's opinion page of record, Scowcroft's piece reinvigorated Powell's diplomacy-first position. It also angered Cheney and then national security advisor Condoleezza Rice.

Powell's cautious approach to Iraq also seemed to carry the day at an August 16 National Security Council video conference with Bush at his Crawford ranch. Cheney's fast track to war was being undermined by diplomats in Foggy Bottom. But he had learned in the Ford administration that speeches shape the policy process. "In reality," Cheney said in

1977, "what happens is that oftentimes the speech process ends up driving the policy process."

Cheney began to drive the policy process when he spoke to the Veterans of Foreign Wars convention in Nashville on August 26—more than two weeks in advance of the president's United Nations speech. Cheney informed Bush that he would be speaking to the VFW. He did not provide the president a copy of his text.

"Don't get me into trouble," Bush told Cheney, according to Bob Woodward's *Plan of Attack*. Considering the speech Cheney delivered—and the disastrous war that followed—Bush's lighthearted admonishment seems laughable.

Cheney's VFW speech stopped short of declaring that the United States would attack Iraq. But the speech was a syllogism leading to the conclusion that not going to war with Iraq put the United States at risk.

> We now know that Saddam has resumed his efforts to acquire nuclear weapons. . . . Many of us are convinced that Saddam will acquire nuclear weapons fairly soon.
>
> Simply stated, there is no doubt that Saddam Hussein now has weapons of mass destruction. There is no doubt he is amassing them to use against our friends, against our allies, and against us. . . .
>
> Yet if we did wait until that moment, Saddam would simply be emboldened, and it would become even harder for us to gather friends and allies to oppose him. As one of those who worked to assemble the Gulf War coalition, I can tell you that our job then would have been infinitely more difficult in the face of a nuclear-armed Saddam Hussein.
>
> And many of those who now argue that we should act only if he gets a nuclear weapon would then turn around and say that we cannot act because he has a nuclear weapon. At bottom, that argument counsels a course of inaction that itself could have devastating consequences for many countries, including our own. . . .
>
> Against that background, a person would be right to question any suggestion that we should just get inspectors back into Iraq, and then our worries will be over. Saddam has perfected the game of cheat and retreat, and is very skilled in the art of denial and decep-

tion. A return of inspectors would provide no assurance whatsoever of his compliance with U.N. resolutions. Many of us are convinced that Saddam will acquire nuclear weapons fairly soon.

How could Bush say "no" to war when Hussein was a nuclear threat? Cheney completely undermined the secretary of state's argument to work with the United Nations and to allow U.N. inspectors time to complete their work on the ground in Iraq.

A week later, on NBC's *Meet the Press,* Cheney reiterated his claim that Hussein had reconstituted a nuclear weapons program. Then Cheney argued that there were connections between Hussein and al-Qaeda, repeating the false claim that Wolfowitz had made at the British embassy five months earlier.

> Well, I want to be very careful about how I say this. I'm not here today to make a specific allegation that Iraq was somehow responsible for 9/11. I can't say that. On the other hand, since we did that interview, new information has come to light. And we spent time looking at that relationship between Iraq, on the one hand, and the al-Qaeda organization on the other. And there has been reporting that suggests that there have been a number of contacts over the years. We've seen in connection with the hijackers, of course, Mohamed Atta, who was the lead hijacker, did apparently travel to Prague on a number of occasions. And on at least one occasion, we have reporting that places him in Prague with a senior Iraqi intelligence official a few months before the attack on the World Trade Center. The debates about, you know, was he there or wasn't he there, again, it's the intelligence business.

Taken together, the vice president's warnings made a compelling case for war. They were, however, entirely untrue. Yet they reframed the terms of the Iraq debate, leading the public to the conclusion that the question should not be "if" but rather "when" the nation goes to war in Iraq.

"The secretary was shocked," Wilkerson says of Powell's reaction to the VFW speech. "Here we were saying one thing out of one side of our mouth and here was the vice president speaking to what you might call a semi-official military audience and he was saying the exact opposite. Undercutting every bit of diplomacy before that diplomacy actually got off the ground. And I remember Powell coming back from a principals' meeting where he had made some remonstrance to the president about what's going on. And the president had said something which he was wont to say about most things like this. He said, 'Oh, that's just Dick.' "

A month later, it was evident that Dick had prevailed when Bush interrupted Condi Rice's West Wing meeting with three senators to say "Fuck Saddam! We're taking him out!"

Cheney was engaged in a tactical rather than a strategic repositioning—a change of mind but not of heart. He'd already become a true believer in the scheme laid out by Wolfowitz, Khalilzad, and Libby—the master plan that envisioned a hegemonic United States making the Middle East safe for democracy and oil and gas production. It had first surfaced in the "Limited Contingency Study" Wolfowitz had handed to Jimmy Carter's secretary of defense, Harold Brown. In the plan's second iteration, Secretary of Defense Cheney embraced it when no one else in the George H. W. Bush administration would. The final version of the plan was informed by the thinking that Cheney and Wolfowitz had developed at the Saturday morning meetings Cheney hosted at the Pentagon when he was defense secretary. With Afghanistan a smashing success, it was time to turn Wolfowitz's bold thinking into a militarized foreign policy. In Iraq, American forces, the vice president predicted, would be "greeted as liberators."

And Bush bought it.

Much has been written about the terrifically smart Cheney easily overwhelming small-bore material like George W. Bush. And while the man-to-man might have brought Bush around on the Iraq War, there's a larger picture. Bush, Rove, Karen Hughes, and Joe Allbaugh did brilliant work in the 2000 campaign—even if Cheney and Bush family consigliere James Baker III had to manage the postelection fight through the Supreme Court. Yet when it was time to govern, Bush and his "Iron Triangle" were out of their league. In Washington, they were indeed the "Mayberry Machiavellians" described by Bush's first faith-based initiatives director, John DiIulio. The president's staff was no match for the disciplined operation Dick Cheney deployed to take care of business and to bureaucratically emasculate George W. Bush.

The public got a rare glimpse of the power and insularity of Cheney and his staff when the vice president shot Austin lawyer Harry Whittington on a South Texas bird hunt in February 2006. Before speaking to Bush about the shooting, Cheney consulted his family, Addington, and his former media aide, Mary Matalin. For the twenty-four hours that lapsed before the ranch owner reported the shooting to a small local news outlet, the president's staff was besieged by reporters demanding an explanation, but Cheney didn't seem to care. On Tuesday, after Cheney had said nothing publicly about the Saturday hunting accident, Bush's beleaguered press flack tried levity to diffuse the issue. At a press conference, Scott McClellan joked about his orange tie and Cheney's hasty trigger finger, unaware that the vice president's staff had been informed earlier that morning that Whittington had suffered a heart attack as a result of the shooting. It was only after a personal appeal from Karl Rove that Cheney made a public statement, in an interview with Fox News anchor Brit Hume five days after the shooting.

Lawrence Wilkerson was Colin Powell's assistant for the four years Powell served as secretary of state. In the Army and at State, Colonel Wilkerson has paid careful attention to bureaucratic structure and power. Watching the White House from the perspective of the State Department, and trying to cover his boss's back, Wilkerson figured out who was in charge.

It wasn't George Bush.

Within the largest vice presidential staff in the history of the office, Dick Cheney set up his own shadow National Security Council staff—something no vice president had ever done before. In this unprecedented arrangement was another glaring peculiarity. The vice president's national security staffers read all the e-mail traffic "in, out, and between" the president's NSC staffers, Wilkerson says. Yet the president's staff isn't allowed to read the communication of Cheney's staffers.

"Members of the president's staff sometimes walk from office to office to avoid Cheney's people monitoring their discussions," says Wilkerson. "Or they use the phone." The arrangement provides a clear demonstration of who is running foreign policy.

During the administration of George H. W. Bush, when Secretary of Defense Cheney reached the end of his tether, he would hear from the president, or the president's secretary of state and friend James Baker. An angry Baker called National Security Advisor Brent Scowcroft on one occasion in 1989 to complain about Cheney's open criticism of Mikhail Gorbachev.

"Dump on Dick with all possible alacrity," Baker demanded.

No one in the current White House is willing to play that role. If someone did, Cheney's staff would devour that person. "Bush's staff is terrified of Cheney's people," says a former White House staffer. To maintain tight control of the national security portfolio, Cheney brought in his loyalists to fill positions on his staff—and on the president's staff. It was a gathering of intellectual and ideological firepower the Texans could never equal. Stephen Hadley became the White House's deputy national security advisor, after working for years with Wolfowitz. Zal Khalilzad was the National Security Council's Middle East agent, until he was shipped to Baghdad to try to salvage the disaster in Iraq. Both foreign policy experts had a long history with Cheney, going back as far as Bush I. Libby, who had been Wolfowitz's deputy, became Cheney's chief of staff. Cheney saw to it that Libby was also special assistant to the president, thus insinuating his chief of staff into the White House staff. Aides from Cheney's NSC staff sat in with White House staff on all major foreign policy deliberations. Cheney had George Bush surrounded. Not only was the president outsmarted by the man he calls "Vice"—he was outstaffed.

At the top of Cheney's staff hierarchy sat the vice president's legal counsel, David Addington, a tall, paunchy workaholic with a gray beard and thatch of gray hair. He would replace Scooter Libby as chief of staff after Libby was indicted in the outing of CIA officer Valerie Plame. Addington, who had been with Cheney since their days together on the House Intelligence Committee, was always the power center in Cheney's office. "Addington would have been [Cheney's] chief of staff from the beginning," says a military officer who worked with both men. "But he didn't want to be tied down. [Addington] is always involved in the issues. But he's always in the background. They are too smart, too powerful for Bush and his team. There's nothing new in this town. There are a lot of smart people who know how to run things. But none of them I've ever seen compare to Addington. Al Gonzales is not going to stand up to him."

Indeed, the attorney general, who followed Bush from Texas, has nowhere near the experience, or, it appears, the intellectual capacity, of David Addington. Gonzales was a Hispanic tabula rasa working in the property rights division of Vinson & Elkins, a Houston-based law firm, when Karl Rove made him Bush's general counsel, then Texas secretary of state in 1997. At that moment, Addington was on his sole brief hiatus from government service, after having worked at the CIA, the House Intelligence Committee, the Iran-Contra Joint Committee, and the Department of Defense. Addington and the team he and Libby directed, the general said, were eating the Bush people alive.

While Cheney was pushing Bush toward war with Iraq, Cheney's cabal in the Office of the Vice President and at the Pentagon were laying the groundwork for that war. They were the nation's best and brightest right-wing policy intellectuals while Bill Clinton was president. Many of them had attended the Saturday policy salon Wolfowitz and Cheney held at the Pentagon, then moved on to the American Enterprise Institute, the Washington Institute for Near East Policy, and the Hudson Institute. Cheney himself spent some time at AEI after he left the administration of Bush père. Lynne Cheney also found a home there, and stayed. The collection of think tanks served as a shadow administration, filled with policy wonks waiting for their return to power.

The think tanks also served as a nexus for Cheney's policy cabal to cultivate their relationship with Iraqi expatriate Ahmed Chalabi and others from the exiled Iraqi National Congress. Those relationships proved to be useful when the administration began preparing for war. Wolfowitz and Libby were often the INC's principal protagonists inside the White House. Wolfowitz was hostile to the CIA because, among other reasons, they did not trust Chalabi, a reservation that seemed reasonable when nothing Chalabi promised in Iraq ever materialized. An INC source who worked with Chalabi while he was trying to sell regime change explained the heart-and-head dichotomy that members of his organization came to understand existed in the Bush-Cheney White House.

"Bush believed the democracy part," the INC official said. "That's where his head was. For Cheney, it was the threat—we cannot live with the threat. Democracy was an afterthought.

"The issue was to take Saddam out. There was a debt to us by the U.S. The spring '91 uprising, chemical weapons sold in the eighties, sanctions that were really hurting the Iraqi people but not Saddam." It was a legitimate and uniquely Iraqi perspective. Americans had sold Hussein feed stock to make chemical weapons during Iran's war with Iraq and failed to live up to promises made after the Gulf War.

"My interest," he said, "was Iraq, not America."

The INC's access to the Office of the Vice President was facilitated by Cheney's NSC director, John Hannah. The argument INC leader Ahmed Chalabi would lay out was appealing and useful for Cheney and his cabal of neocons, who now were convinced that U.S. forces had to go back into Iraq and finish what was left undone by the administration of Bush père ten years earlier. Support for Hussein in Iraq would evaporate after a U.S. invasion. Iraqi exiles returning to govern would be embraced as they began building a democratic system. It provided a large part of the justification for going back into Iraq and getting it right.

George Bush's war was being planned by Dick Cheney's staff and loyalists.

It was predictable that Bush would be displaced by Cheney, who at thirty-four was known to Gerald Ford's security detail as "Backseat"—the chief of staff sitting behind the president and leaning into the deal. Twenty-five years later, "Backseat" would become the vice president whom White House staffers humorously call "Edgar"—a reference to Edgar Bergen, the vaudeville comic who did the talking (and thinking) for the celebrated ventriloquist dummy Charlie McCarthy.

A year before the September 11 attacks, Bush had been engaged in statehouse policy fights over property tax reduction bills and mandatory testing in public schools in Texas. In Washington he found himself confronting what six years as governor of Texas had least prepared him for: a room full of intelligent advisers steeped in the political culture of Washington pressing him for a decision on war.

As formidable as Bush's "Iron Triangle" might have appeared, the war was not so much the work of the Bush White House, but rather what Colonel Lawrence Wilkerson refers to as "the cabal" running American foreign policy out of the vice president's office and the DOD: men who had been working together, in and out of government, for almost thirty years. Cheney, Addington, and Libby, working with Wolfowitz in the Pentagon and several moles in the State Department, drove Iraq War policy.

Cheney and Scooter Libby also cooked the intelligence to justify the Iraq War, and when the moment came to sell the conflict to a reluctant United Nations, the vice president's staff prepared the forty-eight-page backgrounder for Colin Powell's disastrous February 2002 speech to the Security Council. John Hannah wrote the material, and Scooter Libby massaged it. The background paper has not yet been declassified (and few expect to see it declassified any time soon). Wilkerson describes what was handed to Powell as a "movie script." Libby had called it a "Chinese smorgasbord." Powell looked at it, declared it "bullshit," and tossed the entire document. He and his staff turned instead to the National Intelligence Estimate on Iraq as a foundation for the U.N. speech. Wilkerson has since come to believe Libby's smorgasbord was a setup, designed to direct Powell to the NIE—which was better sourced, but almost as flawed as the "bullshit" he had rejected. "These are facts, not allegations," Powell would tell the United Nations and the world. Yet before he announced he wasn't staying on for Bush's second term, each of the foundational "facts" he included in his Security Council speech had been disproved.

"These guys planned to spend ninety days in Baghdad, then move on to Tehran," says a retired general who stays in contact with the Pentagon. "Then Rumsfeld's plan fell apart in Iraq."

Wilkerson also suspects that generals breaking ranks and protocol in 2006 to speak openly against Rumsfeld's failed Iraq war plan had a great deal to do with a planned bombing campaign to take out Iran's nuclear research and development facilities. The generals knew the armed forces were overextended to the point of being broken in Iraq, yet the neocons were planning to move on to the neighboring country. So upon retirement, the generals broke with precedent and publicly criticized the conduct of the Iraq War. Iran was a subtext, and the notion that the United States would bomb rather than negotiate, a serious concern. Even if the administration's position was no more than saber-rattling and coercive diplomacy, which didn't seem likely in Washington in early 2006, the proposed bombing campaign represented a further overextension of the already worn-out military.

"Everybody seems to believe that we'll be bombing Iran after the November elections," said a source at the State Department in April 2006. "It feels like the decision has been made."

The existence of plans to bomb Iran were revealed by *The New Yorker*'s Seymour Hersh. Hersh reported that "the U.S. Strategic Command, supported by the Air Force, had been drawing up plans at the President's direction for a major bombing campaign in Iran." The White House even wanted a nuclear weapon in the mix, to destroy Iran's uranium-enrichment plant at Natanz. Marine General Peter Pace, the chair of the Joint Chiefs of Staff, talked Bush and Cheney out of the nuclear option. Hersh's reporting also supports Wilkerson's thesis that the generals publicly challenging Bush and Cheney on *Iraq* in April were trying to slow the momentum for the campaign to bomb *Iran*. At the Pentagon the campaign was known as "the April Revolution," reports Hersh. By June, it appeared that the generals had stopped, at least for the moment, the administration's plans for preemptive attack on Iran.

The plan to bomb Iran, the centerpiece for the coercive foreign policy that the Cheney cabal had in the works, was complemented by a specific project at the Department of State. The plan, run out of the Bureau of Near Eastern Affairs, involved spending at least $85 million in 2006, much of it distributed to Iranian and Syrian dissidents in their countries and in exile. It bore similarities to the program to support Ahmed Chalabi and the Iraqi National Congress in the run-up to the war in Iraq. The program was widely perceived to be supported by the vice president because it was directed by thirty-nine-year-old Elizabeth Cheney.

The older Cheney daughter is smart, competent, hard-working, and engaging, according to sources who have worked with her. She's also completely unqualified for the job she held: Principal Deputy Assistant for Near Eastern Affairs (known by the acronym PDAS). Liz Cheney was a political appointee to the PDAS position she held until the spring of 2006, just as she was a political appointee to a lower position in the bureau in 2002, when she arrived with a rather thin CV and no prior experience in Middle Eastern affairs. (Prior to hiring on at State, Liz Cheney turned her family name and her University of Chicago law degree into a $170,000-a-year position in the Washington office of the White & Case law firm. Her husband earned $53,000 at another law firm.)

Assistant Secretary of State for Near Eastern Affairs David Welch was Liz Cheney's boss. "But she's the vice president's daughter," says a source who recently worked at State. "There was kind of a parallel universe over there, where David had his projects and Liz had hers. There were some things that David didn't touch." Before returning home to care for her five children, Liz Cheney leveraged her influence by bringing in her own people and changing the character of Near Eastern Affairs: "Until she came in, the NEA bureau always had a variety of people and a variety of perspectives. Under Powell, anyone could voice their opinion, make dissenting arguments, even if it wasn't the policy of the administration. That changed when Liz came to be PDAS. It's now understood that it does you no good to make your views known. In fact, it can hurt you professionally."

The source continued, "She filled a big space here. There's always a fear of the DOD hawks associated with her father, and she's obviously talking to her father and his people."

In her official capacity, Liz Cheney has traveled to several Middle Eastern countries. On at least two occasions she has informed U.S. ambassadors that she was going to see the head of state alone—a complete violation of protocol. "The ambassador is our government's representative in the country," says Wilkerson. "No one meets a head of state without the ambassador." Except for the vice president's daughter.

On one occasion, Cheney's daughter told an ambassador to call Washington if he had a problem with the meeting she had scheduled. She went in solo, and the embarrassed head of state later called in the American ambassador to brief him on the closed, private meeting with Liz Cheney.

Liz Cheney resigned in the spring of 2006, though by summer, sources at State were saying her return was imminent. Once she departed, there was a definite policy shift away from military options and toward negotiation with Iran. "Probably a coincidence, but it would have been much more difficult with her in the building," says the former State Department employee. As Cheney announced her departure and summer arrived in the capital, discussions of bombing Iran's nuclear facilities quieted. Secretary of State Rice seemed to resume some of the State Department functions that had been seized by the OVP. With the vice president's approval numbers falling to 18 percent, it is altogether possible that Bush finally took charge and told his VP "No more war."

Not everyone is hopeful.

While David Welch did accompany Secretary of State Condi Rice to Israel in August 2006, as Israel's bombing of Lebanon spiraled out of control, he wasn't entirely on his own. Somewhat weakened by his forced cohabitation with the vice president's daughter, Welch was accompanied by a figure who might be described as his minder. Elliott Abrams also traveled with Rice for the duration of the Middle East mission, all the while in constant communication with Dick Cheney's office. Cheney and Abrams knew that Welch, if permitted, would try to use the stature he held as former ambassador to Egypt to move the United States closer to a mediator's position in Israel's conflict with the Arab world. That wasn't likely to happen with Abrams looking over Welch's shoulder. "The genius of Elliott Abrams is that he's Elliott Abrams," an unnamed administration official told *The New York Times*. "How can he be accused of not sufficiently supporting Israel?" Not only was Israel familiar territory for Abrams, the deputy assistant to the president and deputy national security advisor for global democracy strategy, he also had an Iranian backstory. Twenty years earlier, Abrams was involved in a policy that included selling missiles to the Iranians as part of a three-way negotiation between the United States, Iran, and Hezbollah. Cheney's support of Abrams in Iran-Contra was finally paying off.

"They are incapable of diplomacy," Larry Wilkerson says of the Cheney cabal within the White House. Not only incapable, but hostile to the notion of diplomacy, particularly in dealing with countries that have adversarial relations with the United States. In such cases, the Cheney cabal considers diplomacy the imposition of its will on a capitulating adversary. It's the same position Cheney described to a stunned Thomas Downey twenty years earlier, saying the Soviets would have to accept "all our terms" in arms talks. Downey's observation describes the marching orders Cheney handed Assistant Secretary of State Jim Kelly for his negotiations with the North Koreans. Afer Kelly confronted the North Koreans in 2003 with U.S. intelligence that proved the Koreans had a nuclear weapons program, Cheney impeded negotiations with Kim Jong Il's government. On two occasions, according to Wilkerson, Cheney changed the terms of negotiations after they had been established by all of the principals who decide American foreign policy.

"A script would be drafted for Jim [Kelly], what he could say and what he could not say, with points elucidated in the margins. And that script would be approved through the statutory process," Wilkerson says. That process involves the consensus of the president, the vice president, the secretary of state, the secretary of defense, the national security advisor, and the chairman of the Joint Chiefs of Staff. On at least two occasions, Cheney rewrote the script after it had been through the statutory process. As Kelly departed for Pyongyang or Beijing, Cheney provided the State Department's negotiator a revised draft outlining a more rigid position. As Wilkerson describes it, the vice president "put handcuffs on our negotiator, so he could say little more than 'welcome and good-bye.' " U.S. negotiations with one of the most dangerous, volatile, and unpredictable nations in the world, which had just rolled out its nuclear arsenal, were defined by one man—Dick Cheney. His negotiating position was that there would be no negotiations.

Cheney's no-negotiation-with-evil position is not limited to North Korea and in fact is a corollary to the neocons' hegemonic foreign policy agenda. Wilkerson points to a critical moment, entirely ignored by the press, that further illustrates the administration's low regard for diplomacy:

In May 2003 the Iranian government approached the U.S. government with an urgent request to open up negotiations. There had been only one other official communication between Iran and the United States since Iranian radicals seized the U.S. embassy in Tehran during the Carter administration. Now the initial U.S. success in Iraq had the Iranians coming to the bargaining table as supplicants.

"The Iranians came to us through the Swiss ambassador after they saw how fast we moved through Afghanistan and Iraq," Wilkerson says. "This was in 2003, right after [the invasion of] Iraq." Mahmoud Ahmadinejad was not yet president and the moderates in charge in Iran wanted to deal.

The letter delivered by Swiss ambassador Tim Guldimann offered concessions on Iran's nuclear program, Israel policy, and al-Qaeda. "Israel policy," of course, involved Tehran's support of Hezbollah. According to Wilkerson, the Iranians offered to exchange al-Qaeda prisoners they held for Mujahedeen e Khalq prisoners the United States had in custody. The MEK was a guerrilla group Saddam Hussein had used in his war against Iran. After the war they engaged in terrorist attacks against Iran and are designated terrorists by the U.S. State Department.

More than a hundred billion dollars, thousands of American and Iraqi lives, America's allies' unflagging opposition to the war, and a deeply divided public. Finally it was all paying off. One of the countries Bush had placed in the Axis of Evil was coming in out of the cold.

"We told them no," Wilkerson says in an interview at George Washington University. "Not only did we tell them no—we wrote a letter of protest to the Swiss for interfering in our foreign policy."

The entire diplomatic endeavor was immediately curtailed. Asked if he knows who made the decision to reject the Iranian request for negotiations, Larry Wilkerson didn't miss a beat.

"Yes, I know," he says. "It was the vice president of the United States."

ELEVEN

The Torture Presidency

I n early 2004, Secretary of State Colin Powell walked into the office of his chief of staff, Colonel Lawrence Wilkerson. A scandal of major proportions was threatening to come to public light. By April, CBS News and *The New Yorker* would release photos of U.S. soldiers abusing Iraqi detainees at Abu Ghraib prison. "He was very concerned and he wanted to make sure State's role was clear, and he wanted to make sure also that we had some idea of the dimensions of the problem," Wilkerson remembers.

Powell told his subordinate: "Get the paperwork. Get everything you can get your hands on."

Wilkerson had worked for Powell for more than a decade, since the general was chairman of the Joint Chiefs of Staff during the first Gulf War. He'd been a soldier for much longer. Not a lot surprised him, but looking at his boss, he quickly realized that Powell had no concept of how big this scandal was going to be nor how widespread it was. Over the coming months, working with the State Department's legal adviser, William Taft IV, and using both classified and unclassified documents, Wilkerson began to assemble the paper trail Powell requested. Eventually, he says, it would make a seven-foot pile of documents, divided into three stacks in Wilkerson's office. It would tell the story of how Bush, Cheney, and Rumsfeld, despite their denials, had made torture the policy of the U.S. government. They had done so in the service of an all-powerful presidency the likes of which America has never seen—a vision that Dick Cheney and David Addington had nurtured for years.

The legal justification began as early as December 2001, with the image of the smoking wreckage of the World Trade Center still fresh enough to smell. By that time the United States had been at war in Afghanistan for almost two months. Army and CIA troops had captured hundreds of suspected Taliban and al-Qaeda fighters. More than anything, everybody in the upper levels of government feared another attack was in the offing. As higher-level captives became available, Bush and Cheney demanded any intelligence they might provide, regardless of what it took to produce it. The Pentagon wanted a place to keep the detainees, a tightly controlled, easily defended environment where interrogations could be conducted far from prying eyes or distractions. As Rumsfeld would say, Guantánamo Bay was "the least worst place."

Yet the War President and his Vice required more than a physical location; they needed a legal framework in which to operate. The administration had the man for the job already in place, a deputy attorney general in the Office of Legal Counsel (OLC) in the Justice Department named John Yoo. Some have compared the OLC to a mini–Supreme Court. Its job is to provide legal interpretations for the executive, but only when asked. Alumni from the office, including William Rehnquist and, more recently, Samuel Alito, Jr., have landed on the actual Supreme Court. While some see the OLC as a place that should be a neutral arbiter of what the executive can constitutionally do, more often than not it's been an aggressive advocate, "the president's law firm."

"The OLC is calculated to defend as robustly as possible presidential authority, that's what it's all about," says Bruce Fein, who worked in the office during the Nixon and Ford administrations.

Dick Cheney learned from a master how the OLC could defend executive privilege against an activist Congress during the Ford administration, when Antonin Scalia ran the office. Cheney knew what he was getting when he placed Yoo, a thirty-five-year-old law professor at the University of California at Berkeley, inside the Bush-Cheney OLC. In

March 1996, Yoo had published a book-length article in the *California Law Review* that tried to make the case that the Constitution gave wider authority to the president in war-making than had been previously understood. The only role Congress had, Yoo argued, was the power of the purse and impeachment. The federal courts were excluded entirely. When Cheney and Addington had made the call for a similarly strong executive during Iran-Contra, Yoo had been just an undergraduate at Harvard. He went on to Yale Law School and then to clerk for Justice Clarence Thomas at the U.S. Supreme Court, where he worked on issues of national security and separation of powers.

Within weeks of 9/11, Addington and Yoo had started to create the legal architecture for an all-powerful wartime commander in chief. Cheney knew the ruling he wanted—he just needed to ask the OLC the right question. "You have asked for our opinion as to the scope of the President's authority to take military action in response to the terrorist attacks on the United States on September 11, 2001," wrote Yoo in a memo to the president on September 25, 2001.

It would come as no surprise to the vice president and his legal counsel, David Addington, that Yoo determined the scope was practically unlimited.

"The President may deploy military forces preemptively against terrorist organizations or the States that harbor or support them, whether or not they can be linked to the specific terrorist incidents of September 11," wrote Yoo in the memo. Given that criterion, Bush and Cheney don't need congressional approval to attack Cuba, Iran, Libya, North Korea, Sudan, or Syria—all identified as state sponsors of terror by the Office of the Coordinator for Counterterrorism of the State Department. Throw in "terrorist safe havens"—logically, given how permissive this legal interpretation is—and the war powers extend to Venezuela, Yemen, and the Mediterranean, among other locales. But they had no intention of stopping with states. Yoo determined that the president's powers in the never-ending war on "terror" extended to people and organizations as well.

This wasn't a statutory right. Yoo claimed that Congress, when it passed its resolution authorizing the use of military force against terrorists a week after 9/11, only gave the president what he already had—in fact, just a sliver of the nearly unlimited power the wartime president possessed. "The President's broad constitutional power to use military force to defend the Nation, recognized by the Joint Resolution itself, would allow the President to take whatever actions he deems appropriate to pre-empt or respond to terrorist threats from new quarters."

Two days later, Yoo wrote another memo, this time with Patrick Philbin, a fellow deputy attorney general. (Philbin would later have second thoughts about Addington and Cheney's executive power grab. As a result, although Alberto Gonzales, by then the attorney general, had tapped Philbin for the job of deputy solicitor general, Addington blocked the appointment.) The December 28 memo argued that non-U.S.-citizen detainees at Guantánamo would not have access to that most basic of American rights, habeas corpus, the right of an individual to appear before a judge after detention. Almost two weeks later, Yoo coauthored a memo with Office of Legal Counsel attorney Robert J. Delahunty, concluding that the Geneva Conventions and other international agreements against torture "do not protect members of the al Qaeda organization, which as a non-State actor cannot be a party to the international agreements governing war." Furthermore, if Congress acted to "restrict presidential authority" by legislating that the U.S. armed forces had to obey the Geneva Conventions, it "would represent a possible infringement on presidential discretion to direct the military." It didn't matter that Congress had ratified the Geneva Conventions; executive power superseded that authority. White House chief counsel Alberto Gonzales—whose legal experience as a transactional lawyer and short tenure on the Texas Supreme Court had not exactly prepared him for national security law—wrote a memorandum upholding Yoo's conclusions. (The Justice Department won't release the memo, but a draft copy is public.)

The State Department had tried to rein the White House back into the international human rights standards that had been accepted for almost half a century. State Department counsel William Taft argued to Gonzales that if the United States used torture, then when American troops were captured, they could expect the same in return. Furthermore, torture would inflame anti-Americanism in the Muslim world. Addington was working overtime to marginalize or bully any lawyer at Justice or the National Security Council who might disagree with this new approach, but enough dissent existed for Gonzales to write Bush the memo on January 25 laying out the various arguments for and against whether the Geneva Conventions should apply to al-Qaeda and Taliban prisoners. On the side of the ledger against adhering to the Conventions, Gonzales added the federal

War Crimes Act of 1996. The act provides for strict sanctions, including the death penalty, for American officials convicted of serious war crimes as defined by the Geneva Conventions. Gonzales argued that if they dispensed with the Geneva Conventions, technically there would be no war crimes.

In February, Bush decided to split the baby. In a memo on February 7, he wrote, "I have the authority under the Constitution to suspend Geneva as between the United States and Afghanistan, but I decline to exercise that authority at this time." While declaring that al-Qaeda detainees did not qualify as prisoners of war under Geneva, he allowed that "as a matter of policy, the United States Armed Forces shall continue to treat detainees humanely and, to the extent appropriate and consistent with military necessity, in a manner consistent with the principles of Geneva."

And yet, some time after the West Wing meeting that produced that memo, Dick Cheney and Donald Rumsfeld agreed to ignore the part about humane treatment. "In going back and looking at the deliberations, it was clear to me that what the president had decided was one thing and what was implemented was quite another thing," says Wilkerson. The policy would be implemented as Cheney had "briefed it" to the president.

The message filtered down, and it was unmistakable to everyone from Army reservists to highly trained CIA interrogators. The results at Abu Ghraib were murder, rape, and a menu of sadistic acts that ranged from sexual humiliation to physical maiming. For CIA interrogators, it included, among other torture tactics, "waterboarding," a simulated drowning of the victim that is essentially a mock execution.

"The complicity of everyone down the line was mind-boggling to me, including the commander in the field, Rick Sanchez," says Wilkerson. "In some cases, Rumsfeld would protect himself very carefully. For example, I have his memo with appendixes and annexes where he goes from A to double D, telling them what they can do. When you read this, you read for example, that dogs can be used but they have to be muzzled. Well, I'm a soldier. I know what that means to an E-6 [noncommissioned officer] that is trying to question a guy and he's got a German shepherd with a muzzle on there. If that doesn't work, the muzzle comes off. If that doesn't work, you kind of let the dog leap at the guy and maybe every now and then take a bite out of him. It's a very careful crafting of a memo that would probably never get [Rumsfeld] in a court of law or get him convicted at the International

Criminal Court, but it's damn sure apparent to me that things were different, things had changed. And I can't imagine Rumsfeld doing that without at least having his head covered by the vice president."

In other words, Cheney not only had to know, he had to make it clear this was his and the president's policy.

Six months after Bush's memo about humane treatment, the head of the Office of Legal Counsel, Jay Bybee, wrote what has become known as "the torture memo." Yoo is credited with ghostwriting the fifty-page document for Bybee, who today sits on the U.S. Court of Appeals for the Ninth Circuit as a Bush appointee. How much input Cheney and Addington had into the document is unknown, but they would certainly have been aware of and had veto power over its contents.

In order for it to qualify as torture, the memo said, "Where the pain is physical, it must be of an intensity akin to that which accompanies serious physical injury such as death or organ failure."

Short of homicide, everything was fair game.

Shrouded behind his antipathy toward congressional prerogatives is a little-known fact about Dick Cheney. When it comes to lobbying the Hill, he is one of the Bush administration's most effective weapons. Consistently, it is Cheney, as negotiator in chief, who has taken the lead role in binding GOP legislators to the White House. Even as this administration has drifted away from long-standing conservative principles like deficit reduction and limited government, the Republican Congress has meekly followed.

As vice president, Cheney serves as the president of the Senate. While his main constitutional responsibility is to break tie votes, he has used his position to quietly insinuate himself into the very fabric of Senate deliberations and leadership. Cheney is a regular participant in the Senate GOP Tuesday meetings, where he mostly sits quietly and observes. When the White House refused to support Senate majority leader Trent Lott after he made a racist comment in 2002, Cheney didn't rise to the defense of his former House rival. Incoming Tennessee senator Bill Frist would be an infinitely more pliable leader for the White House, and thanks to the vice presidential search, Cheney already knew every skeleton that hung in Frist's closet. Yet Cheney's reach extends beyond S-214, his traditional ceremonial office in the Senate, and into areas of Congress where no vice president in American history has ever dared to tread.

The Founding Fathers were quite explicit on the matter of how independent each branch of government should be from the other. Members of Congress cannot be employed by or receive benefit from the executive branch. While the vice president has a role in the Senate, there is no comparable position for a member of the executive in the House of Representatives. This is because the House was modeled after the British House of Commons, where the monarch has been unwelcome for four centuries.

But shortly before President Bush's inauguration in January 2001, Speaker Dennis Hastert quietly, and without public notice, chucked aside 212 years of American tradition. He offered Vice President Dick Cheney a second office in the U.S. Capitol, on the House side. In the cramped domed building, workspace exists at a premium that would make even space-conscious New Yorkers wince. (In Manhattan, the average cost of real estate is more than a thousand dollars a square foot.) To make room for the vice president, Hastert ejected Representative Bill Thomas, chairman of the Ways and Means Committee, from part of his suite of committee offices just steps from the House chamber. Now, even in their own wing of the Capitol, when House members negotiate with Cheney, legislators come to him, and not the other way around. "Offering office space to the vice president represented more than a breach in the symbolism concerning the powers and autonomy of the House of Representatives," notes Scott Lilly, a former House Appropriations Committee clerk. "Hastert's plan was to convert the House into a compliant and subservient role player inside the White House political organization."

Hastert succeeded in placing party over principle.

The vice president further cemented his influence by being attentive to the one thing that matters to congressmen above all: campaign cash. No one in the administration headlines more fundraisers for individual GOP members of Congress than Cheney. Strategically, this is understandable, but it's also tactically smart. Cheney knows better than anyone else the peril an emboldened Democratic Congress represents for a Republican administration. It boils down to two words: subpoena power. A Democratic Senate or House would allow Democratic committee chairs to subpoena documents (and individuals) that would reveal the workings of the Bush-Cheney administration. Every fundraising event Cheney attends not only helps keep Congress under GOP control, it's an individual chit waiting to be called by the vice president at the appropriate moment. Still, despite Cheney's considerable pull in Congress, when it came to the issue of torture, in 2005 the vice president finally hit a wall of immovable moral authority even he couldn't push through head-on.

As the pictures from Abu Ghraib and other details of detainee abuse filtered out, Arizona Republican senator John McCain experienced an almost visceral reaction. Shot down over Vietnam in 1967, McCain spent five and a half years as a prisoner of war, most of it in the infamous "Hanoi Hilton" prison camp. When his captors discovered that he was the son of the admiral in charge of the Pacific Command at the time, the North Vietnamese offered him freedom if he would cooperate in their propaganda efforts. McCain refused and was repeatedly tortured, leaving him physically incapacitated for life.

The senator knows from experience that torture doesn't work. At one point during his captivity, the North Vietnamese tortured McCain for the names of the members of his flight squadron. Under the physical abuse he "confessed" and gave them the Green Bay Packers' offensive line instead. McCain also understands how devastatingly corrosive government-sponsored torture is to the standing and authority of the United States government both at home and abroad. He would write in an article for *Newsweek:* "What I do mourn is what we lose when by official policy or official neglect we allow, confuse or encourage our soldiers to forget that best sense of ourselves, that which is our greatest strength—that we are different and better than our enemies, that we fight for an idea, not a tribe, not a land, not a king, not a twisted interpretation of an ancient religion, but for an idea that all men are created equal and endowed by their Creator with inalienable rights."

In the summer of 2005, McCain offered several bills to prohibit torture by U.S. forces. For the next six months, Dick Cheney would tenaciously fight to defeat them. Cheney started his campaign with two meetings in July, including a thirty-minute nighttime session with the most powerful Republican members of the Armed Services Committee: McCain, Senator Lindsey Graham of South Carolina, and the chairman, Senator John Warner of Virginia. The vice president was explicit in making the case that if McCain's amendments passed, they would encroach on the authority of the president and make America more vulnerable to attacks by terrorists. His arguments failed to convince. A steady, sickening barrage of evidence of abuses spoke louder.

On October 5, McCain attached an anti-torture amendment to a $440 billion defense appropriations bill. The amendment prohibited cruel, inhumane, and degrading treatment of prisoners held in detention by the U.S. government. It also decreed that the Army Field Manual would be the uniform standard for the interrogation of Department of Defense detainees. The field manual was at that time going through revisions, and Pentagon sources had said that it would include a section on the importance of following the Geneva Conventions in the treatment of prisoners.

On the floor of the Senate, McCain read a letter from the now retired Colin Powell. Under Powell, the State Department had fought Cheney on torture. As with most of his battles against the vice president, Powell had lost. "Our troops need to hear from Congress," he wrote. "The world will note that America is making a clear statement with respect to the expected future behavior of our soldiers."

The Senate passed McCain's amendment by a vote of 90 to 9.

But it wasn't to be that clear. Cheney wouldn't give up. The White House threatened to veto the bill, which would have been Bush's first veto ever. The vice president reportedly circulated pro-torture talking points to friendly Republicans on the Hill. A few weeks after the Senate vote, Cheney approached McCain again, this time with the hapless new CIA director Porter Goss in tow. As chairman of the House Intelligence Committee, Goss had refused Democratic pleas to hold hearings on the Valerie Plame case. His appointment to head the CIA set off an exodus of talented senior staff officers who recognized they had far better prospects in the private sector than in an agency that was beginning to suffer from institutional battered-spouse syndrome. By the end of his tenure in 2006, Goss was spending more time at his farm in Virginia than in the office at Langley as he waited for his inevitable departure. At the meeting with Cheney, the CIA Director asked McCain to exempt agency personnel from his anti-torture amendment when the president believed such procedures were necessary. McCain refused.

In what should be ranked as one of the more distinguished moments in American journalism since Bush and Cheney took power, editorial writers from Anchorage to Miami condemned in the strongest possible terms the administration's practice of torture. Public opinion began to have an effect even on the ostrichlike Republican House. On November 4, the House leadership postponed a vote on a resolution endorsing McCain's amendment after they realized the measure would pass overwhelmingly.

A few days earlier, Cheney had taken a last run at Senate Republicans. During the Tuesday meeting, he had Senate staffers leave the room before giving what was described to reporters as an impassioned plea to let the CIA torture when necessary. The president needed the flexibility. If the Senate moved forward on the amendment, it could result in the loss of "thousands of lives," he said. As part of his argument, Cheney pointed to the capture of al-Qaeda leader Khalid Sheikh Mohammed. Aggressive interrogations of Mohammed had led to important disclosures, he insisted.

Cheney didn't tell the senators anything about Mohammed's wife—or his son and daughter, ages seven and nine. They were also in custody and interrogators had told Mohammed they would be harmed if he didn't talk. Cheney didn't convey to the senators that rather than make Mohammed more talkative, the threats and the torture seemed to harden the terrorist. He likely didn't tell the senators about Abu Zubaydah and Ibn al-Sheikh al-Libi, two midlevel al-Qaeda leaders who gave false and misleading information under torture. (They started torturing Zubaydah, who suffered from split personality disorder, in May 2002. Made to think he was going to be killed, he reeled off lists of targets—supermarkets, banks, shopping malls, apartment buildings—with each new disclosure sending the U.S. government scurrying in fear to safeguard sites that defied protection.)

At the meeting, McCain challenged Cheney, saying, "This is killing us around the world."

By the middle of November, Cheney stepped away from trying to negotiate with McCain. Bush tapped National Security Advisor Stephen Hadley to continue discussions with the senator in Cheney's place. On December 15, the House passed its resolution in support of McCain's amendment 308 to 122. The next day, Bush met with McCain in the Oval Office. Cheney was not there. In a startling reversal, Bush endorsed the McCain amendment. In exchange, the senator agreed to language that would allow intelligence officers to present a defense that a "reasonable" person could conclude they were following a lawful order. The media billed it as a major setback for the vice president.

Three days later, an unbowed vice president gave a startling interview to *Nightline*'s Terry Moran. When asked where the president drew the line on torture, Cheney said the rule, according to court decisions, was "whether or not it shocks the conscience."

Here was how Cheney could say with a straight face that America didn't torture: "Now you can get into a debate about what shocks the conscience and what is cruel and inhuman. And to some extent, I suppose, that's in the eye of the beholder."

There he was, Dick Cheney, nakedly amoral, and driven by fear: "We think it's important to remember that we are in a war against a group of individuals, a terrorist organization that did in fact slaughter three thousand innocent Americans on 9/11; that it's important for us to be able to have effective interrogation of these people when we capture them," Cheney continued.

Unspoken was the concern that 9/11 was just a beginning, a prelude to much more terrifying attacks—a dirty bomb, poison gas in a subway, the release of a biological agent—in which as many as half a million could die. Future attacks could visit a degree of death on America not seen since the Civil War. It wasn't a matter of *if* as much as *when*. The fear of the big attack gave birth to a new doctrine. Ron Suskind, in his remarkably insightful book *The One Percent Doctrine*, describes the epiphany Cheney experienced: "If there was even a one percent chance of terrorists getting a weapon of mass destruction—and there has been a small probability of such an occurrence for some time—the United States must now act as if it was a certainty." It was prevention based on suspicion, dealt with by the application of overwhelming blunt force. The end justified any means necessary. It didn't matter how effective torture was as long as it provided even a remote chance that it might save American lives.

"That one percent drove Cheney and Bush nuts," says Wilkerson. "In certain respects, they became paranoids, willing to sacrifice every element of our civil liberties, even our republic, to save the republic."

A lifetime of experience had influenced the development of Cheney's new doctrine, not just the events of 9/11. Dick Cheney had thought about worst-case scenarios for almost half a century. What else would make a young man who supported the Vietnam War seek five deferments to avoid it, other than a fear of a personal worst-case scenario? Cheney's first heart attack at thirty-seven brought him face to face with his own mortality. As vice president, he lives with it every day. A device implanted near his heart keeps him from sudden death. An ambulance trails him wherever he goes, as does a team of the most sophisticated armed guards on the planet. He travels with a bioterrorism suit in case of an attack and spends time in undisclosed locations deep underground, practicing for Armageddon.

Cheney is one of the few people alive who has prepared for the possibility of a nuclear attack on the United States. In fact, he regularly simulated the experience during the 1980s. The highly classified program went by the nondescript title of "the National Program Office," but it had a budget of hundreds of millions of dollars. About once a year, Cheney would make his way to Andrews Air Force Base in the middle of the night. There he joined forty to sixty federal officials and a member of Reagan's cabinet on one of three teams that would fly or drive to secret bunkers. Lead-lined trucks with sophisticated communications hardware followed. For three or four days they would pretend that nuclear catastrophe with the Soviets had occurred. What they wanted was speed of decision-making. Rather then follow federal law and the constitutional order of presidential succession, they planned for a different future. The former chiefs of staff, a very short list that included Cheney and Rumsfeld, would provide experience to the cabinet member–leader, who owing to circumstances would most likely be a figurehead at the start. They discussed what to do about Congress, according to James Mann, then a writer at the Center for Strategic and International Studies, who was the first to write extensively about the program. "One of the awkward questions we faced," Mann quoted one participant, "was whether to reconstitute Congress after a nuclear attack. It was decided that no, it would be easier to operate without them." They also failed to involve Congress in these post-doomsday plans, making no effort to keep the constitutional framework intact.

After the trauma of 9/11, the Bush administration ramped up the government exercises in which Cheney had been involved under Reagan. The specifics of the government's current doomsday plans are some of its most tightly held secrets. For the first time, high-level officials including the vice president participated in the exercises. Millions of dollars went into renovating secure living quarters and updating communication capabilities. For many members of the administration, and particularly for Cheney, the nightmare scenario is ever present, and it warps their thinking.

During the Ford administration, Cheney told an interviewer about how best to serve a president. It was essential "to see to it that the president has the information he needs to make an intelligent decision so that he doesn't have a blind center," Cheney said. The blind center was that crucial factor you couldn't see but absolutely needed to know.

Fear has become Dick Cheney's blind center, although maybe it always was. And now, all the adults who throughout his career helped keep his darker impulses in check—Gerald Ford, Ed Levi, Tip O'Neill, Jim Baker, George H. W. Bush—are gone. Cheney is in charge, with the highly effective David Addington, his super-id, cracking heads to force compliance.

Cheney could afford to be cavalier about McCain's amendment. In the end, it proved largely meaningless. The vice president retreated back into the shadows, the place where he has always operated most effectively. The Army Field Manual that would spell out the principle that U.S. forces do not torture would be delayed if not outright suppressed. By early July 2006, the Pentagon still had not produced the manual. In classic Cheney-Addington form, torture advocates wanted a classified appendix that would include more savage interrogation techniques. Even Army commanders opposed that idea, as did McCain and the other Senate leaders on the Armed Services Committee. Cheney was getting increasing flak from within the administration as public disclosure led to stronger resistance; but he and Addington were ready. For decades, they had closely studied the mechanisms for increasing executive power.

Bush signed the bill enacting McCain's amendment into law on December 28. Two days later, the White House press office "put out the trash." The Friday before one of the biggest holiday weekends of the year, it released seven bland-sounding press releases covering various statements, memoranda, and the Presidential Message for New Year's Day 2006. Buried deep in a statement that accompanied the signing of H.R. 2863, the "Department of Defense, Emergency Supplemental Appropriations to Address Hurricanes in the Gulf of Mexico, and Pandemic Influenza Act, 2006," was a comment on the McCain Amendment.

"The executive branch shall construe Title X in Division A of the Act, relating to detainees, in a manner consistent with the constitutional authority of the President to supervise the unitary executive branch as Commander in Chief and consistent with the constitutional limitations on the judicial power, which will assist in achieving the shared objective of the

Congress and the President, evidenced in Title X, of protecting the American people from further terrorist attacks."

Testifying before Congress months later, Bruce Fein, Cheney's legal eagle from Iran-Contra days, would describe that paragraph. "While to the layman, the language of the signing statement may seem both Delphic and innocuous, to the initiated the words referring to a unitary executive and commander in chief powers clearly signify that President Bush is asserting that he is constitutionally entitled to commit torture if he believes it would assist the gathering of foreign intelligence," Fein testified. "President Bush has nullified a provision of statute that he had signed into law and which he was then obliged to faithfully execute."

With his signing statement, Bush apparently once again winked at allowing torture, as he had with his February 7, 2002, memo. As before, the mixed message was aimed at the federal bureaucracy that would carry out his orders.

The first reporter to catch Bush's sleight of hand was Charlie Savage of *The Boston Globe*, who reported on the signing statement on January 4. Later in April, the *Globe* published another stunner by Savage: The torture memo was just one of what was at the time 750 written challenges by the Bush administration in which the president reserved the right to ignore the will of Congress. In subsequent stories by Savage and other reporters, the man behind many of these signing statements was identified as David Addington. Cheney had finally found an end-run around the congressional prerogatives he despised so much.

Since the early 1800s, presidents have occasionally included a statement when they signed a large bill asserting a specific provision was unconstitutional. But it wasn't until the Reagan administration that an American president started issuing signing statements as a deliberate strategy to expand executive power. In 1986, a twenty-six-year-old Justice Department lawyer named Samuel Alito, Jr., wrote a strategy memo explaining how to make fuller use of the statements. (The memo surfaced in late 2005, when Bush nominated Alito for the Supreme Court, but during the hearings, his critics, Senate Democrats, decided to focus on the nominee's opposition to affirmative action rather than issues of executive privilege.) Subsequent presidents used this newfound form of power, but none to the extent of Bush and Cheney. Before 2000, all the presidents combined had issued fewer than six hundred such challenges. In one and a half terms, President George W. Bush would produce more than eight hundred. At the same time, in a first in modern American history, the president went almost six years without issuing a veto and sending a bill back to Congress, the way the Founders envisioned the system of checks and balances working. (Bush broke that streak with a veto on July 19 of a bill that relaxed restrictions on federal financing of stem cell research.)

Bruce Fein, a lifelong Republican, has called on Congress to censure Bush for disregarding the Constitution. "The key to our system is that it ultimately collapses unless there is self-restraint by all branches," he says. "At least at present, a sense of balance and restraint is gone."

Among the hundreds of laws that involve congressional oversight of the executive, Bush has decided to ignore ones involving war, whistleblowers, civil rights, and even whether his administration is required to provide environmental maps to Congress. In 2003, Congress passed a law prohibiting the administration from obstructing corruption investigations of the Iraq Coalition Provisional Authority without notifying the legislative branch. Bush declared that any Pentagon investigation took precedence over a civilian one and that he would follow the law on his own terms: "The executive branch shall construe these sections in a manner consistent with the constitutional authority of the President to classify and control access to information bearing on the national security." When Congress limited the number of U.S. troops stationed in Colombia and forbade them from fighting in that country's war unless in self-defense, Bush interpreted the law as "advisory," asserting that only the president has control over U.S. forces. When Congress passed a law saying Bush couldn't fire whistleblowers from the Department of Energy and the Nuclear Regulatory Agency if they testified before legislators, Bush maintained that only he and his appointees had the right to decide who gives information to Congress. In March 2006, after intense debate, Congress renewed the USA Patriot Act, giving the administration unprecedented powers to violate the privacy of Americans. As a compromise, Congress decreed that the Justice Department had to report regularly how the FBI was using the act. Bush declared that he could order Justice to withhold information from Congress if he decided that it might impair national security or the functioning of the executive branch.

Eighty-two of the signing statements mention "the unitary executive." In an interview, Fein is dismissive of this concept favored by David

Addington and John Yoo that holds that there is no check on the executive powers of the president particularly when it involves his commander in chief responsibilities. "All it is, is sloganeering," Fein believes, a catchall to cloak an executive power grab.

Some have argued that the signing statements are empty symbolism, mere executive posturing by Cheney and Addington. The administration has yet to be challenged in court for following one of the statements rather than the law as written by Congress. And in an administration obsessed by secrecy, it will be hard to discover if and when the statements have been invoked. Still, as history has demonstrated, those who underestimate Cheney do so at their own peril.

The vice president's expansive view of executive power and his sweeping mandate under his new doctrine of doing anything he believes necessary to protect the nation, preferably in secret, spilled out onto the front pages of *The New York Times* in December 2005. The *Times* revealed that the administration had been conducting secret wiretapping of Americans without a judicial warrant since at least 9/11. Cheney has insisted that the classified program targets only al-Qaeda suspects, but subsequent news reports have revealed that the government is intercepting and monitoring the calls and e-mails of possibly millions of Americans in a sweeping fishing expedition. The truth is classified, and while eight congressional leaders have been briefed on the program, it's unclear how extensive the information is that they have been given.

As part of the Watergate reforms, Congress had set up a special tribunal, the Foreign Intelligence Surveillance Court, to review warrants for wiretapping, even providing for making the warrants retroactive in order to give the government maximum flexibility. Congress had shown its willingness to meet post-9/11 security concerns by increasing the time the administration could wait before seeking the warrant from forty-eight to seventy-two hours. It still wasn't enough. Cheney had never demonstrated any enthusiasm for Congress's role in this arena, not when Attorney General Ed Levi had proposed a version of the Foreign Intelligence Surveillance Act (FISA) during the Ford administration nor when it was enacted under President Carter. Rather than use the media revelations to begin a serious debate—as befits a democracy—on what's required to protect the nation, the Bush administration, with Cheney at the forefront, has threatened to prosecute the press, and particularly *The New York Times*.

Sitting in his office at the Library of Congress, Louis Fisher can marshal endless arguments using the Constitution, the deliberations of the Founding Fathers, and U.S. Supreme Court precedents to poke holes in Cheney and Addington's legal case in favor of broad executive privilege. As one of the nation's foremost experts on separation of powers, he has been countering their arguments since his days as a House researcher for the majority side on the Iran-Contra Committee. Yet he recognizes that there is another level at work here that defies reason. "It's emotional after a while, not intellectual," he says as he tries to sum up their argument. What does it boil down to? "In an insecure society, [they] feel more secure when power is in one place."

By the summer of 2006, the carte blanche bestowed on the administration after 9/11 had largely worn off, and Cheney's push for near unlimited power was meeting with resistance—most notably from the Supreme Court. Even a reluctant Republican Congress had started to bleat, however ineffectually. The American Bar Association (ABA) appointed a blue-ribbon panel to review Bush's signing statements. Among its members were Mickey Edwards and Bruce Fein. In a report released in late July, the panel condemned signing statements that disregard the intent of Congress as "contrary to the rule of law and our constitutional system of separation of powers." Fein drafted legislation for Senate Judiciary Committee chairman Arlen Specter that would give Congress the standing to sue the administration over the signing statements. But the most surprising challenge to Cheney's imperial presidency has come from within the administration. Despite Addington's attempts to bully lawyers at Justice into submission, a few have opposed the executive power grab. Administration lawyers fought Addington on the torture memo and on warrantless wiretapping. They lost more battles than they won, but at the very least, they left a trail of dissent. (For example, Jack Goldsmith, who replaced Bybee at the OLC in 2003, withdrew the August 2002 torture memo. He would only last a year in his position, leaving the Justice Department for a teaching post at Harvard Law School.) Amid the infighting, Yoo departed the administration and returned to Boalt Hall at Berkeley.

In June 2004, the U.S. Supreme Court ruled in *Hamdi v. Rumsfeld* that U.S. citizen Yaser Esam Hamdi could not be detained indefinitely without access to the judicial system. Hamdi had started out at Guantánamo, but upon the discovery of his American citizenship, his captors transferred him to a Navy brig. The justices had restored that most sacred of American rights, habeas corpus. The same day, the court also ruled in *Rasul v. Bush* that the judicial system had the authority to decide whether individual non-U.S. citizens held at Guantánamo were illegally imprisoned. A year later, in *Hamdan v. Rumsfeld*, a divided Supreme Court invalidated administration plans to establish special military tribunals to prosecute those at Guantánamo. The authority to do so rested with Congress, the court ruled. And on August 16, District Judge Anna Diggs Taylor in Detroit became the first federal judge to rule that the administration's program of warrantless wiretapping was unconstitutional. "It was never the intent of the Framers to give the President such unfettered control, particularly where his actions blatantly disregard the parameters clearly enumerated in the Bill of Rights," Taylor wrote in her opinion, before pointing something out that in another age might seem obvious. "The three separate branches of government were developed as a check and balance for one another."

The pendulum seems to be swinging against the imperial presidency, but Cheney doesn't give up—that's not the Wyoming way. Despite the recent rulings, the administration is probably only one or two aging justices away from having its views upheld by the Supreme Court. While time might take care of that, the more pressing concern would be the congressional elections looming in November. In the first half of 2006, Cheney raced around the country attending fundraisers for Republican congressional candidates. By early August, three months before the most important midterm election of his career, Cheney had already attended eighty fundraisers for the cycle, netting Republicans more than $24 million.

At each event, he gives more or less the same speech. He begins by saying, "It's important that we keep proven leaders like [X] because these are times of incredible consequence for the nation." The speech dwells on national security and how "America is a stronger and better nation thanks to the leadership of our president."

It's a questionable statement, right down to whether the leadership is coming from the president or from Cheney himself. What is certain is that today the vice president is changing America's system of government in the service of his doctrine of fear. If al-Qaeda strikes again, this time with a weapon of mass destruction, the imperial presidency now in its infancy will harden and grow more robust.

"What will happen if it does happen?" asks Wilkerson rhetorically. "We have tyranny. We have military law established. I think we bomb whomever. We don't care what the intelligence says. It may be nuclear. And I think the president after that has got no maneuvering room with the American people, other than executive power to the max for whatever purpose it might be used."

TWELVE

What Dick Knew—and When He Knew It

Some time in 2007, Dick Cheney will leave his White House office for a short ride west on Constitution Avenue. Accompanied by his lawyer and a security detail, he will walk into a federal courthouse that bears the name of a judge who once settled a crisis that involved the presidency, the CIA, and American military adventurism gone bad.

E. Barrett Prettyman was sent to Havana in 1962 to negotiate the release of a battalion of the CIA's Cuban insurgents captured by Fidel Castro at the Bay of Pigs. The United States and USSR were entangled in the Cold War. John F. Kennedy had just been elected president. Castro's communist government was consolidating its power in Cuba. And Kennedy decided to act, even as the military and the CIA disagreed about the wisdom of the plan. His proxy invasion of Cuba was the sort of muscular foreign policy Cheney would support in Central America twenty years later—even if by Cheney's standards Kennedy was a little light on the muscle.

In a courtroom on the second floor of the E. Barrett Prettyman Courthouse, Vice President Cheney will be confronted by the consequences of a failed military adventure in Iraq. More precisely, he will confront the consequences of his distortion of the intelligence used to sell that war to the American people. The trial will focus on the cover-up Cheney and his staff undertook when it was revealed that he fabricated the central pretext for a war that by summer 2006 had killed more than twenty-five hundred American soldiers, injured some twenty-five thousand, and killed more than thirty thousand Iraqi civilians. If the vice president avoids the ride to the courthouse and testifies by closed-circuit television—as Ronald Reagan did in Iran-Contra—he will be answering questions under an oath administered by a no-nonsense federal judge. Cheney will be called to testify as a fact witness to a crime allegedly committed by a colleague and friend. The trial of Cheney's former chief of staff, Scooter Libby, will hinge not only on how the vice president answers the questions. In a very real sense, the largest legacy of the Bush-Cheney administration—the Iraq War—will be on trial in Judge Reggie Walton's courtroom.

The Scooter Libby affair began immediately after retired diplomat Joseph Wilson refuted President Bush's claim that Iraq was purchasing uranium from Niger. Bush had made the sixteen-word claim in his January 2003 State of the Union address: *"The British government has learned that Saddam Hussein recently sought significant quantities of uranium from Africa."* Wilson, who had traveled to Niger at the CIA's request, found that the claim was false and tried to inform the White House and the State Department. Getting no response, he published a July 2003 op-ed piece in *The New York Times*, under the headline "What I Didn't Find in Africa." On the following day, says Wilson, "the White House admitted that the sixteen words did not rise to the level of inclusion in the State of the Union." Having backed away from the false claim, the administration should have moved on. "That would have been the end of it," Wilson says. His fifteen-hundred-word op-ed piece would have been a "two- or three-day news story."

But to Cheney and Libby, Wilson's talking to reporters and then challenging the administration in *The New York Times* was an attack on the vice presidency. So Libby, White House senior adviser Karl Rove, and others began quietly plotting to discredit Wilson. It is for lying about his role in that scheme, and obstructing a federal investigation, that Dick Cheney's friend, adviser, and chief of staff, Scooter Libby, was indicted.

It wasn't that Wilson's article specifically attacked Cheney; but the facts he marshaled undermined the closed foreign policy operation run out of Cheney's office. Wilson's account of his trip to Niger put to rest the fabrication Cheney and Bush used to send 220,000 Americans to war in Iraq. It challenged the near absolute right to secrecy Cheney and other advocates of the "unitary presidency" claim for the executive branch—in particular in time of war. It confronted Cheney's ideas about the authority of the executive branch to "create" its own intelligence, to direct its own foreign policy, to wage war. It was an affront to everything Dick Cheney has fought for since he was a thirty-five-year-old chief of staff for President Gerald Ford. At that time, Cheney saw "the presidency at its nadir" as Congress reclaimed its power after Watergate. His entire career has been dedicated to the restoration of the executive branch. He wasn't going to let some retired ambassador get in his way.

Wilson wryly observed that at some point in the summer of 2003, Dick Cheney must have turned to his staff and whispered: "Will no one rid me of this troublesome priest?" If appropriating the martyr's mantle of Thomas à Becket was over the top, Wilson was closer to the truth than was the administration. Joe Wilson had to be silenced in a way that demonstrated the consequences of challenging the administration. Yet Wilson's op-ed piece was unassailable. Its truth had already been borne out early in the summer of 2003, by the fact that American troops found no nuclear weapons program (indeed, no weapons of mass destruction) in Iraq.

Cheney understands that the White House is a court, and courtiers can be manipulated to eliminate adversaries. As a young chief of staff for Gerald Ford, Cheney, as consort to Donald Rumsfeld, undermined the power Henry Kissinger held in the Ford administration and ended the career of Ford vice president Nelson Rockefeller. Joe Wilson was smaller game. Cheney moved with the same methodical efficiency he employed when he took out Nelson Rockefeller. "On or about June 12, 2003, Libby was advised by the Vice President that Wilson's wife worked for the Central Intelligence Agency in the Counterproliferation Division," reads one line from the five-page chronology that sets up Libby's indictment. The troublesome priest would be silenced by an attack on his wife.

The criminal case styled *United States of America v. I. Lewis Libby, also known as "Scooter Libby"* is one chapter of a story much larger than the outing of

CIA agent Valerie Plame Wilson. "It was Dick Cheney's contempt for the CIA," says Mel Goodman, who spent twenty-five years at the agency. "For him the CIA just gets in the way." Valerie Plame Wilson was another casualty of Dick Cheney's lifelong campaign to weaken the agency.

Cheney's contempt for the Central Intelligence Agency has its roots in the Ford administration. Cheney believed the agency, like Dr. Kissinger, was soft on the Soviet Union. So Cheney and Rumsfeld colluded with a clique of right-wing academics—which would grow into the neocon movement that did the big thinking on the war in Iraq—to prove how bad the agency was. They proposed that a group of foreign policy experts—"Team B"—would match wits and skills with the agency, "Team A." The "comparative intelligence analysis" would ensure that the agency wasn't missing the mark. CIA director William Colby wouldn't buy it. He insisted that no "ad hoc independent group of analysts could prepare a more thorough analysis of the Soviet strategic capabilities." Colby's commitment to truth in intelligence became a liability, and the president asked for his resignation. Ford replaced Colby with George H. W. Bush, a perennial team player who eagerly embraced Team B. Harvard historian Richard Pipes directed the group, which included Paul Wolfowitz, Scooter Libby, and other disciples of Cold War theorist Albert Wohlstetter. Cheney and Rumsfeld provided White House backing for the enterprise. (They even brought in Edward Teller for tech support.) "They wanted to toughen up the agency's estimates," Goodman says. "Cheney wanted to drive it so far to the right it would never say no to the generals."

The game was rigged. It was hard for CIA analysts to stand up to someone like Pipes, a Harvard professor and prominent policy intellectual. Team B looked at the same raw intelligence agency analysts used and arrived at conclusions consistent with their ideology:

- The Soviet Union's military capacity was far greater than what the CIA reported;
- Russian military spending was far beyond CIA estimates;
- Advances in Soviet submarine warfare technology made first-strike capacity against the United States far more likely;
- The Soviets were quietly accelerating the arms race, in a calculated attempt to surpass the United States.

Most of Team B's findings would ultimately prove to be hyperbole and way off the mark. But their "intelligence" was leaked to *The New York Times* and laid out in a December 26, 1976, front page story. The timing of the leak, less than a month before Jimmy Carter's inauguration, was aimed at the former governor of Georgia, who had little foreign policy experience. Cheney's flawed decisions in the Ford campaign contributed to Ford's loss to Carter. But with a cooked intelligence document leaked to a *Times* reporter, he won the foreign policy debate. Carter was locked into military spending defined by Dick Cheney, Donald Rumsfeld, and their intelligence B team.

And the CIA was housebroken.

But not sufficiently housebroken.

Almost thirty years later, as a vice president resolved to topple Saddam Hussein, Cheney was again frustrated by what he believed to be timid CIA analysts. He and Bush began considering regime change in Iraq before the September 11 terrorist attacks. But even after 9/11, the hard intelligence got in the way. The CIA had understated Hussein's WMD ten years earlier in the run-up to the first Gulf War. To make a war happen, Cheney would again have to neutralize the Central Intelligence Agency.

The CIA is the only federal agency that makes regular house calls to the White House. It delivers the President's Daily Briefing, a closely guarded report made available to six or seven people at the top of the administration. The principals who get the PDB are assigned briefers. The briefers are sometimes sent back to the "raw traffic" at the agency to provide additional information, or a different interpretation of information. They often develop a close relationship with their principals, based on daily contact and the sharing of classified information. In the run-up to the Iraq War, Cheney's briefer got a workout as the vice president demanded intelligence to justify attacking Iraq. When the intelligence wasn't there, Cheney took an unprecedented step: He fired his briefer. "I've never heard of anyone firing a briefer in all the time I've been associated with the agency," says Mel Goodman, who maintains contacts with CIA staffers. "It is absolutely unprecedented." But Cheney has never been a slave to precedent. In fact, he is so liberated from precedent that he fired the second briefer the CIA sent over. "Cheney was hard as nails," Goodman says. "He knew the kind of intelligence he wanted on these issues.

And he couldn't get that information from them." The firings sent a chilling signal to CIA employees.

There was more shattering of precedent. Cheney made repeated visits to the CIA headquarters at Langley, Virginia. Goodman, who is working on his second book on the agency, says that one visit to Langley is beyond what anyone at the agency considers reasonable for a vice president. Cheney made at least eight, perhaps as many as fifteen, according to Goodman and another source with contacts in the intelligence agency. "That's the only time I've ever heard of a principal going to headquarters that way," Goodman says. "When they go it's usually for some ceremonial function. To hand out an award or cut a ribbon. Then they get the hell out."

Cheney wasn't handing out awards. "He wanted them to make a connection between Iraq and al-Qaeda," says the second source interviewed. "He already got them to agree on nuclear weapons. But he wanted the al-Qaeda connection." Accompanying Cheney on some of the trips was Libby, who had muscled CIA employees thirty years earlier when he was a player on Team B. The repeated visits by Cheney and Libby placed enormous pressure on agency analysts. In a report commissioned by the agency, Richard Kerr, a retired CIA officer retained to study intelligence failures, wrote that "questions of weapons of mass destruction and Saddam's links to al-Qa'ida . . . in the months leading up to the war were numerous and intense." Kerr described "overwhelming consumer demand" on agency analysts, which resulted in flawed intelligence. A second source following the vice president's Langley visits was more direct. The pressure Cheney and Libby brought to bear on agency analysts "was brutal."

While he was beating up on CIA analysts, Cheney was also gathering his own intelligence—which would lead to the conflict between his office and Joe Wilson. In early 2002—more than a year before Bush was to make the accusation—Cheney obtained from the British a file of Italian origin that claimed Iraq had tried to purchase uranium from Niger. This "intelligence" provided the underpinnings for the sixteen words in the State of the Union speech.

When Cheney sent the Niger documents to the CIA, analysts in Langley recognized them as crude forgeries. But because of the pressure from the vice president, the CIA initially asked French intelligence to check into the claims that Iraq was buying five hundred metric tons of uranium "yellow cake" from Niger. French intelligence had debunked this rumor once before. In response to this second CIA request, the French sent five investigators to their former colony and again determined there was no merit to the claim. Alain Chouet, director of French intelligence, told the *Los Angeles Times* that he had no doubt about what his agents found. "We told the Americans, 'Bullshit, it doesn't make any sense.' "

In fact, debunking the Niger yellow cake documents required no travel whatsoever. International Atomic Energy Agency (IAEA) inspector Jacques Baute had spent months in Iraq and found nothing to suggest that Saddam Hussein had a nuclear weapons program. So Baute had his doubts about the Niger documents. To look into their authenticity, he used a sophisticated tool known outside the intelligence community as Google. In the dozen pages the Bush administration provided him, Baute found glaring errors. The president of Niger referred to "the constitution of 1965," though the country was governed under a constitution ratified in 1999. There was a letter signed by a foreign minister who hadn't been in office for eleven years. There were bogus letterheads, forged signatures, and other evident flaws. The CIA had the same material, because Cheney had sent it to the agency. They also had Google. Cheney's dishonesty in justifying the war in Iraq was becoming painfully evident.

The first three months of 2003 were a race between the International Atomic Energy Agency and the United Nations—both committed to inspections and diplomacy—and an American administration that had already decided to attack Iraq. The Bush-Cheney administration was marching inexorably toward war. On January 28, Bush delivered his "sixteen words" State of the Union speech. On February 5, Secretary of State Colin Powell went to the Security Council to lay out U.S. proof of Iraq's WMD programs. On March 7, IAEA director general Mohamed ElBaradei responded, delivering Baute's report on the Niger documents to the Security Council. The U.S. representatives at the Security Council privately agreed that there was no evidence that Iraq had a nuclear weapons program. Cheney personally attacked ElBaradei and the IAEA. On March 16, he told NBC's Tim Russert: "I think ElBaradei, frankly, is wrong. I think if you look at the record of the International Atomic Energy Agency on this issue, especially where Iraq is concerned, they have constantly underestimated or missed what it was Saddam Hussein was doing. I don't have any reason to believe they're any more valid at this time than they've been in the past." (Cheney had a legitimate complaint about the IAEA's missing weapons locations in the past, but Iraq had since been bombed and boycotted and IAEA inspectors were on the ground filling the gaps that they and intelligence agencies had missed ten years earlier.)

Speaking to Russert, Cheney even went nuclear on Hussein: "And we believe he has, in fact, reconstituted nuclear weapons."

That statement was, in a word, bullshit.

Yet on March 16, President Bush gave Hussein an ultimatum to leave Iraq or face attack by U.S. forces. On March 17, Bush declared war on Iraq. On March 20, U.S. airplanes began bombing Baghdad.

By May, U.S. and British forces combing Iraq had found no nuclear weapons or any other weapons of mass destruction. It was becoming evident that the administration had misled Congress and the American people. Joe Wilson was about to become a part of that story.

On May 5, *The New York Times*'s Nicholas Kristof wrote a column about an unnamed ambassador's trip to Niger and *Washington Post* veteran reporter Walter Pincus then tracked down Wilson. On June 12, Pincus wrote the first news article questioning the administration's pretext for war, citing an unnamed retired ambassador who had gone to Niger for the CIA and found that the uranium story was without merit. When Kristof's column appeared in mid-May, Cheney's office, in concert with Bush senior adviser Karl Rove, began discussing the problem the article presented. When Pincus's hard-news story ran in the *Post*, the discussions became a coordinated campaign against Joe Wilson and the truth. The vice president played a critical role in that campaign, which seemed to grow in intensity with each news report.

And the news stories continued, *The New Republic* following the *Post* with a seven-thousand-word investigative feature. It included a quote from an unnamed ambassador who said administration officials "knew the Niger story was a flat-out lie."

On July 6, Joe Wilson went public with his own account of the trip to Niger, publishing his *New York Times* op-ed. Wilson immediately got one odd warning of the smear campaign that was about to consume him and his wife. On July 8, a friend told him he had seen right-wing columnist Robert Novak on Pennsylvania Avenue. "He said Novak called me an asshole," Wilson says. "He said 'Wilson is an asshole. His wife works for the CIA.' "

When Wilson called Novak—at seventy-five, the dark doyen of conservative journalism in Washington—Novak asked whether the call was confirmation that Wilson's wife was a CIA agent. In his July 14 column, Novak, whom Cheney once referred to as "No Facts," outed Valerie Plame Wilson. Because the Intelligence Identities Protection Act makes it illegal to reveal the identity of an undercover CIA agent, the agency requested an investigation. The Department of Justice started the two-year inquiry that resulted in Scooter Libby's indictment and resignation in October 2005. (Cheney took his swipe at "No Facts" Novak in a 1977 *Casper Star-Tribune* article under the headline "Cheney: Altering Foreign Elections a Possible Option.")

Coincidentally, the entire process was set in motion by Cheney. "Wilson was asked to go to Niger for one specific purpose," Goodman says. "It was the CIA's idea to get Cheney off their backs. Cheney would not get off their backs about the yellow cake documents. They couldn't get Cheney to stop pressing the issue. He insisted that was the proof of reconstitution of their program."

Someone at the agency took the vice president at his word and called Joe Wilson to investigate. Wilson had been an ambassador in Africa, spoke fluent French, and knew many of the players—including the directors of the French uranium consortium. In fact, Wilson had been the last American diplomat in Iraq when the United States invaded it the first time, in 1991; the senior George Bush had commended him for his courage and service to his country. Wilson went to Niger to check out the intelligence that few but the vice president considered anything other than a fraud. In fact, it is hard to believe that Cheney himself believed the Niger documents were anything other than a fraudulent though useful tool to make the case for war. If he initially thought they were legitimate, he also knew that *New Yorker* reporter Seymour Hersh had thoroughly debunked them soon after they surfaced. Cheney then participated in a plan to discredit Wilson. All will be played out in federal court—and in the court of public opinion—in 2007, unless Bush takes the unlikely step of pardoning Scooter Libby before the trial.

The man prosecuting Scooter Libby is Patrick Fitzgerald.

The U.S. attorney in Chicago was a loyal lieutenant in an administration that had declared a war on terror. Fitzgerald convicted Sheikh Omar

Abdel Rahman for his role in the 1993 World Trade Center bombings. In June 1998, he handed down a sealed indictment against Osama bin Laden after investigating him and his terrorist network for two years. That same year, he was in Nairobi two days after the bombing of the American embassy there, directing five hundred FBI agents sifting through evidence. Three years later, in federal court in Manhattan, Fitzgerald won convictions against the Nairobi bombers, two of whom were sentenced to death. "His brain was like a computer," Manhattan U.S. attorney Mary Jo White told *Vanity Fair.* "You had 224 victims, you had lots of al-Qaeda names, Arabic names that sound alike. He could recite these names and knew the links, knew the history. I thought I'd seen everything. . . . But watching him in that case was just head-jerking." Adored by magazine feature writers, who described his workaholic habits, his indifference to the world around him, and his uncanny mind (he keeps his suits, underwear, and socks in his office; once left a pan of lasagna in his oven for three months; memorized entire case files), Fitzgerald was the Bush administration's fed from Central Casting.

Then he was appointed to investigate them—at which point he became the prosecutor described in an *Irish Times* headline: "Scary Irish-American." After Bush's first attorney general, John Ashcroft, recused himself, and Assistant Attorney General Patrick Comey appointed Fitzgerald to investigate the criminal betrayal of CIA agent Valerie Plame's name, the scary forty-five-year-old Irish American prosecutor became the administration's worst nightmare. An attorney representing reporters whom Fitzgerald was pressuring for information about Libby said that after just one meeting with the prosecutor, he knew it would be bad for the press. Fitzgerald did put Judith Miller in jail for three months when she refused to reveal her sources. The lawyer said he walked away from his meeting with Fitzgerald realizing that Libby and the vice president were in far greater trouble: "I don't think these guys had any idea what they are in for."

Fitzgerald's appointment was another unintended consequence of the excessive and endogamous partisanship of the Bush-Cheney administration. Attorney General John Ashcroft was the only incumbent U.S. senator in U.S. history to lose his seat to a dead man, coming in second after Democratic challenger Mel Carnahan was killed in a plane crash. Ashcroft's one term in the Senate had been fairly unremarkable. But he had been a client of Karl Rove. He was the darling of the extreme Christian right. And he was out of work. For the Bush team, he was a natural choice for AG. And Cheney had eliminated Oklahoma governor Frank Keating, who as AG could have directed the investigation with no "Rove conflict."

Because Rove had directed Ashcroft's Senate campaign and was also a possible target of the leak investigation, Ashcroft, as they say at the courthouse, was "conflicted out." He was too close to one of the subjects he would be investigating. Once Ashcroft designated his assistant AG to appoint a special investigator, the White House was saddled with Fitzgerald, a prosecutor so dedicated to the law that he's become a cult hero among his peers.

Fitzgerald deposed and jailed journalists, questioned the president, engaged in a broad and protracted discovery process, and began to follow a testimonial and documentary trail into the Vice President's Office. He became the Javert of the DOJ, following Libby from reporter to reporter and building a case based on what he extracted in what one witness described as "precise and persistent interrogation." In most instances, Fitzgerald knew the answer to the question he would ask each subject he called before the grand jury.

Fitzgerald's indictment provides a narrative that tells a story and defines a motive. He starts at Bush's sixteen words on January 28 and proceeds to Nicholas Kristof's May 5 column. By May 29, Fitzgerald has Libby on the phone with the State Department inquiring about the trip. On June 9, he has Libby receiving faxed classified documents from the CIA, with "Wilson" noted in Libby's handwriting on one page. On June 11, he finds Undersecretary of State Marc Grossman telling Libby that Wilson's wife works for the CIA. On June 11, the CIA advises Libby that Wilson's wife works at the agency. On June 12, the vice president appears on the crime scene, telling Libby that Wilson's wife works for the CIA in the Counterproliferation Division, information Cheney has gotten out of the CIA. On June 14, Libby is meeting with his CIA briefer, discussing Joe Wilson and his wife, Valerie Wilson.

Fitzgerald's detailed indictment also tracks Libby to a long meeting with *New York Times* reporter Judith Miller at the St. Regis Hotel—a Washington institution a few blocks from the White House. The St. Regis meeting occurred two days after Wilson's op-ed ran. When asked by the FBI and later under oath, Libby says he first learned about Valerie Wilson's CIA status from "reporters." He says he told each reporter he spoke to that he heard about Valerie Wilson "from reporters." Fitzgerald's investigation, however, established that Libby was working official government sources from his office in the White House. Based on Libby's response, Fitzgerald makes a prosecutorial decision that will make 2007 a difficult year for Scooter Libby and Dick Cheney. Rather than prosecute him under the Intelligence Identities Protection Act, Fitzgerald puts Libby in a very small box. He charges him with perjury and obstruction of justice.

Behind the narrative is a clear motive. Cheney, according to one CIA source, was furious when he learned that the CIA had revealed the Niger documents as a forgery, because they were "the very core" of his argument for war in Iraq. Further fueling the vice president's anger was the man the agency sent out to investigate the story: Joe Wilson, a flamboyant Francophile and a Democrat. And the timing, just as American troops in Iraq were finding there were no weapons of mass destruction of any kind, made a bad moment for the vice president even worse. For the White House, the story of the 2004 campaign *could not be* about missing weapons of mass destruction. Scooter Libby went after Valerie Plame Wilson.

Trying to get to the bottom of what essentially was an act of treason committed in the White House, Fitzgerald relentlessly worked the paper trail that led to the Vice President's Office. Two years and six months into the investigation, the persistent U.S. attorney from Chicago walked into the clerk's office in the E. Barrett Prettyman Courthouse and filed a piece of evidence that literally bore the fingerprints of the vice president—an original clipping of Joe Wilson's *New York Times* op-ed piece of July 6, 2003. Written in the margin are pointed questions about Wilson's mission to Iraq and his wife's role at the CIA. The handwriting—on the wall as well as on the op-ed page of the *Times*—is Dick Cheney's. "Have they done this sort of thing before?" Cheney wrote. "Send an Amb. to answer a question. Do we ordinarily send people out to do pro bono work for us? Or did his wife send him on a junket?" The annotation places Cheney at the center of the campaign to discredit Wilson, aware early on that Wilson's wife was a CIA agent.

Judge Reginald Walton is a Republican. George W. Bush appointed him to the District Court bench in Washington, D.C. He's one of the party's African American stars, first brought to Washington to work in the White House by George Bush the elder. Unfortunately for Scooter Libby and Dick Cheney, Reggie Walton is a hardass when it comes to criminals.

A trim man with a sprinkling of gray in his hair, an intense and focused face, and a dry, sometimes witty demeanor, he has yielded little ground to Libby's attorneys. In a pretrial hearing in May, Libby sat taking notes as Walton refused to order the State Department and CIA to turn over documents to the defense team. He repeatedly reminded Libby's attorneys that the case is about perjury and obstruction of justice. His standard for what is relevant in the trial was clearly defined in one reply to the defense counsel:

"I just don't see how that helps the jury decide whether Mr. Libby lied. . . ."

Speaking from the bench in the stark, cavernous courthouse, the judge also spelled out what the case is not about:

"I'm not willing to let this case end up to be a judicial resolution on the war or the statements the president made."

Yet when the trial begins in January, the court of public opinion will be focused on the issue Judge Walton promises not to put on trial. The subtext has become the text. It is evident that Dick Cheney was made aware of Wilson's findings in Niger. Yet he and others at the CIA and on the White House staff allowed the president to utter those sixteen words—which were put to the lie by Joe Wilson's fifteen-hundred words in *The New York Times*.

When the criminal case is done with, Scooter Libby will again be compelled to answer the same questions Fitzgerald is asking. In July, Joseph Wilson and Valerie Plame filed suit, naming Dick Cheney, Scooter Libby, Karl Rove, and ten unnamed defendants in a suit that makes the same charges Fitzgerald did. Fitzgerald, in fact, had done much of the legwork for Wilson and Plame, providing through his criminal investigation pretrial "discovery" that would have cost Wilson and Plame hundreds of thousands of dollars. Their suit was filed in the E. Barrett Prettyman Courthouse on Judiciary Square in Washington.

Scooter Libby can be pardoned. The president can plead ignorance. Dick Cheney cannot. He knew when he decided to take the country into war that Iraq was not buying uranium from Niger. As secretary of defense in the first Gulf War, he presided over the bombing of all the suspected nuclear weapons facilities in Iraq, each one identified with precise targeting coordinates. He knew that U.N. inspectors had been all over the country. He knew that German and French intelligence services had concluded there were no nuclear weapons in Iraq. And he knew that the CIA had concluded there were no nuclear weapons in Iraq. Yet he sent American soldiers into what has turned out to be a prolonged, failed, and unpopular war, with a cost that will exceed $300 billion and the death or disfigurement of tens of thousands of Americans and Iraqis.

His justification for doing so was a handful of forged documents that he knew were bullshit.

EPILOGUE

In a hotel restaurant at Pentagon City, a retired general wears a grimace on his face as he speaks. "The Army is broken," he says. "It will take decades to fix." He had seen the first Gulf War up close, watching Dick Cheney and Colin Powell ensure that there were adequate forces deployed before they commenced hostilities. He knew the vice president when Cheney was secretary of defense.

"It was different then," he says. "The staffs were apolitical. And the military was taken care of. If we made a mistake, we did no irreparable harm. Cheney now seems oblivious to what the military needs. That's because he trusts Rumsfeld. . . .

"So we have an army that is broken. The DOD is broken. And the process is broken. Rumsfeld has left us with the smallest army since 1941. First time in the history of the country that we haven't surged up the Army in time of war. We have *never* not surged up the Army in time of war. They can't recruit. So we redeploy, and redeploy, and redeploy, and break down the Army.

"They're not surging up, and they're burning through equipment in Iraq." Dick Cheney and Donald Rumsfeld have done, he says, "irreparable harm" to the Army.

Across the river in Foggy Bottom, Larry Wilkerson makes a similar argument. "They have gone through so much equipment in Iraq," Wilkerson says. He argues that the real test the military faces will not be on a foreign battlefield, but in Washington. "The first challenge," he says, "is going to be the reconstitution bill that will confront the next president. I mean bringing the ground forces, and to a certain extent the Air Force, back to levels pre-Iraq. They have burned up Abrams tanks, Humvees, wheeled vehicles, five-tons, eight-tons, Apache helicopters, Chinook helicopters, all very expensive hardware, at a rate which is astronomical." This will all be left for the next Congress to repair. Wilkerson also believes recruiting an army after this war is going to be very difficult.

Another institution that will be in need of repair when Dick Cheney and George W. Bush return to the private sector is the CIA. The vice president's visits to the agency's Langley, Virginia, headquarters in the run-up to the Iraq War, accompanied by his chief of staff, Scooter Libby, and others from the OVP, will adversely affect the agency's ability to provide accurate intelligence for decades.

Former CIA analyst Mel Goodman, who spent twenty-five years at the agency, says the damage is lasting, if not permanent. "The CIA is a brittle bureaucracy, fragile as any other," he says. "It's now broken."

"In the history of the agency, I've never heard of a vice president making specific demands of analysts," says a former deputy director of the agency. "It's never occurred. It's without precedent." It will, he says, change the way the CIA functions. Analysts and supervisors are bureaucrats, sensitive to the complaint that bureaucracies are unresponsive.

He shares Goodman's concerns. "The mere fact that [Cheney and Libby] were out there will generate in the bureaucracy—and the CIA is a bureaucracy—a sort of thinking that says 'Gee, can we make them happy, can we continue to satisfy them?' That's not the sort of thinking you want in any intelligence agency."

The agency, he says, already had morale and organizational problems.

The damage didn't end with the visits to Langley, but continued through the outing of CIA agent Valerie Plame Wilson and the appointment of Porter Goss as director of the agency.

An impaired intelligence agency and an impaired military are the contradictory legacy of the Bush-Cheney administration. Contradictory if only because Bush described himself as a "war president" who would fix the intelligence system that failed the nation on September 11, 2001. Yet the problems are identifiable, and they can be fixed—if a president and a Congress can summon the political courage and imagination to address them.

Over coffee at the University Club a few blocks from the White House, constitutional lawyer Bruce Fein has a lot to say about the assault under way on the safeguards America's founders created to keep the nation free. Fein has been around the block a few times in Washington. He has argued cases before the Supreme Court, so he understands the importance of saying all that needs to be said while the clock is running. On this particular morning he is speaking at a Gilbert-and-Sullivanesque pace, trope after pressurized trope, delivering a magisterial defense of a Constitution under attack by Vice President Dick Cheney.

"Dick Cheney exercises all the powers of the presidency," Fein says. "He has great contempt for Congress. You can get pretty cynical about Congress. Some of these people are yahoos. But that's not the point. You don't have to be brilliant to provide the checks and balances. You just need the constant questioning, the restraint."

Fein dismisses Cheney's argument that Congress overreached when it requested the names of participants in his energy task force meetings. "Bogus" and "Specious," he says. He's equally dismissive of the administration's defense of its warrantless wiretapping. "This is a crime," Fein states flatly. "FISA says if you operate or undertake electronic surveillance on American citizens, it's illegal. They don't need to do this to spy on al-Qaeda outside the country. It's not necessary. . . . The president could have asked for changes in FISA. They've amended it five times. . . . The important thing is to get the constitutional issues right. These are crimes against the constitutional architecture."

Fein doesn't expect Congress to set things right. "Congress is too philosophically ignorant to know how much of their power is being usurped," he says. He also sees the current congressional majority as accommodating the president because they belong to the same party. "They don't think about the future. The destiny of the nation is too long-term for them." After spending almost half of the last century in the minority, the Republican majorities in both houses of Congress reached a tacit agreement with the executive branch: Congress surrendered much of its constitutional authority to the president in exchange for partisan political dominance. It's particularly unfortunate that they did so on the eve of a terrorist attack that has made fear a political campaign tool.

Waiving away the waiter, Fein continues to describe the larger and more lasting structural damage done by the vice president—damage to the Constitution and the system of government it has defined for two hundred and thirty years. In the decade that followed Watergate, the Congress reasserted the authority vested in it by the Framers and redefined constitutional limits for an executive branch that refused to recognize them. It did so in response to a very evident constitutional crisis. What the vice president refers to as "the post-9/11 world" has delivered the country into another, although still largely invisible, constitutional crisis—in this case, an executive branch that has very low regard for the Bill of Rights, or for the Congress.

Whether the Democrats can take control of Congress, and, should they do so, whether they would somehow find the vision and political courage to confront the current constitutional crisis, are questions that, unfortunately, address our last best hope. The account of Ben Franklin emerging from the Pennsylvania State House after the ratification of the Constitution has been told so many times it is now a part of our received historical wisdom. As the story has it, a woman in the crowd gathered on the Philadelphia street shouted out to Franklin: "What sort of government have you given us?"

Franklin's reply was brief:

"A republic, if you can keep it."

The intersection of Dick Cheney, a supine Republican Congress, and four commercial jetliners transformed into terrorist weapons give Ben Franklin's response a currency it has not had since the Civil War.

25 QUESTIONS FOR DICK CHENEY

1. Why was your energy task force reviewing maps of Iraqi oilfields in 2001, two years prior to the Iraq War, while Iraq oil was embargoed?

2. After the initial military success in Afghanistan and Iraq in 2003, the Iranian government offered to negotiate with the United States regarding al-Qaeda, relations with Israel, and the Iranian nuclear energy and weapons program. Why did you kill the negotiations before they began?

3. Do you believe that in wartime there are any limits on the powers of the commander in chief, and if so, what are they?

4. What was the extent of your participation in the awarding of the no-bid single source contracts the Army Corps of Engineers awarded to Halliburton?

5. What were your intentions when you scribbled in the margins of *The New York Times* on July 6, 2003, "did his wife send him on a junket?"

6. At what point were you aware that Niger was not providing large quantities of uranium "yellow cake" to Iraq?

7. Exactly how many times did you visit CIA headquarters prior to the Iraq War, and what did you ask of the CIA analysts with whom you met?

8. How do you explain the complete reversal of your position on invading and occupying Iraq, a course of action you unequivocally opposed as George H. W. Bush's secretary of defense?

9. How do you justify ignoring CIA pleas for more U.S. forces when American and Northern Alliance forces had Osama bin Laden trapped in a cave complex in Tora Bora?

10. Was it your expectation leading up to the Iraq War that Ahmed Chalabi would replace Saddam Hussein, and did you or your staff discuss the organization of a provisional or future government of Iraq with Chalabi?

11. Considering that American and European intelligence sources were discounting the idea at the time, where did you get the information on which you based your claim that the Iraqi government was developing nuclear weapons in 2002?

12. What foreign policy instructions did you convey to your daughter Elizabeth while she was in the number two spot at the Bureau of Near Eastern Affairs of the State Department?

13. Considering the North Korean missile tests in June 2006 and North Korea's development of nuclear weapons, how do you justify the constraints you personally imposed on a negotiation agenda that had been drafted and approved by the president and secretary of state in 2004?

14. Do you believe that human-caused global warming is a reality? If so, do you believe the U.S. government has an obligation to do something about it?

15. Why doesn't the public have a right to know who serves on the vice president's staff and the size and details of the staff budget office and how many documents it has classified?

16. How long do you envision continuing warrantless wiretapping of American citizens, surveillance of their financial and telephone records, and other extraordinary domestic measures your administration has put in place to fight the "global war against terror"?

17. If there were to be a major attack on the United States involving weapons of mass destruction, what plans are in place for continuity of government, and will they comply with the constitutional statutory line of succession?

18. Do you believe the administration's signing statements take precedence over congressional statutes? How have these signing statements been put into effect in executive branch actions?

19. What was your involvement, either independently or through David Addington, in the drafting of the Yoo and Bybee memos justifying torture?

20. Are you still receiving any compensation of any kind from Halliburton, and would you provide an account of all Halliburton compensation you have received since you became George Bush's vice presidential nominee?

21. What request did Ken Lay make of you regarding Enron and the California electricity markets in 2001?

22. Did you have any discussions with Jack Stanley about bribing Nigerian officials while you were CEO at Halliburton?

23. Will you release the full list of names of the donors to the 2000 Presidential Transition Foundation and the amounts they gave?

24. Is the public subsidizing in any way your frequent travel to and attendance at fundraising events for congressional candidates?

25. Why won't you release your complete medical history and list of medications you take?

ACKNOWLEDGMENTS

This book would have not been possible without the generous support of colleagues and friends.

Nancy Miller at Random House conceived this project, offered us the opportunity to undertake it, helped shape it, and indulged our requests for deadline extensions. Her assistant, Lea Beresford, was indispensable in keeping editor and authors on the same page. And Random House production editor Beth Pearson and copy editor Emily DeHuff ensured that our grammatical and typographical errors didn't make it into the published text. Our agent, Dan Green, was as good a critical reader of our manuscript as he was a guide through the paper processes and decisions involved in any book contract.

In Washington, D.C., Ann Geracimos provided lodging and insight into the social and power centers of our nation's capital. Frank Smyth also offered a congenial space, which came with insight, advice, moral support, and a foldout couch. Amy Southerland offered us her good counsel as well as the friendship of a fellow writer. In Austin, the editorial staff of *The Texas Observer* allowed one of the editors the freedom to work on this project while other staff bore the extra burden involved in writing and editing an issue every two weeks. Jeanne Goka tolerated the extended absence of a spouse who set up a temporary residence in Washington. And Molly Ivins was generous enough to suspend a collaborative project with one of the authors so that this book could happen. Finally, we are deeply indebted to Peter Lindstrom, a researcher and insightful editor whose collaboration helped make this project possible.

Any nonfiction work rests on a foundation laid by those who have come before. The nature of this book required us to lean heavily on the work of others. Fortunately, despite frequent and often valid criticism of the Fourth Estate, investigative journalism is alive and well in the United States. We are indebted to a number of dedicated and fearless reporters who have faced the threat of prosecution in order to expose the inner workings of the most secretive administration in American history. Sy Hersh, Michael Isikoff, Jane Mayer, Walter Pincus, Dana Priest, James Risen, Charlie Savage, Evan Thomas, and Murray Waas come to mind, but there are many more. Charlie Cray of Halliburton Watch also provided us direction and hard data on the company Dick Cheney directed before Bush selected him as a running mate.

In the course of reporting this book, we have had the good fortune to meet a number of American heroes; some were willing to attach their names to their comments, but many spoke off the record out of fear of reprisal. A number of them are lifelong Republicans who are horrified by the direction in which Dick Cheney is taking our nation. While we do not have the time or space to name them all, three true patriots we feel must be mentioned are Colonel Larry Wilkerson, Bruce Fein, and Lou Fisher. Even when the substance of our discussion with them was grim, their passion and commitment to the American ideal left us filled with hope.

SOURCE NOTES

CHAPTER ONE
A Man, a Plan—and Names Named

ABC News *This Week*. Interview with Dick Cheney. January 28, 2002.

Abraham, Spencer (Secretary of Energy). Schedule. April 17, 2001.

Barbour, Haley. Memo to Vice President Dick Cheney. March 2, 2001.

Browning, Stephen. E-mail (recipient's name redacted). February 2, 2001.

Buccino, Sharon. Author interview. March 24, 2006.

Contratto, Dana. E-mail to Joseph Kelliher. March 22, 2001.

Fineman, Howard, and Michael Isikoff. "Enron Continues to Roil Washington." *Time*, February 11, 2002.

Fitton, Tom. Author interview. March 27, 2006.

Grodner, Nicole. E-mail to John Flaherty et al. April 2, 2001.

Hagel, Chuck (U.S. senator). Memo and floor remarks text to Energy Secretary Spencer Abraham. May 11, 2001.

Halsted, T. J. "Walker v. Cheney: Legal Insulation of Vice President Cheney from GAO Investigations." *Presidential Studies Quarterly*, September 2003.

In Re: Richard v. Cheney, Vice President of the United States, et al., Petitioners. United States Court of Appeals for the District of Columbia Circuit, May 10, 2005.

Johnson, Jim (Barbour Griffith & Rogers). Memo to Cheryl Alford (Office of the Secretary of Energy), March 20, 2001.

Judicial Watch et al. v. United States Department of Energy, United States District Court for the District of Columbia. July 1, 2002.

Kelliher, Joseph. E-mail to Kyle McSlarrow et al. April 13, 2001.

———. E-mail to Kyle McSlarrow et al. April 16, 2001.

Knight, Danielle. "Congress Sues White House to Get Cheney Docs." *Global Information Network*, January 31, 2002.

Koppel, Ted. Interview with Dick Cheney. ABC News. *Nightline*, July 26, 2001.

Landsberg, Mitchell, and Miguel Bustillo. "Legislators Unite over Energy Price Issue." *Los Angeles Times*, April 20, 2001.

Lewis, Charles. *The Buying of the President 2004: Who's Really Bankrolling Bush and His Democratic Challengers—and What They Expect in Return.* New York: HarperCollins, 2004.

Linehan, LouAnn (Chief of Staff to Sen. Chuck Hagel). Memo to Kyle McSlarrow. March 20, 2001.

Marshall, Joshua Micah. "Vice Grip: Dick Cheney Is a Man of Principles. Disastrous Principles." *Washington Monthly*, January 1, 2003.

Milbank, Dana. "Is Judge's Past Prelude in Cheney Case?" *The Washington Post*, November 26, 2002.

————, and Justin Blum. "Document Shows Cheney Aides, Oil Executives Met." *The Washington Post*, November 16, 2005.

National Energy Policy Development Group. Final Schedule for Chief of Staff. April 15, 2001.

————. "Foreign Suitors for Iraqi Oil Fields Contracts." March 5, 2001.

————. "Iraqi Oilfields Exploration Blocks." March 5, 2001.

————. "Iraqi Oil Gas Projects." March 5, 2001.

————. "Selected Oil Facilities of the United Arab Emirates." March 2005.

Nichols, John. "What Dick Cheney Knew: An Investigation of the Company's White House Ties Should Begin at His Door." *The Nation*, April 15, 2002.

Pasternak, Judy. "Energy Plan Bares Industry Clout." *Los Angeles Times*, April 26, 2001.

Pianin, Eric, and Dan Morgan. "Oil Executives Lobbied Cheney on Drilling." *The Washington Post*, February 27, 2002.

Shogren, Elizabeth. "President Drops Plans to Curb Carbon." *Los Angeles Times*, March 14, 2001.

Simendinger, Alexis. "Power Plays." *National Journal*, April 17, 2004.

Skelton, George. E-mail response to authors' query. February 9, 2003.

————. "Price Caps Don't Fit in Cheney's Head for Figures." *Los Angeles Times*, April 19, 2001.

Stone, Peter H. "Big Oil's White House Pipelines." *National Journal*, April 7, 2001.

Suskind, Ron. *The Price of Loyalty: George W. Bush, the White House, and the Education of Paul O'Neill*. New York: Simon & Schuster, 2004.

Tidrick, Donald. "An Interview with Donald Walker." *The CPA Journal*, February 2003.

Van Natta, Don, Jr. "Agency Files Suit for Cheney Papers on Energy." *The Washington Post*, February 23, 2002.

————. "Energy Chief Met Envoys from Industry." *The Washington Post*, March 25, 2001.

————, and Neela Banerjee. "Top GOP Donors in Energy Panel Meet Cheney Panel." *The Washington Post*, March 1, 2002.

Waxman, Henry M. United States House of Representatives Committee on Government Reform—Minority Staff Division of Special Investigations. "Congressional Oversight of the Bush Administration." January 17, 2006.

————. United States House of Representatives Committee on Government Reform—Minority Staff Division of Special Investigations. "Congressional Oversight of the Clinton Administration." January 17, 2006.

Weisskopf, Michael, and Adam Zagorin. "Getting the Ear of Dick Cheney." *Time*, February 11, 2002.

York, Byron. "GAO v. Cheney." *The National Review*, January 31, 2003.

————. "Is Cheney Lying?" *National Review Online*, February 1, 2002.

CHAPTER TWO
The Education of Richard B. Cheney

Ashcroft, John. (Office of the Attorney General, Department of Justice). Memo to Heads of All Federal Departments and Agencies. October 12, 2001.

Background Memorandum for Oversight Hearings of the Government Information and Individual Rights Subcommittee on the Interception of Non-Verbal Communications by Intelligence Agencies. February 20, 1976. Max L. Friedersdorf Files, box 10, Gerald R. Ford Library.

Blanton, Thomas. Author interview. March 2006.

Buchen, Philip. Memo for the President. Subject: Chairman of the Federal Trade Commission. February 3, 1976. Richard B. Cheney Files, 1974–1977, box 5, folder "Federal Trade Commission," Gerald R. Ford Library.

Cannon, James M. Author interview. May 18, 2006.

Cheney, Dick. Handwritten notes. May 29, 1975. Richard B. Cheney Files 1974–1977, box 6, folder "Intelligence—*New York Times* Article by Seymour Hersh (1)," Gerald R. Ford Library.

———. Interview, June 27, 1975. James F. C. Hyde and Stephen J. Wayne collection, Gerald R. Ford Library.

———. Interview, February 8, 1977. James F. C. Hyde and Stephen J. Wayne collection, Gerald R. Ford Library.

———. Memo to Don Rumsfeld. May 22, 1974. Subject: Senator Ted Stevens's Request to Visit Camp David. Richard B. Cheney Files 1974–1977, General Subject File, box 1, folder "Camp David," Gerald R. Ford Library.

———. Memo to Don Rumsfeld. July 8, 1975. Richard B. Cheney Files, 1974–1977, box 10, folder "Solzhenitsyn, Alexander," Gerald R. Ford Library.

———. Memo to Don Rumsfeld. Subject: Status Report—*New York Times* Story on Sunday, May 25, 1975. Richard B. Cheney Files 1974–1977, box 6, folder "Intelligence—*New York Times* Article by Seymour Hersh (2)," Gerald R. Ford Library.

———. Memo to Don Rumsfeld. Subject: Domestic Council Meeting Scheduled for Tuesday, June 10. June 9, 1975. Richard B. Cheney Files 1974–1977, General Subject File, box 3, folder "Domestic Council Folder," Gerald R. Ford Library.

———. Memo to Don Rumsfeld. February 15, 1975. Richard B. Cheney Files 1974–1977, General Subject File, box 13, folder "Voting Rights Act Extension," Gerald R. Ford Library.

———. Memo to Don Rumsfeld. May 17, 1975. Subject: Social Security. Richard B. Cheney Files 1974–1977, General Subject File, box 10, folder "Social Security Finances," Gerald R. Ford Library.

———. Memo to Jerry Jones. December 24, 1974. Jerry H. Jones Files 1974–1977, Staff Secretary Files, box 10, folder "White House Memos—Cheney, Dick," Gerald R. Ford Library.

———. Memo to Jerry Jones. January 25, 1975. Jerry H. Jones Files 1974–1977, Staff Secretary Files, box 10, folder "White House Memos—Cheney, Dick (16)," Gerald R. Ford Library.

———. Memo to Jerry Jones. February 14, 1975. Jerry H. Jones Files 1974–1977, Staff Secretary Files, box 10, folder "White House Memos—Cheney, Dick (8)," Gerald R. Ford Library.

———. Memo to Jerry Jones. April 7, 1975. Jerry H. Jones Files 1974–1977, Staff Secretary Files, box 11, folder "White House Memos—Cheney, Dick," Gerald R. Ford Library.

———. Speech. Hofstra University, April 7, 1989.

———. Question and Answer. National Press Club, Washington, D.C., June 19, 2006.

———. Speech. Waldorf-Astoria, New York, June 30, 2006.

Dean, John. Author interview. May 2006.

Firestone, Bernard J., and Alexej Ugrinsky, eds. *Gerald R. Ford and the Politics of Post-Watergate America*. Westport, Conn.: Greenwood Press, 1993.

Ford, President Gerald R. July 21, 1976. Letter to W. L. Lindholm, president of AT&T. Presidential Handwriting File, box 51. Gerald R. Ford Library.

———. June 2, 1976. National Security Advisor Memorandum of Conversation. National Security Advisor Memoranda of Conversations, box 19, Gerald R. Ford Library.

———, et al. October 13, 1975, Memorandum of Conversation, National Security Advisor Memoranda of Conversations, box 16, Gerald R. Ford Library.

Hartmann, Robert T. Author interview. May 5, 2006.

———. *Palace Politics: An Inside Account of the Ford Years.* New York: McGraw-Hill, 1980.

Hersh, Seymour. "Huge C.I.A. Operation Reported in U.S. Against Anti-War Forces, Other Dissidents in Nixon Years." *The New York Times,* December 22, 1974.

Hersh, Seymour M. "Submarines of U.S. Stage Spy Missions Inside Soviet Waters." *The New York Times,* May 25, 1975.

———. "The Pardon: Nixon, Ford, Haig, and the Transfer of Power." *The Atlantic,* August 1983.

Levi, Edward H. " Assertion of Executive Privilege with Respect to a House Committee Subpoena to American Telephone and Telegraph Company." Memorandum. Presidential Handwriting File, box 51, folder "Utilities; Telephone," Gerald R. Ford Library.

Lopez, Dan, Thomas Blanton, Meredith Fuchs, and Barbara Elias, eds. National Security Archive Electronic Briefing Book No. 142, November 23, 2004.

Mann, James. *Rise of the Vulcans: The History of Bush's War Cabinet.* New York: Viking, 2004.

Marsh, Jack. Author interview. June 1, 2006.

———. Memorandum for the President. Subject: Proposed Legislation on Electronic Surveillance. March 16, 1976. Presidential Handwriting File, box 31, folder "NSI (14–15)," Gerald R. Ford Library.

McCormack, Bruce. "Cheney Says Carter Needs Success in Middle East." *Casper Star-Tribune,* October 5, 1977.

Miller Center of Public Affairs Staff at the University of Virginia. *The Ford White House: A Miller Center Conference Chaired by Herbert J. Storing.* Lanham, Mass.: University Press of America, 1986.

Nessen, Ron. *It Sure Looks Different on the Inside.* Chicago: Playboy Paperbacks, 1979.

Nunn, Lee R. Letter to Bo Callaway. October 2, 1975. Richard B. Cheney Files 1974–1977, Campaign Subject File, box 18, folder "Lee Nunn—Resignation as Political Director 10/12/75," Gerald R. Ford Library.

Ornstein, Norman. Author interview. May 8, 2006.

Osborne, John. *White House Watch: The Ford Years.* New York: New Republic Books, 1977.

Republican Party Platform. "Morality in Foreign Policy." Republican National Convention, 1976.

Richelson, Jeffrey, and Thomas Blanton, eds. National Security Archive Electronic Briefing Book No. 178. February 4, 2006.

Risen, James, and Eric Lichtblau. "Bush Lets U.S. Spy on Callers Without Courts." *The New York Times,* December 16, 2005.

Scalia, Antonin. Memorandum for the Honorable Philip W. Buchen, re: Claim of Executive Privilege with respect to materials subpoenaed by the Committee on Government Operations, House of Representatives. February 17, 1976. Presidential Handwriting File, box 31, Gerald R. Ford Library.

Shabecoff, Philip. "Ford's Primary Losses Split White House Staff as Factions Trade Charges of Laxity," *The New York Times,* May 24, 1976.

Smith, Donald. "Richard B. Cheney: Rumsfeld's Alter Ego." *Congressional Quarterly,* November 8, 1975.

Thompson, Kenneth W., ed. *The Ford Presidency: Twenty-two Intimate Perspectives of Gerald Ford*, Portraits of American Presidents, vols. VI and VII. Lanham, Mass.: University Press of America, 1988.

Train, Russell E. *Politics, Pollution, and Pandas: An Environmental Memoir.* Washington, D.C.: Island Press, November 2003.

Wilderotter, James A. (Associate Deputy Attorney General). Memo for the File. Subject: CIA Matters. January 3, 1975, Richard B. Cheney Files 1974–1977, box 6, Gerald R. Ford Library.

CHAPTER THREE

Long Strange Trip: Washington to Wyoming to Washington

American Embassy of Nicaragua. Flash Memo to Secretary of State Cyrus Vance. June 7, 1979.

Associated Press. "Congressman Says MX Is in Trouble." March 13, 1984.

Barlow, John Perry. Author interview. May 16, 2006.

Barnes, Michael. Author interview. June 26, 2006.

Broder, David S. "Cheney: Cutting Defense 'Unsafe.' " *The Washington Post*, November 17, 1982.

Cannon, Lou. "From the White House to the Hustings: Richard Cheney Wants to Work on Capitol Hill." *The Washington Post*, October 16, 1978.

———. "Reagan Urges 'Dense Pack' in Wyoming." *The Washington Post*, November 23, 1982.

———. "Soviet Hill Speech Blocked; White House Denies Making Invitation." *The Washington Post*, November 21, 1987.

Casper Star-Tribune. "Cheney Back Home in Casper." June 30, 1978.

———. "Cheney Has 'Lost Patience.' " November 5, 1978.

———. "Cheney Outspends Democrat Bagley." October 12, 1978.

———. "Cheney Outspends GOP Primary Opponents by Comfortable Margin." September 6, 1978.

———. "Cheney War Chest Healthy but Bagley Campaign in Debt." November 1, 1978.

———. "Cheney Will Run After Heart Attack." July 12, 1978.

———. "Dick Cheney Thinking About Job in Casper." January 11, 1976.

———. "Ford and Cheney." October 26, 1978.

———. "GOP Candidate Says Polls Put Him in the Lead." October 10, 1978.

———. "House Candidate Hospitalized." June 20, 1978.

———. "Restaurants Serve Up Campaign Money to GOP." November 1, 1978.

Cheney, Dick. Floor Remarks. Congressional Record, October 14, 1981.

———. Floor Remarks. Congressional Record, June 12, 1985.

———. Floor Remarks. Congressional Record, July 18, 1985.

———. Floor Remarks. Congressional Record, September 17, 1986.

———. Floor Remarks. Congressional Record, May 26, 1988.

Cheney, Mary. *Now It's My Turn: A Daughter's Chronicle of Political Life.* New York: Simon & Schuster, 2006.

Cohen, Richard. "Full Speed Ahead." *National Journal*, January 30, 1988.

Downey, Thomas. Author interview. July 28, 2006.

Dubose, Lou, and Jan Reid. *The Hammer: Tom DeLay, God, Money, and the Rise of the Republican Congress.* New York: Public Affairs, 2004.

Edwards, Mickey. Author interview. March 24, 2006.

Evans, Rowland, and Robert Novak. "House Democratic Leaders Compromise." *Chicago Sun-Times*, December 28, 1987.

———. "Reagan's in a Bind in Nicaragua." *Chicago Sun-Times*, May 13, 1986.

Gutman, Roy. "Behind Wright vs. Regan." *Newsday*, September 23, 1988.

Haas, Cliff. "Speaker's Partisan Tactics Provoke House GOP." *Minneapolis Star Tribune*, May 22, 1988.

Hunter-Gault, Charlene. Interview with Dick Cheney. *The MacNeil/Lehrer NewsHour*, September 30, 1988.

Inside Energy. "Oil Firms Edgy as Wyoming Congressman Faces Pressure to Close Wilderness." July 20, 1981.

———. "Wyoming Wilderness Approved by Senate, Sent Back to House for Amending." October 8, 1984.

Kentworthy, Tom. "House Republicans Promote Cheney; Conference Chief Succeeds Kemp." *The Washington Post*, June 5, 1987.

Mann, Thomas E., and Norman Ornstein. *The Broken Branch: How Congress Is Failing America and How to Get It Back on Track*. New York: Oxford University Press, 2006.

McCormack, Bruce. "Cheney Will Run." *Casper Star-Tribune*, December 15, 1977.

McGrory, Mary. "Lame Ducks Take Flight." *The Washington Post*, December 19, 1985.

Ornstein, Norman. Author interview. May 8, 2006.

———. "Minority Report: Ignored by Their President, Ill-Used by Their Democratic Colleagues, House Republicans Are in a Mutinous Mood." *The Atlantic*, December 1985.

Parry, Robert. "Congressional Trip to Grenada Boosts Reagan." Associated Press, November 8, 1983.

Parry, Robert. "House Loosens Rules on Nicaraguan Rebel Aid." Associated Press, November 19, 1985.

Partridge, Dan. "Town Welcomes Cheney." *Casper Star-Tribune*, April 2, 1976.

Roberts, Steven. "O'Neill Criticizes President." *The New York Times*, October 28, 1983.

Russakoff, Dale. "Unlikely Wyoming Posse Saddles Up for Energy Fight." *The Washington Post*, August 26, 1982.

Salisbury, David. "Reagan Begins Turning Key to 'Unlock' US Wilderness." *The Christian Science Monitor*, December 8, 1981.

Schmemann, Serge. "U.S. Lawmakers, in Moscow, Disagree About a 'Signal' on Missiles," *The New York Times*, July 8, 1983.

Shabecoff, Philip. "House Studies Ban on Oil Leases in Wilderness Areas." *The New York Times*, November 18, 1981.

Swardson, Anne, and Tom Kentworthy. "Wright Ekes Out Tax Bill's Passage; Speaker Literally Turns Back Clock to Overcome Party Rebellion." *The Washington Post*, October 30, 1987.

Tolchin, Martin. "Congressional Fellowship: Up a Golden Ladder." *The New York Times*, February 3, 1984.

United Press International. "Cheney's Good Fortune Due to Luck, Even He Admits." October 29, 1978.

Wilson, Warren. "Cheney May Have Violated Campaign Law." *Casper Star-Tribune*, November 4, 1978.

Wright, Jim. Author interview. February 27, 2006.

———. *Worth It All: My War for Peace*. McLean, Va.: Brassey's (US) / Maxwell Macmillan, 1993.

CHAPTER FOUR
Covert Cover-up

Abshire, David M. *Saving the Reagan Presidency: Trust Is the Coin of the Realm.* College Station, Tex.: Texas A&M University Press, 2005.

Cheney, Dick. Question and Answer. Air Force Two en route to Muscat, Oman, December 20, 2005.

Department of State. Memo for the Record. Subject: Testimony before the House Permanent Select Committee on Intelligence Regarding the Crash of a C-123 in Nicaragua. National Security Archives, October 14, 1986.

Fein, Bruce. Author interview. July 21, 2006.

Fisher, Louis. Author interview. June 9, 2006.

———. *The Politics of Executive Privilege.* Durham, N.C.: Carolina Academic Press, 2004.

Fuerbringer, Jonathan. "Democrats Dispute Reagan View on Iran Dealings." *The New York Times,* November 14, 1986.

Hamilton, Lee. Author interview. June 23, 2006.

Hoffman, David. "North Drew Rodriguez into Contra Operation: Ex–CIA Operative Was Friend of Bush Aide." *The Washington Post,* April 26, 1987.

Iran-Contra Committee hearing transcripts, vols. 1–8, Library of Congress, Washington, D.C., 1987.

Kornbluh, Peter, and Malcolm Byrne, eds. "The Iran-Contra Scandal: The Declassified History." *A National Security Archive Documents Reader,* 1993.

Liman, Arthur L. *Lawyer: A Life of Counsel and Controversy.* New York: PublicAffairs, February 2003.

Locy, Toni. "Experts Say Cheney Can't Avoid Testifying." Associated Press, May 26, 2006.

The MacNeil/Lehrer NewsHour, July 7, 1987.

———, July 24, 1987.

McNamee, Wally. "Two Leaks, but by Whom?" *Newsweek,* July 27, 1987.

Osterlund, Peter. "GOP Congressman Warns Against Limiting Presidential Power." *The Christian Science Monitor,* November 24, 1987.

Report on the Congressional Committees Investigating the Iran-Contra Affair, with Supplemental, Minority, and Additional Views. Washington, D.C.: U.S. Government Printing Office, November 1987.

Roland, Neil. "Reagan Urged Limited Disclosure of Iran Arms Deals." United Press International, July 31, 1987.

Rudman, Warren. Author interview. June 6, 2006.

Shales, Tom. "What a Difference a Day Makes: Lawmakers Pull Out Kid Gloves for North." *The Washington Post,* July 11, 1987.

Shenon, Philip. "G.O.P. Iran Report Defends President." *The New York Times,* November 17, 1987.

Thatcher, Gary. "Minority Report Takes Strong Issue." *The Christian Science Monitor,* November 19, 1987.

United States v. Curtiss-Wright Export Corp. Supreme Court of the United States, December 21, 1936.

Walker, Dana. "Cheney: Iran-Contra Scandal Will Be a Footnote in History." United Press International, April 7, 1987.

Walsh, Lawrence E. *Firewall: The Iran-Contra Conspiracy and Cover-up.* New York: W.W. Norton, 1997.

Wright, Jim. Author interview. February 27, 2006.

———. *Worth It All: My War for Peace.* McLean, Va.: Brassey's (US) / Maxwell Macmillan, 1993.

CHAPTER FIVE
Secretary of War

Bernstein, James. "Dick Cheney Goes on the Offensive." *Newsday,* January 14, 1991.

Broder, John H., and Ralph Vartabedian. "Cheney Cancels Navy's $57-Billion Attack Jet." *Los Angeles Times,* January 1, 1981.

Church, George J. "How Much Is Too Much?" *Time,* February 12, 1990.

———. "Towering Troubles: Bush's Pick for the Pentagon Faces Questions About His Conduct." *Time,* February 13, 1989.

Clancy, Paul. "Congress Would OK Use of Force." *USA Today,* January 7, 1991.

Cohen, Richard E. "The Unhappy Few Lose Another Chief." *National Journal,* March 18, 1989.

Congressional Budget Office. *Defense Spending, 1969–2005.*

Duffy, Brian. "Desert Storm." *U.S. News & World Report,* January 28, 1991.

The Economist, "Central Intelligence Agency: Meaning to Kill People Is Wrong," October 28, 1989.

———. "Dick Cheney's Pentagon." January 19, 1991.

Elson, John. "Just Who Can Lead Us to War: A Legal Dilemma Pits the White House Against Congress," *Time,* December 17, 1990.

Galtney, Liz, and Charles Fenyvesi. "What Did the Swallows Learn in Geneva?" *Business Week,* February 20, 1989.

Gordon, Michael R. "Cheney Blamed for Press Problems in Panama." *The New York Times,* March 20, 1990.

Hall, John. "Cheney Tackles Pentagon Waste by Sweeping Away Admiral." *Richmond Times,* December 13, 1990.

Lacayo, Richard. "The Insider." *The New York Times,* August 7, 2000.

Los Angeles Times. "Cheney, Powell Back from Gulf, Meet with Bush Military: 'America Is Behind You,' President Tells Troops in a Broadcast Message for the Holiday." December 25, 1990.

Mann, James. "Colin Powell, Forever the 'Good Soldier.' " *Los Angeles Times,* March 28, 2004.

Matthews, Thomas. "The Secret History of the War." *Newsweek,* March 18, 1991.

———. "War in the Gulf: The Road to War." *Newsweek,* January 28, 1991.

Meyer, Peter. "A Week in the Life of Dick Cheney." *Time,* February 25, 1991.

Morganthau, Tom, and Russell Watson. "War in the Gulf: The War: Desert Storm." *Newsweek,* March 4, 1991.

Morrison, David C. " 'Whiz Kids' Rebound." *National Journal,* November 11, 1989.

Nelan, Bruce W. "Ready for Action: Dick Cheney and Colin Powell Are the Savviest Pair to Lead the Pentagon in Years." *Time,* November 12, 1990.

Nelson, Lars-Erik. "Defense Contractors Learn Business as Usual Too Costly for Cheney." *Minneapolis Star Tribune,* January 11, 1991.

Perry, Nancy. "How Defense Will Change." *Fortune,* March 25, 1991.

Romano, Lois. "The Pentagon's Dapper Spokesman: Pete Williams Has Regained Confidence of Media After Panama Fiasco." *San Francisco Chronicle,* January 24, 1991.

San Francisco Chronicle. "Cheney 'Livid' About Confusion over Bombing." April 11, 1990.

Schneider, William. "The In-box President: George Bush Is a Master of Unheroic Politics in Which Everything, or Almost Everything, Is Negotiable." *The Atlantic*, January 1990.

Shanker, Thom, and Elaine Povich. "Cheney Dodges Growing Flak over Uprising." *Chicago Tribune*, October 6, 1989.

Walsh, Kenneth T. "The Brief Eclipse of James Baker." *U.S. News & World Report*, March 4, 1991.

Walte, Juan J. "Cheney to Congress: Hands Off Foreign Crisis." *USA Today*, October 11, 1989.

Wartzman, Rick, and Bob Davis. "Cheney's Bomb Rattles Aerospace World—No Ready Replacement Seen for Canceled Navy Program." *The Wall Street Journal*, January 9, 1991.

Wildstrom, Stephen. "The Loneliness of the Last Cold Warrior." *Business Week*, May 7, 1990.

Wilkerson, Lawrence, Col. Author interview. June 16, 2006.

———. Speech to New American Foundation. October 19, 2005.

Woodward, Bob. *The Commanders: The Pentagon and the First Gulf War, 1989–1991.* New York: Touchstone, 2002.

CHAPTER SIX
Lawless CEO: The Halliburton Years

ABC News *This Week.* Interview with Dick Cheney. July 30, 2000.

Berenson, Alex, and Lowell Bergman. "Under Cheney, Halliburton Altered Policy on Accounting." *The New York Times*, May 22, 2002.

Bergman, Lowell, et al. "The 2000 Campaign: The Republican Running Mate: Cheney Is Said to Be Receiving $20 Million Retirement Package." *The New York Times*, August 12, 2000.

Briody, Dan. *The Halliburton Agenda: The Politics of Oil and Money.* New York: John Wiley & Sons, Inc., 2004.

Bruno, Kenny, and Jim Vallette. "Halliburton's Destructive Engagement." A report by EarthRights International, October 2000.

Bryce, Robert. "Halliburton's Boss from Hell." Salon.com, July 21, 2004 (http://dir.salon.com/story/news/feature/2004/07/21/halliburton/index.html).

CBS News *60 Minutes.* "Doing Business with the Enemy." August 29, 2004.

Cheney, Dick. "Defending Liberty in a Global Economy." Collateral Damage Conference, Cato Institute, Washington, D.C., June 23, 1998.

———. Speech. Astana, Kazakhstan, May 5, 2006.

———. Speech. Vilnius, Lithuania, May 4, 2006.

DeFrank, Thomas M., and Kenneth R. Bazinet. "Putin Takes Poke at 'Bad Shot' Veep." New York *Daily News*, July 13, 2006.

Elkind, Peter. "The Truth About Halliburton." *Fortune*, April 18, 2005.

Gerth, Jeff, and Richard W. Stevenson. "Cheney's Role in Acquisition Under Scrutiny." *The New York Times*, August 1, 2002.

Gold, Russell. "Halliburton to Put KBR Unit on the Auction Block." *The Wall Street Journal*, January 31, 2005.

Gwynne, S. C. "Did Dick Cheney Sink Halliburton (and Will It Sink Him)?" *Texas Monthly*, October 2002.

Halliburton Earnings Conference Call. Q2 2002. FDCHeMedia, Inc., July 24, 2002.

Halliburton Watch, http://halliburtonwatch.org.

Hays, Kristen. "Halliburton Bribery Investigation Expands." Associated Press, March 2, 2005.

Hearing of the Senate Armed Services Committee on Secretary of Defense Confirmation, March 14, 1989.

Highland Insurance Group, Inc., et al. v. Halliburton Company, et al. Court of Chancery of Delaware, March 21, 2001.

Ivanovich, David, and Tom Fowler. "Cheney at Halliburton." *Houston Chronicle*, August 29, 2004.

KBR, Inc. Prospectus. April 14, 2006.

King, John. "With an Eye on White House, GOP Prospects Gear Up Fund-Raising." Associated Press, September 2, 1994.

Landers, Jim. "Halliburton Chief Calls U.S. 'Sanctions-Happy': Cheney Criticizes Government Policy in Cato Institute Address." *The Dallas Morning News*, June 24, 1998.

———, and Richard Whittle. "Details Emerge in Bribery Probe: Cheney Isn't Focus of French Inquiry of Nigerian Gas Project." *The Dallas Morning News*, January 25, 2004.

Linzer, Dafna. "Past Arguments Don't Square with Current Iran Policy." *The Washington Post*, March 27, 2005.

Lynch, Colum. "Firm's Iraq Deals Greater Than Cheney Has Said." *The Washington Post*, June 23, 2001.

Mayer, Jane. "Contract Sport: Why Did the Vice President Go to Halliburton?" *The New Yorker*, February 16, 2004.

Murray, Brendan. "Bushes' Assets May Top $20 Million; Cheneys', $94 million." Bloomberg News, May 16, 2006.

Teeter, Bob. NBC / *Wall Street Journal* National Public Opinion Survey Data, December 1992–March 1994. Gerald R. Ford Library.

Vice presidential debate. Danville, Kentucky, October 5, 2000.

CHAPTER SEVEN
Lady MacCheney

ABC News *This Week*. Interview with Lynne Cheney. July 30, 2000.

Alonso-Zaldivar, Ricardo, and Jean Merl. "Booklet That Upset Mrs. Cheney Is History: The Department of Education Destroys 300,000 Parent Guides to Remove References to National Standards." *Los Angeles Times*, October 8, 2004.

Barlow, John Perry. Author interview. May 16, 2006.

Cheney, Dick. Speech. Fort Myers, Florida. October 14, 2004.

———, and Lynne Cheney. Speech. Coraopolis, Pennsylvania, October 13, 2004.

———. Interview. *Missile Defense*, April/May 2001.

———. Town Hall Meeting. Duluth, Minnesota, September 29, 2004.

———. Town Hall Meeting. Milwaukee, Wisconsin, September 10, 2004.

Cheney, Lynne. *Executive Privilege*. New York: Simon & Schuster, 1979.

———. "Kill My Old Agency, Please." *The Wall Street Journal*, January 24, 1995.

———. Prepared Testimony. House Interior Appropriations Subcommittee, January 24, 1995.

———. *Sisters*. New York: New American Library, 1981.

———. "The End of History." *The Wall Street Journal*, October 20, 1994.

———. *Telling the Truth*. New York: Touchstone, 1996.

Cheney, Lynne V. Memo to All NEH Staff. December 1, 1992.

Cheney, Mary. *Now It's My Turn: A Daughter's Chronicle of Political Life.* New York: Simon & Schuster, 2006.

CNN *Larry King Live.* Interview with Mary Cheney. May 10, 2006.

Davidson, Lee. "Lynne Cheney's Ancestors." *Deseret Morning News,* January 22, 2006.

Fox News *On the Record with Greta Van Susteren.* Interview with Lynne Cheney. November 28, 2002.

Gibson, Don. Author interview. May 11, 2006.

Hackney, Sheldon. Author interview. May 1, 2006.

———. *The Politics of Presidential Appointment: A Memoir of the Culture War.* Montgomery, Ala.: NewSouth Books, 2002.

Hammer, John. Author interview. May 7, 2006.

Hughes, Robert. "Pulling the Fuse on Culture: The Conservatives' All-Out Assault on Federal Funding Is Unenlightened, Uneconomic and Undemocratic." *Time,* August 7, 1995.

Jacoby, Mary. "Madame Cheney's Cultural Revolution." Salon.com, August 26, 2004 (http://dir.salon.com/story/news/feature/2004/08/26/lynne_cheney/index.html).

Katz, Stanley. Author interview. May 1, 2006.

Kemper, Bob. "Mary Cheney Urged to Speak Out: Activists Appeal to VP's Gay Daughter." *Chicago Tribune,* March 7, 2004.

Lemann, Nicholas. "The Quiet Man: Dick Cheney's Discreet Rise to Unprecedented Power." *The New Yorker,* May 7, 2001.

Martin, Jerry L., and Anne D. Neal. "Defending Civilization: How Our Universities Are Failing America and What Can Be Done About It." American Council of Trustees and Alumni, November 2001.

Nash, Gary. Author interview. May 1, 2006.

———, et al. *History on Trial.* New York: Alfred A. Knopf, 1997.

Presidential debate. Tempe, Arizona, October 13, 2004.

Rawlins Daily Times. "Lynne Cheney Plugs 'Executive Privilege.' " August 8, 1979.

Scigliano, Eric. "Naming—and Un-naming—Names: A Report from the American Council of Trustees and Alumni." *The Nation,* December 31, 2001.

Segal, David. "Cheney's Command." *Lingua Franca,* September/October 1992.

The NewsHour with Jim Lehrer. Interview with Lynne Cheney. October 1, 2003.

Weiss, Mike. "Landing the Lineman: Lynne Cheney Knew What It Took to Get Her Man—from Wyoming to Washington." *San Francisco Chronicle,* October 3, 2004.

CHAPTER EIGHT

Back to the White House

ABC News *This Week.* Interview with Dick Cheney, July 30, 2000.

ABC *World News Now.* Interview with Dick Cheney, July 26, 2001.

Altman, Lawrence K. "His Own E.R. in His Chest." *The New York Times,* June 30, 2001.

———. "The State of Haig's Health: News Analysis." *The New York Times,* January 8, 1981.

Associated Press. "Cheney Says He Would Not Join Bush Administration." May 17, 2000.

Bowden, Mark, et al. "How Bush Selected Cheney." *The Philadelphia Inquirer,* July 26, 2000.

Bresnahan, John, and Mark Preston. "Congressional Republicans Blast Bush Team's Failure to Be Prepared for Attacks on VP Candidate Cheney." *Roll Call,* July 31, 2000.

Bruni, Frank. "The 2000 Campaign: The Search; Bush's List of Possible Running Mates Getting Shorter, but Not Clearer." *The New York Times,* June 19, 2000.

Cannon, James M. Author interview. May 18, 2006.

Cheney, Mary. *Now It's My Turn: A Daughter's Chronicle of Political Life.* New York: Simon & Schuster, 2006.

CNN *Larry King Live.* Interview with Dick Cheney. July 25, 2000.

Cooper, Michael. "The 2000 Campaign: The Republican Running Mate; In Harshest Attack Yet, Cheney Accuses Gore of Fabrications." *The New York Times,* September 20, 2000.

Dart, Bob. "GOP Raising Funds to Ease Forced Delay in Transition." *The Atlanta Journal Constitution,* November 28, 2000.

DeFrank, Thomas M. "Bush Taps Cheney to Head Running Mate Search." *New York Daily News,* April 20, 2000.

———, and Joe Mahoney. "Cheney's in Veep Chase." New York *Daily News,* July 21, 2000.

Fournier, Ron. "Bush Picks Cheney as Running Mate; Former Defense Secretary Accepts, GOP Source Says." Associated Press, July 25, 2000.

Gamboa, Suzanne. "Bush, Cheney Meet to Scour Running Mate Data." Associated Press, July 3, 2000.

George W. Bush, et al., Petitioners v. Albert Gore, Jr., et al. Supreme Court of the United States, December 12, 2000.

Gullo, Karen. "Cheney: Cabinet Appointments Coming," Associated Press, December 15, 2000.

———. "Cheney Retirement Package Worth $20 Million Approved." Associated Press, August 12, 2000.

Harris, Leon, et al. "Cheney Released from George Washington University Hospital." CNN, November 24, 2000.

Isikoff, Michael. "Why Keating Didn't Cut It." *Newsweek,* January 15, 2001.

Johnson, Glen. "Bush Picks Cheney to Head Running Mate Selection." Associated Press, April 25, 2000.

Kurtz, Howard. "Speculation Hardly Idle in Veepstakes." *The Washington Post,* July 26, 2000.

Macintyre, Ben. "Bush Retreats to Select a Running Mate." *The Times* (London), July 6, 2000.

Mann, James. *Rise of the Vulcans: The History of Bush's War Cabinet.* New York: Viking, 2004.

Mashek, John W. "Bush Advisers Tout Cheney for Chief of Staff: Campaign '92." *Boston Globe,* June 1, 1992.

Miller, Karin. "Alexander Was Among 'Handful' of Serious Veep Candidates." Associated Press, July 25, 2000.

Mittelstadt, Michelle. "Bush Builds Campaign Brain Trust." Associated Press, February 25, 1999.

NBC News *Meet the Press.* Interview with Dick Cheney, July 30, 2000.

Neal, Steve, and Lynn Sweet. "Cheney on the Offensive: 'It Is Time for Them to Go,' Republican Candidate Says in Acceptance Speech." *Chicago Sun-Times,* August 4, 2000.

Neal, Terry M., and Dan Balz. "GOP Hails Cheney's Inclusion on Ticket; Democrats Prepare to Fight 'Big Oil.' " *The Washington Post,* July 26, 2000.

The NewsHour with Jim Lehrer. Interview with Dick Cheney, November 8, 2000.

Pearson, Rick. "Cheney Defends Record as Democrats Scramble to Attack." *Chicago Tribune,* July 27, 2000.

Raum, Tom. "Cheney's Health Poses New Uncertainty for GOP Planning." Associated Press, November 24, 2000.

Sanger, David E., and Lawrence K. Altman. "Cheney Gets Heart Device and Declares, 'I Feel Good.' " *The New York Times*, July 1, 2001.

Slater, Wayne, and Sam Attlesey. "Bush Picks Cheney to Be GOP Running Mate." *The Dallas Morning News*, July 26, 2000.

Stevens, Stuart. *The Big Enchilada: Campaign Adventures with the Cockeyed Optimists from Texas Who Won the Biggest Prize in Politics*. New York: Free Press, 2001.

Tapper, Jake. "I Pick Me!" Salon.com, July 26, 2000 (http://archive.salon.com/politics/feature/2000/07/26/nominee).

Texas Monthly. "Fantastic Four." August 1999.

Wetzstein, Cheryl. "Oklahoma's Keating Claims Comfort in Any Role for Bush; Ready to 'Serve Iced Tea' If Needed." *The Washington Times*, July 21, 2000.

The White House Bulletin. "Bush Transition Team Begins to Take Shape." December 12, 2000.

CHAPTER NINE
Soldiers of Fortune

Bolton, Claude M., Jr. (Assistant Secretary of the Army). Justification and Approval Memorandum for Commander Army Corps of Engineers. Department of the Army, February 28, 2003.

Business Wire. "Partner Joins Stroock & Stroock & Lavan Growing International Practice." May 13, 1990.

Callister, Fiona. "Eversheds' Moscow Office Poaches McDermotts [*sic*] Team." *The Lawyer*, April 19, 1999.

Defense Contract Audit Agency. Audit Report, September 16, 2004.

———. Audit Report, October 8, 2004.

Flowers, Robert B., Lt. Gen. Letter to Rep. Henry Waxman. May 2, 2003.

Fox News *Biography*. "Michael Mobbs," April 23, 2003 (www.foxnews.com/story/0,2933,84942,00.html).

Hamdi et al. v. Rumsfeld, Secretary of Defense, et al. Supreme Court of the United States, June 28, 2004.

Hansen, Susan. "Lost in the Ruble." *The American Lawyer*, November 1988.

Hecker, Charles. "Peanut Butter Process to Defuse Toxic Fuel." *The Moscow Times*, July 13, 1995.

Holland, Steve. "Cheney Took $178,473 from Halliburton in 2003." Reuters, April 13, 2004.

House Government Reform Committee. Hearing: "Efforts to Build Iraq," July 22, 2004.

The International Lawyer. "Squire, Sanders & Dempsey Opens Moscow Office." June 1995.

Kohn, Michael D., et al. Letter to Acting Secretary of the Army Les Browning, October 21, 2004.

KBR, Inc. Prospectus. April 14, 2006.

Legal Times. "Mobbs Scene." April 7, 2003.

Lowenberg, Sam. "Defensive Touch." *International Business*, June 1996.

NBC News *Meet the Press*. Interview with Dick Cheney, September 14, 2003.

O'Harrow, Robert. "E-Mail Lists Cheney's Office Contact; Officials Say Only Involvement with Halliburton Contract Was Announcing It." *The Washington Post*, June 2, 2004.

Shnayerson, Michael. "Oh! What a Lucrative War." *Vanity Fair*, April 2005.

Tappan, Sheryl Elam. Author interview. March 22, 2006.

———. *Shock and Awe in Fort Worth: How the U.S. Army Rigged the "Free and Open Competition" to Replace Halliburton's Sole-Source Oil Field Contract in Iraq*. San Mateo, Cal.: Pourquoi Press, 2004.

———. Testimony. Senate Democratic Policy Committee, September 10, 2004.

United Press International. "Defense Secretary Caspar Weinberger Announces the Appointment of Michael Mobbs." April 16, 1982.

———. "Michael Mobbs, assistant director of the U.S. Arms Control and Disarmament Agency, announced his resignation." June 4, 1987.

Waxman, Henry. Committee on Government Reform, U.S. House of Representatives. Fact Sheet: "Halliburton Contracts Worth $10 Billion." December 9, 2004.

———. Committee on Government Reform, U.S. House of Representatives. Letter to Christopher Shays, Chair, Subcommittee on National Security, Emerging Threats, and International Relations, U.S. House of Representatives. March 15, 2005.

———. Committee on Government Reform, U.S. House of Representatives. Letter to Lt. Gen. Robert Flowers. March 26, 2003.

———. Committee on Government Reform, U.S. House of Representatives. Letter to Lt. Gen. Robert Flowers. April 10, 2003.

———. Committee on Government Reform, U.S. House of Representatives. Letter to Rep. Tom Davis. February 27, 2006.

———. Committee on Government Reform, U.S. House of Representatives. Letter to Vice President Dick Cheney. June 13, 2004.

Wolfowitz, Paul (Assistant Secretary of Defense). "Determination and Findings." December 5, 2005.

CHAPTER TEN
Dick Cheney's War

Ackerman, Spencer, and Franklin Foer. "The Radical." *The New Republic*, December 1, 2003.

Cheney, Dick. Speech. Discovery Institute, August 14, 1992.

———. Speech. Vietnam Veterans of Foreign Wars Convention, August 26, 2002.

Cheney, Elizabeth. Financial Disclosure Report, 2002.

Clarke, Richard A. *Against All Enemies: Inside America's War on Terror*. New York: Free Press, 2004.

Cooper, Helene. "Rice's Hurdles in Mideast Begin at Home." *The New York Times*, August 10, 2006.

"Downing Street Memos." David Manning to Prime Minister Tony Blair, March 14, 2002.

———. Christopher Meyer to David Manning, March 18, 2002.

Dreyfuss, Robert. "Vice Squad." *The American Prospect*, May 2006.

Eisendrath, Craig R., and Melvin A. Goodman. *Bush League Diplomacy: How the Neoconservatives Are Putting the World at Risk*. Amherst, N.Y.: Prometheus Books, 2004.

Ereli, J. Adam. State Department Regular News Briefing, November 21, 2003.

Hersh, Seymour, "Last Stand: The Military's Problem with the President's Iran Policy." *The New Yorker*, July 10, 2006.

Hoagland, Jim. "Bush's Gamble on Iran." *The Washington Post*, June 4, 2006.

Hosenball, Mark, and Michael Isikoff. "What Went Wrong." *Newsweek*, February 9, 2004.

Isikoff, Michael, and Evan Thomas. "Cheney's Long Path to War." *Newsweek*, November 17, 2003.

Lake, Eli. "Cheney's Daughter Offered State Dept. Job." United Press International, February 28, 2002.

Lemann, Nicholas. "The Quiet Man: Dick Cheney's Discreet Rise to Unprecedented Power." *The New Yorker*, May 7, 2001.

Mann, James. *Rise of the Vulcans: The History of Bush's War Cabinet.* New York: Viking, 2004.

Milbank, Dana. "In Cheney's Shadow, Counsel Pushes the Conservative Cause." *The Washington Post*, October 11, 2004.

Nessen, Ron. *It Sure Looks Different from the Inside.* Chicago: Playboy Press, 1979.

Powell, Colin. *My American Journey.* New York: Random House, 1995.

Suskind, Ron. *The One Percent Doctrine: Deep Inside America's Pursuit of Its Enemies Since 9/11.* New York: Simon & Schuster, 2006.

Tyler, Patrick. "U.S. Strategy Plan Calls for Insuring No Rivals Develop." *The New York Times*, March 8, 1992.

Unger, Craig. "The War They Wanted, the Lies They Needed." *Vanity Fair*, June 2006.

Wilkerson, Col. Lawrence. Author interview. June 16, 2006.

———. Speech to the New American Foundation, October 19, 2005.

Woodward, Bob. *Plan of Attack.* New York: Simon & Schuster, 2004.

CHAPTER ELEVEN
The Torture Presidency

ABC *Nightline*. Interview by Terry Moran with Vice President Richard Cheney at Al Asad Air Base, Al Anbar Province, Iraq, December 20, 2005.

American Bar Association Task Force on Presidential Signing Statements and the Separation of Powers Doctrine. Report with Recommendations. July 24, 2006.

American Civil Liberties Union et al. v. National Security Agency/Central Security Service et al. Memorandum of Opinion, Hon. Anna Diggs Taylor. United States District Court for the Eastern District of Michigan, August 17, 2006.

Benac, Nancy. "Despite Image, Cheney a GOP Rock Star." Associated Press, August 5, 2006.

Bush, George W. "Humane Treatment of al Qaeda and Taliban Detainees." Memo to Vice President et al. February 7, 2002.

Bush, George W. Statement on Signing the Department of Defense Emergency Supplemental Appropriations to Address Hurricanes in the Gulf of Mexico and Pandemic Influenza Act of 2006, December 30, 2005.

Bybee, Jay S. (Office of Legal Counsel, Department of Justice). Memo to Alberto R. Gonzales, Counsel to the President. "Standards of Conduct for Interrogation under 18 U.S.C. §§ 2340–2340A." August 1, 2002.

Cheney, Dick. Interview, June 27, 1975. James F. C. Hyde and Stephen J. Wayne collection, Gerald R. Ford Library.

Croghan, Lore. "Sales Slow Down in Steep New York Apartment Market." New York *Daily News*, July 7, 2006.

Fein, Bruce. Author interview. April 26, 2006.

Fisher, Louis. Author interview. June 9, 2006.

———. "Lost Constitutional Moorings: Recovering the War Power." *Indiana Law Review*, Fall 2006.

Gonzales, Alberto R. Memorandum for the President. Subject: Decision re Application of the Geneva Convention on Prisoners of War to the Conflict with al Qaeda and the Taliban. January 25, 2002.

Hamdan v. Rumsfeld, Secretary of Defense, et al., Supreme Court of the United States, June 29, 2006.

Hamdi et al v. Rumsfeld, Secretary of Defense, et al., Supreme Court of the United States, June 28, 2004.

Kelley, Matt. "U.S. to Bring Taliban, al-Qaida Prisoners to Navy Base in Cuba, Rumsfeld Says." Associated Press, December 27, 2001.

Klaidman, Daniel, and Michael Isikoff. "Cheney in the Bunker: Bloodied but Unbowed, the Veep Has a New Number Two." *Newsweek,* November 14, 2005.

Klaidman, Daniel, Stuart Taylor, Jr., and Evan Thomas. "Palace Revolt." *Newsweek,* January 29, 2006.

Lilly, Scott. Author interview. April 27, 2006.

Mann, James. "The Armageddon Plan." *The Atlantic,* March 1, 2004.

McCain, John. "Torture's Terrible Toll: Abusive Interrogation Tactics Produce Bad Intel, and Undermine the Values We Hold Dear." *Newsweek,* November 21, 2005.

———, and Mark Salter. *Faith of My Fathers.* New York: Random House, 1999.

Philbin, Patrick F., and John C. Yoo. Office of Legal Counsel, Department of Justice. Memo to William J. Haynes II, General Counsel, Department of Defense. "Possible Habeas Jurisdiction over Aliens Held in Guantanamo Bay, Cuba." December 28, 2001.

Powell, Colin. Letter to Senator John McCain, October 5, 2005.

Priest, Dana, and Robin Wright. "Cheney Fights for Detainee Policy; as Pressure Mounts to Limit Handling of Terror Suspects, He Holds Hard Line." *The Washington Post,* November 7, 2005.

Purdum, Todd. "A Face Only a President Could Love." *Vanity Fair,* June 2006.

Ragavan, Chitra. "Cheney's Guy." *U.S. News & World Report,* May 29, 2006.

Rasul et al. v. Bush, President of the United States, et al., Supreme Court of the United States. June 28, 2004.

Risen, James, and Eric Lichtblau. "Bush Lets U.S. Spy on Callers Without Courts." *The New York Times,* December 16, 2005.

Savage, Charlie. "Bush Could Bypass New Torture Ban." *The Boston Globe,* January 4, 2006.

Schmitt, Eric. "Pentagon Rethinking Manual with Interrogation Methods." *The New York Times,* June 14, 2006.

———, et al. "President Backs McCain on Abuse." *The New York Times,* December 16, 2005.

Smith, R. Jeffrey, and Josh White. "Cheney Plan Exempts CIA from Bill Barring Abuse of Detainees." *The Washington Post,* October 25, 2005.

Suskind, Ron. *The One Percent Doctrine: Deep Inside America's Pursuit of Its Enemies Since 9/11.* New York: Simon & Schuster, 2006.

Taft, William H. IV (Legal Adviser, Department of State). Memo to Alberto R. Gonzales, Counsel to the President, "Comments on Your Paper on the Geneva Convention," February 2, 2002.

Yoo, John C. "The President's Constitutional Authority to Conduct Military Operations Against Terrorists and Nations Supporting Them." Memorandum Opinion for the Deputy Counsel to the President, Office of Legal Counsel, Department of Justice, September 25, 2001.

————, and Robert J. Delahunty. Office of Legal Counsel, Department of Justice. Memo to William J. Haynes II, General Counsel, Department of Defense. "Application of Treaties and Laws to al Qaeda and Taliban Detainees." January 9, 2002.

Wilkerson, Lawrence. Author interview. June 16, 2006.

Woolley, John, and Gerhard Peters. "Presidential Signing Statements." The American Presidency Project, University of California at Santa Barbara, www.presidency.ucsb.edu.

CHAPTER TWELVE
What Dick Knew—and When He Knew It

Ackerman, Spencer, and John B. Judis. "The First Casualty." *The New Republic,* June 30, 2003.

Clinton, Bill. Executive Order 12958, "Classified National Security Information." April 17, 1995.

Dreyfuss, Robert. "The March of the Spooks." *The Dreyfuss Report,* November 3, 2005.

————. "The Commissar's in Town." *The American Prospect,* June 2006.

Eisendrath, Craig R., and Melvin A. Goodman. *Bush League Diplomacy: How the Neoconservatives Are Putting the World at Risk.* Amherst, N.Y.: Prometheus Books, 2004.

Fein, Bruce. Author interview, April 26, 2006.

Goodman, Melvin. Author interview, April 20, 2006.

Hume, Brit. "Vice President Cheney Interviewed." Fox News, February 15, 2006.

Isikoff, Michael, and Evan Thomas. "The Leaker in Chief?" *Newsweek,* April 17, 2006.

Kerr, Robert. "Intelligence and Analysis on Iraq: Report for CIA, Issues for the Intelligence Community." July 29, 2004.

Margolick, David. "Mr. Fitz Goes to Washington." *Vanity Fair,* February 2006.

McCormack, Bruce. "Cheney: Altering Foreign Elections Possible Option." *Casper Star-Tribune,* December 9, 1977.

Scherer, Michael. "Secrets and Lies." Salon.com, October 26, 2005 (http://dir.salon.com/story/news/feature/2005/10/26/questions/index.html).

United States of America v. I. Lewis Libby, also known as "SCOOTER LIBBY." Indictment, October 28, 2005.

United States of America v. I. Lewis Libby, also known as "Scooter Libby." Reply to the Response of I. Lewis Libby to Government's Response to Court's Inquiry. . . . United States District Court for the District of Columbia, May 24, 2006.

United States of America v. I. Lewis Libby, also known as "Scooter Libby." Pretrial hearing on defendant's motions, May 5, 2006.

United States of America v. I. Lewis Libby (also known as "Scooter Libby"). Government's Response to Defendant's Third Motion to Compel Discovery. United States District Court for the District of Columbia, April 5, 2006.

Valerie Plame Wilson and Joseph C. Wilson IV v. I. Lewis (a/k/a "Scooter") Libby, Jr., Karl Rove, Richard Cheney, and John Does No. 1–10, United States District Court for the District of Columbia, July 13, 2006.

Wallsten, Peter, and Tom Hamburger. "Bush Critic Became Target of Libby, Former Aides Say." *Los Angeles Times,* October 21, 2005.

Waas, Murray. "Bush Directed Cheney to Counter War Critic." *National Journal,* July 3, 2006.

————. "Cheney 'Authorized' Libby to Leak Classified Information." *National Journal*, February 9, 2006.

————. "Insulating Bush." *National Journal*, March 30, 2006.

————. "Iraq, Niger, and the CIA." *National Journal*, February 6, 2006.

Wilson, Joseph. Author interview. April 18, 2006.

————. *The Politics of Truth.* New York: Carroll & Graf, 2004.

————. "What I Didn't Find in Africa." *The New York Times*, July 6, 2003.

INDEX

ABOUT THE AUTHORS

Lou Dubose has covered Texas politics for twenty-five years. He is the co-author (with Molly Ivins) of two *New York Times* bestsellers, *Shrub: The Short but Happy Political Life of George W. Bush* and *Bushwhacked: Life in George W. Bush's America*. In 2003 he wrote (with *Texas Monthly* writer Jan Reid) *The Hammer: Tom DeLay, God, Money, and the Rise of the Republican Congress*. He has also written a political biography of Karl Rove. He lives in Austin, Texas, with his wife, Jeanne Goka.

Texas Observer executive editor Jake Bernstein has chronicled stories from Washington, D.C., to the jungles of Central America. As a weekly reporter in Miami, he covered the 2000 Florida recount and the Elián González story. While working as a freelancer in Guatemala and El Salvador, he wrote about the destruction of the rain forest and the end of guerrilla insurgencies. In Texas, Bernstein's work on Tom DeLay's campaign-finance scandals has won multiple journalism awards. He lives in Austin.